£5:00

Other books by
Jeffrey Ethell and Alfred Price

The German Jets in Combat

Target Berlin

Air War South Atlantic

Target Berlin: Mission 250, 6th March 1944

Other books by Jeffrey Ethell

Komet: The Messerschmitt 163

Escort to Berlin: 4th Fighter Group in WW2

P-38 Lightning at War

P-40 Hawks at War

Mustang: A Documentary History of the P51

Amelia Earhart: The Final Story

Other books by Alfred Price

Instruments of Darkness

Aircraft Versus Submarine

The Hardest Day

The Spitfire Story

Spitfire at War

Harrier at War

Panavia Tornado

The History of US Electronic Warfare

Battle of Britain Day

ONE DAY IN A LONG WAR

ONE DAY IN A LONG WAR

MAY 10, 1972
AIR WAR,
NORTH
VIETNAM

JEFFREY ETHELL
AND ALFRED PRICE

GUILD PUBLISHING
LONDON · NEW YORK · SYDNEY · TORONTO

This edition published 1990
by Guild Publishing
by arrangement with Greenhill Books
Lionel Leventhal Limited

CN 9966

Printed in Great Britain by
Redwood Press Limited, Melksham, Wiltshire

AUTHORS' NOTE

The primary sources of material for this book were official and unofficial documents and diaries written at the time, cockpit voice recordings, and tape-recorded interviews with those who participated in the actions on May 10, 1972. Unless otherwise stated, all passages quoted verbatim are from transcripts of cockpit tapes or interviews made by the authors. Nowhere have we "re-created" conversations for dramatic effect.

Two of the participants, Steve Rudloff and Garrett Olinde, wrote lengthy personal accounts of their experiences, which they made available to the authors. Randy Cunningham recounted his experiences in the book he wrote. with co-author Jeff Ethell, *Fox Two.* The French journalist Théodore Ronco and Claude Julien observed the actions and wrote lengthy reports for *L'Humanité* and *Le Monde,* respectively, translated sections of which have been included. Where quoted, these are credited accordingly.

Unless otherwise stated, all times are given in North Vietnam local time, time zone G; this is seven hours ahead of Greenwich mean time and twelve hours ahead of Washington, D.C. U.S. bases in Thailand were in time zone G, U.S. carriers on Yankee Station were in zone H, one hour later.

All distances are given in nautical miles; speeds are given in knots. Weights and liquids are measured in U.S. tons and U.S. gallons, respectively. The speed of sound, Mach 1, is approximately 660 knots at sea level.

Wherever possible the authors have avoided using military acronyms, except for such terms as SAM (for surface-to-air missile) that have become part of the English language. The acronym is a generic term for all such weapons, but during the action on May 10 it referred to one specific type: the Soviet-built Dvina (NATO code name SA-2). Wherever SAM is used in this text, it refers to this specific system.

ACKNOWLEDGMENTS

It would have been impossible to write this book without the generous assistance of many people. In particular the authors wish to convey their thanks to Major William Austin and Lieutenant Colonel Joseph Wagovich from the USAF Magazines and Books Division; to William Heimdahl and Roger Jernigan from the Office of Air Force History; to Captain Richard Knott, Captain Rosario Rausa, Roy Grossnick, Ed Marolda, Wes Pryce and Mike Brown at the Naval Historical Center; to Barrett Tillman and Robert Lawson from the Tailhook Association; to Tran Van Hung and the staff of the Vietnamese embassy in London and Tran Trong Khanh at the Vietnamese delegation to the United Nations in New York.

Special thanks are also due to John Gresham for access to his own detailed research on the action on May 10, 1972, to Vance Mitchell for invaluable help, to Patti Sheridan and Tom Halley of the Red River Valley Fighter Pilots Association (the River Rats), to Bob Dorr for the use of photographs from his collection, to Mike Spick for analyzing the air actions and passing useful comments on the manuscript, to Dr. Nguyen Thi Dieu for researching the Vietnamese open literature and translating passages into English, to Trung Huynh for supplying useful material, to Arnold Lye for his excellent photos of the Paul Doumer Bridge, and to David and Joan Yuile and Liz Hodgkin for much useful help and advice. Others who assisted were Harley Copic, Warren Thurn, Peter Mersky, Captain Kent Ewing USN, Walter Boyne, James Mulquin, Mike France, Mike Humphreys, Peter Sowers and Linda Pinegar Dark.

The authors have a special debt of gratitude to those who participated in or observed the events of May 10, 1972, and generously allowed us to intrude into their lives to probe their memories and record their stories. The research for this book was crucially dependent on the interviews and the diaries, papers, recording tapes and photographs these people kindly made available. Their names are given in the section that follows, "The Witnesses."

Jeff Ethell,   Alfred Price,
Front Royal,   Uppingham,
Virginia   Leicestershire
U.S.A   England

Ranks, titles, unit locations, positions in formation and names (in the case of women who later married) were those on May 10, 1972.

Lieutenant Commander Hank Allen USN, A-6 pilot, VA-52, USS *Kitty Hawk*.

Captain James Allen USAF, F-4 pilot, Biloxi 2, 25th Tactical Fighter Squadron, 8th TFW, Ubon, Thailand.

Lieutenant John Anderson USN, F-4 pilot, VF-96, USS *Constellation*.

Commander Fred Baldwin USN, A-7 pilot, Executive Officer VA-146, USS *Constellation*.

Lieutenant Rick Bates USAF, F-4 WSO, Napkin 4, 433rd Tactical Fighter Squadron, 8 TFW, Ubon, Thailand.

Airman Loren Bidwell USN, V-2 Division (Catapults and Arrester Gear), USS *Constellation*.

Lieutenant Norman Birzer USN, A-7 pilot, VA-147, USS *Constellation*.

Lieutenant Michael Bolier USN, F-4 pilot, VF-92, USS *Constellation*.

Captain William Byrns USAF, F-4 pilot, Hitest 2, 435th Tactical Fighter Squadron, 8th TFW, Ubon, Thailand.

Lieutenant Commander Jim Campbell USN, F-4 pilot, VF-92, USS *Constellation*.

Lieutenant Kenneth Cannon USN, F-4 pilot, VF-51, USS *Coral Sea*.

Lieutenant Matt Connelly USN, F-4 pilot, VF-96, USS *Constellation*.

Lieutenant Keith Crenshaw USN, F-4 RIO, VF-96, USS *Constellation*.

Lieutenant Charles Crisp USAF, F-4 WSO, Dingus 3, 433rd Tactical Fighter Squadron, 8th TFW, Ubon, Thailand.

Lieutenant Randall Cunningham USN, F-4 pilot, VF-96, USS *Constellation*.

Lieutenant Brent Danner USAF, F-105G EWO, Galore 5, 17th Wild Weasel Squadron, 388th TFW, Korat, Thailand.

Captain Charles DeBellevue USAF, F-4 WSO, Oyster 3, 555th Tactical Fighter Squadron, 432nd TRW, Udorn, Thailand.

Lieutenant Curtis Dosé USN, F-4 pilot, VF-92, USS *Constellation*.

Major William Driggers USAF, F-4 pilot, Napkin 4, 433rd Tactical Fighter Squadron, 8th TFW, Ubon, Thailand.

Lieutenant James Dunn USAF, F-4 pilot, Dingus 2, 433rd Tactical Fighter Squadron, 8th TFW, Ubon, Thailand.

Captain Harry Edwards USAF, F-4 WSO, Jingle 2, 433rd Tactical Fighter Squadron, 8th TFW, Ubon, Thailand.

Commander Lowell "Gus" Eggert USN, Commander Carrier Air Wing 9, USS *Constellation.*

Lieutenant Thomas Feezel USAF, F-4 pilot, Oyster 4, 555th Tactical Fighter Squadron, 432nd TRW, Udorn, Thailand.

Lieutenant Randy Foltz USN, A-6 pilot, VA-165, USS *Constellation.*

Lieutenant Jim Fox USN, F-4 RIO, VF-96, USS *Constellation.*

Lieutenant George Goryanec USN, A-7 pilot, VA-147, USS *Constellation.*

Lieutenant Brian Grant USN, F-4 pilot, VF-96, USS *Constellation.*

Lieutenant Ralph Griffiths USN, A-6 weapon systems officer, VA-165, USS *Constellation.*

Captain Lynn High USAF, F-4 pilot, Biloxi Leader, 25th Tactical Fighter Squadron, 8th TFW, Ubon, Thailand.

Lieutenant Colonel Rick Hilton USAF, F-4 pilot, Jingle Leader, 433rd Tactical Fighter Squadron, 8th TFW, Ubon, Thailand.

Major Kelly Irving USAF, F-4 pilot, Gigolo Leader, 25th Tactical Fighter Squadron, 8th TFW, Ubon, Thailand.

Lieutenant Laird Johnson USAF, F-4 WSO, Gopher 2, 25th Tactical Fighter Squadron, 8th TFW, Ubon, Thailand.

Lieutenant Dave Jordan USN, F-4 pilot, VF-92, USS *Constellation.*

Mr. Claude Julien, journalist, correspondent to French newspaper *Le Monde,* Hanoi, North Vietnam.

Lieutenant Al Junker USN, A-7 pilot, VA-146, USS *Constellation.*

Major Donald Kilgus USAF, F-105G pilot, 561st Tactical Fighter Squadron, 388th TFW, Korat, Thailand.

Captain Robert King USAF, F-105G electronic warfare officer, Calgon 2, 561st Tactical Fighter Squadron, 388th TFW, Korat, Thailand.

Lieutenant Steve Kuhar USN, EKA-3B naval flight officer, VAQ-135, USS *Coral Sea.*

Captain Roger Locher USAF, F-4 WSO, Oyster Leader, 555th Tactical Fighter Squadron, 432nd TRW, Udorn, Thailand.

Admiral William Mack USN, commander in chief 7th Fleet.

Lieutenant Terry Marecic USN, intelligence officer, VF-96, USS *Constellation.*

Lieutenant John Markle USAF, F-4 pilot, Oyster #2, 555th Tactical Fighter Squadron, 432nd TRW, Udorn, Thailand.

Lieutenant Commander Lonny McClung USN, F-4 pilot, VF-92, USS *Constellation.*

Captain Eugene McDaniel USN, prisoner of war, Hoa Lo prison, Hanoi, North Vietnam.

Captain Thomas McNamara USN, captain USS *Chicago.*

Captain Thomas "Mike" Messett USAF, F-4 pilot, Jingle 3, 433rd Tactical Fighter Squadron, 8th TFW, Ubon, Thailand.

Colonel Carl Miller USAF, F-4 pilot, Goatee Leader and Commander 8th Tactical Fighter Wing, Ubon, Thailand.

Lieutenant Ron Moore USAF, F-4 pilot, 435th Tactical Fighter Squadron, 8th TFW, Ubon, Thailand.

Lieutenant Barry Morgan USAF, F-4 pilot, Dingus 4, 433rd Tactical Fighter Squadron, 8th TFW, Udorn, Thailand.

Captain Jim Mulligan USN, prisoner of war, Hoa Lo prison, Hanoi, North Vietnam.

Major Daniel Nesbett USAF, F-4 pilot, Icebag 3, 334th Tactical Fighter Squadron, 8th TFW, Ubon, Thailand.

Commander Al Neuman USN, F-4 pilot, commanding officer VF-96, USS *Constellation.*

Captain Douglas Nix USAF, F-4 pilot, Gigolo 4, 25th Tactical Fighter Squadron, 8th TFW, Ubon, Thailand.

Chief Radarman Larry Nowell USN, air intercept controller, USS *Chicago.*

Lieutenant Colonel James O'Neil USAF, F-105G pilot, Fletch Leader, 17th Tactical Fighter Squadron, 388th TFW, Korat, Thailand.

Aviation Boatswain's Mate Engineer Third Class Garrett Olinde USN, V-2 Division (Catapults and Arrester Gear), USS *Constellation.*

Lieutenant John Olsen USN, F-4 pilot, VF-92, USS *Constellation.*

Lieutenant Ron Pearson USN, A-6 pilot, VA-165, USS *Constellation.*

Captain Larry Pettit USAF, F-4 WSO, Oyster 4, 555th Tactical Fighter Squadron, 432nd TRW, Udorn, Thailand.

Madame Phan thi Tran, gynecologist, St. Paul's Hospital, Hanoi, North Vietnam.

Captain Don Pickard USAF, RF-4 pilot, Cousin 2, 14th Tactical Reconnaissance Squadron, 432nd TRW, Udorn, Thailand.

Lieutenant Michael Pomphrey USAF, F-4 WSO, Biloxi 3, 25th Tactical Fighter Squadron, 8th TFW, Ubon, Thailand.

Lieutenant Colonel Jerry Potter USAF, Deputy Chief of Staff Operations Electronic Warfare, 7th Air Force Headquarters, Tan Son Nhut, Saigon, Vietnam.

Lieutenant Steve Queen, Landing Signals Officer, USS *Constellation.*

Lieutenant Gary Reed USAF, F-4 pilot, 8th TFW, Ubon, Thailand.

Captain Bill Ridge USAF, F-4 pilot, Balter 4, 13th Tactical Fighter Squadron, 432nd TRW, Udorn, Thailand.

Major Don Rigg USAF, F-4 pilot, Napkin 2, Staff Officer on 8th TFW, Udorn, Thailand.

Captain Steve Ritchie USAF, F-4 pilot, Oyster 3, 555th Tactical Fighter Squadron, 432nd TRW, Udorn, Thailand.

Mr. Théodore Ronco, journalist, correspondent to French newspaper *L'Humanité,* Hanoi, North Vietnam.

Lieutenant Steve Rudloff USN, F-4 WSO, VF-92, USS *Constellation.*

Lieutenant Michael Ruth USN, A-7 pilot, VA-195, USS *Kitty Hawk.*

Captain Clara "Patty" Schneider USAF, intelligence officer, 432nd Tactical Reconnaissance Wing, Udorn, Thailand.

Lieutenant Commander Phil Scott USN, F-4 pilot, Commander VF-92, USS *Constellation.*

Lieutenant Colonel Brad Sharp USAF, F-4 pilot, Operations Officer, 25th Tactical Fighter Squadron, 8th TFW, Ubon, Thailand.

Lieutenant Brewster Shaw USAF, F-4 pilot, 8th TFW, Ubon, Thailand.

Captain Jim Shaw USAF, F-4 WSO, Gopher 4, 25th Tactical Fighter Squadron, 8th TFW, Ubon, Thailand.

Lieutenant Steve Shoemaker USN, F-4 pilot, VF-96, USS *Constellation.*

Mr. David Simmons, vice consul, British consulate, Hanoi, North Vietnam.

Signalman Greg Slavonic USN, lookout, signal bridge, USS *Constellation.*

Captain Ron Smith USAF, A-1 pilot, 56th Special Operations Wing, Nakhon Phanom, Thailand.

Lieutenant Mike Stansel USN, F-4 Radar Intercept Officer, VF-92, USS *Constellation.*

Captain Dale Stovall USAF, HH-53B pilot, 40th Rescue and Recovery Squadron, Nakhon Phanom, Thailand.

Lieutenant Guy Thomas USN, Officer in Charge Special Detachment, USS *Chicago.*

Commander Dwight Timm USN, F-4 pilot and executive officer, VF-96, USS *Constellation.*

Lieutenant Charles Tinker USN, F-4 RIO, VF-92, USS *Constellation.*

Lieutenant Lanny Toups USAF, F-4 WSO, Hitest 4, 435th Tactical Fighter Squadron, 8th TFW, Ubon, Thailand.

Lieutenant Commander William Townsend USN, F-4 pilot, VF-92, USS *Constellation.*

Captain Mike Van Wagenen USAF, F-4 pilot, Jingle 4, 433rd Tactical Fighter Squadron, 8th TFW, Ubon, Thailand.

Major Donald "Dean" White USAF, F-4 pilot, Balter Leader, 13th Tactical Fighter Squadron, 432nd TRW, Udorn, Thailand.

General John W. Vogt Jr. USAF, commanding general 7th Air Force, 7th Air Force Headquarters, Tan Son Nhut, Saigon, South Vietnam.

Lieutenant John Walsh USAF, F-4 WSO, Bertha 2, 336th Tactical Fighter Squadron, 8th TFW, Ubon, Thailand.

Lieutenant Warren Weaver USAF, KC-135 co-pilot, 376th Strategic Wing, detached to U-Tapao, Thailand.

Mr. Joe Wright, consul general, British consulate, Hanoi, North Vietnam.

Mrs. Pat Wright, British consulate, Hanoi, North Vietnam.

Admiral Elmo R. Zumwalt Jr. USN, chief of naval operations, The Pentagon, Washington, D.C.

CONTENTS

Authors' Note   vii
Acknowledgments   ix
The Witnesses   xi

Prologue: Southeast Asia, Spring 1972
    March 30–May 9   3
1   Morning, May 10, Midnight–7:00 A.M.   19
2   Target Haiphong, 6:45–9:15 A.M.   30
3   The Action Around Hanoi, the Opening Phase
    8:00–9:50 A.M.   49
4   The Action Around Hanoi, Softening the Defenses
    9:40–10:00A.M.   64
5   The Action Around Hanoi,
    the Paul Doumer Bridge Strike
    9:55–11:30 A.M.   78
6   The Action over Hai Duong, 11:00 A.M.–2:15 P.M.   102
7   The Afternoon Action, and Later, 3:15 P.M.–Midnight   137
8   Man on the Run, May 11–June 2   151
9   The May 10, 1972, Action Analyzed   165
10   Afterward   179
11   Conflicting Evidence   185

Glossary   193
Appendix A: Aircraft Types in Action on
    May 10, 1972   195
Appendix B: 8th Tactical Fighter Wing F-4 Crews
    Who Took Part in Attacks on the Hanoi Area on
    May 10, 1972   199
Appendix C: U.S. Navy Task Groups off
    North Vietnam on May 10, 1972   203

Appendix D: North Vietnamese Fighter and
Antiaircraft Defense Units on May 10, 1972   205
Bibliography   207
Index   209

ONE
DAY
IN A
LONG
WAR

SOUTHEAST ASIA, SPRING 1972

March 30–May 9

Soldiers of Vietnam, we go forward,
With the one will to save our Fatherland
Our hurried steps sound on the long and arduous road.
Our flag, red with the blood of victory, bears the spirit
    of our country.
The distant rumbling of the guns mingles with our
    marching song.
The path to glory passes over the bodies of our foes.
Overcoming all hardships, together we build up our
    resistance
Ceaselessly for the people's cause we struggle,
Hastening to the battlefield!
Forward! All together advancing!
Our Vietnam is strong, eternal.
        —National anthem of the Democratic
            Republic of Vietnam (North Vietnam)

DURING THE early morning darkness of March 30, 1972, three regular divisions of the North Vietnamese Army stormed across the Demilitarized Zone separating the two halves of Vietnam. Simultaneously, throughout South Vietnam, there was an upsurge of guerrilla activity. With low cloud shielding them from retaliatory air strikes, the invaders quickly secured their initial objectives. In the first three days they overran the northern half of Quang Tri Province. On April 5 three more North Vietnamese divisions launched a new offensive northwest of Saigon. A few days later a third front opened in the Central Highlands.

From the political standpoint, the North Vietnamese had timed the invasion with great care. It was a presidential election year and Richard Nixon was campaigning for a second term in the White House. Three years earlier he had given his promise to pull all U.S. ground forces from Southeast Asia, and the withdrawal was about to enter its final phase. From a peak of more than half a million U.S. troops in South Vietnam in 1969, only 95,000 remained and most of those were scheduled to leave within six months. The ground fighting had already been handed over to the South Vietnamese Army, and U.S. combat troops had orders not to engage the enemy unless they were first attacked.

WITH THE SPRING invasion, the air war in Southeast Asia entered a new phase. U.S. planes had first attacked targets in North Vietnam in August 1964, and during the next four years the aerial bombardment of that country had steadily escalated in ferocity. Then in October 1968, in the hope that it would assist in securing peace by diplomatic means, President Johnson had ordered a halt to the bombing of North Vietnam. Although there were minor breaches, in general the moratorium against air attacks on targets in the north had held.

With the steady withdrawal of U.S. forces from the area, by March 1972 the number of U.S. combat planes remaining in Southeast Asia was well below its peak. In South Vietnam there were three squadrons of F-4 Phantoms and a single squadron of A-37s, a total of seventy-six fighter-bomber and light attack aircraft. In Thailand there were 161 Phantoms, fifty-two B-52 heavy bombers, sixteen F-105 defense suppression planes and twenty-eight gunships. On Guam were a further thirty-one B-52s which could reach targets in Vietnam. Off the coast of

Vietnam cruised two Navy carriers, *Coral Sea* and *Hancock,* each with some seventy planes.

Early in April, as the North Vietnamese troops thrust further into the South, the skies cleared and bombers and attack planes struck back hard. For the first time over South Vietnam, planes were targeted against large-scale conventional military opera-tions rather than hit-and-run guerrilla attacks.

Meanwhile, there was a large-scale transfusion of U.S. air strength back into Southeast Asia. Between the beginning of April and the end of the first week in May, five squadrons of Phantoms, one of F-105s and one of EB-66s—a total of 110 com-bat planes—deployed to bases in Thailand. Fifty-eight more B-52s moved to the West Pacific, and the Navy dispatched two large carriers, *Kitty Hawk* and *Constellation,* to stiffen the force in the Gulf of Tonkin. As each new combat squadron arrived in the area it was hurled into the fray.

ONCE IT was clear that the North Vietnamese were intent on a full-scale invasion of the South, President Nixon allowed air strikes into North Vietnam. By April 4 planes were permitted to attack targets up to eighty miles from the Demilitarized Zone.

Early in April General John Vogt was appointed commander of the Seventh Air Force, and assumed responsibility for directing Air Force operations in Southeast Asia. On April 6, immediately before he left for Saigon, he was summoned to meet with the President at the Executive Offices Building, next to the White House. Vogt, a fighter ace in World War II, told the authors: "The meeting lasted about an hour and there were three of us there: the President, Henry Kissinger and myself. The President gave me the objects of the military campaign he wanted me to pursue. In effect he said we were not going to sell out our friends, we were going to stay and fight. However we were going to continue to withdraw U.S. ground forces from Vietnam, because he had given his promise to the American people. He told me to go over there and do whatever was necessary to keep the Vietnamese war effort going, and turn the war around in the South."

The President told the general that if he required more planes, he had only to ask. Vogt replied that when the Air Force units on the way to the theater were in place, he thought he would have sufficient aircraft to carry out the tasks entrusted to him.

Bit by bit the restrictions on the use of U.S. bombers over North Vietnam were lifted, and on April 16 they attacked petroleum-storage facilities close to Hanoi and Haiphong. Still the President held back from a full-scale resumption of attacks against the North, however, preferring to retain this option a little longer.

IN HANOI the North Vietnamese government had accepted, and discounted, the risk of aerial bombardment against its cities before it ordered the invasion of the South. Yet although the North Vietnamese government was prepared to accept casualties, it did not court them, and it implemented contingency plans to reduce the impact of renewed air attacks. Joe Wright, British consul general in Hanoi at the time, witnessed some of the moves. "After the raids in April 1972 Hanoi was partially evacuated. Many children, old people and others not necessary to keep the city going were moved to the surrounding villages. The government offices and ministries were reduced to the bare minimum of people necessary to run them, and parallel organizations were set up outside Hanoi." To reduce their vulnerability to air attack, supplies and munitions were dispersed in small quantities at numerous sites clear of populated areas. "Supplies were dotted around the countryside. Wherever there were a few trees you would see small piles of ammunition, stores, spare parts, etc. Apparently they had just been left there, but of course the people responsible knew exactly where they were."

ALTHOUGH it was slowed by the air attacks, the North Vietnamese advance into the South continued. On April 25 Kontom was attacked and on May 1 Quang Tri fell.

Forced on by the passage of events, President Nixon felt the time was fast approaching when he would have to order the resumption of full-scale bombing attacks on North Vietnam. Even so, there were limits to the ways he could use the awesome power at his command. In his book *No More Vietnams* he wrote:

> Only two strategies existed that might have won the war at a single stroke. We could have bombed the elaborate system of irrigation dikes in North Vietnam, though this would have resulted in floods that would have killed hundreds of thousands of civilians. Or we could have used tactical nuclear weapons against enemy forces. Like Eisenhower in 1954 [when it was suggested that atomic bombs be dropped to assist the French during the battle of Dien Bien Phu], I gave no serious consideration to the nuclear option. I also categorically rejected the bombing of dikes. . . . If we had chosen to go for a knockout blow by bombing the dikes or using tactical nuclear weapons, the resulting domestic and international uproar would have damaged our foreign policy on all fronts.

A third option, to mount a series of heavy attacks on Hanoi and other cities, was also rejected by the President. That course offered the worst of both worlds: it would cause as much international uproar as nuclear attacks or the bombing of dikes, with no certainty of producing the required decisive result.

Another limiting factor was the need to avoid incidents involving other nations, particularly China and the Soviet Union with whom the President was anxious to improve relations. Attacks were prohibited on targets within ten miles of the Chinese border, or on foreign ships in Vietnamese waters. That ruled out the bombing of ports where such ships were unloading.

Taking these constraints into account, the Joint Chiefs of Staff updated their contingency plan for the large-scale attack of targets throughout North Vietnam, Operation Linebacker. The aims of the operation were threefold:

—to restrict supplies entering that country from abroad,

—to destroy internal stockpiles of military supplies and equipment,

—to restrict the flow of forces and supplies to South Vietnam.

The plan included a strict directive that everything possible be done to avoid civilian casualties. If this rule was violated, operational commanders were to be informed that they would be held personally accountable.

Within the above limitations, Operation Linebacker would permit attacks on military and transportation targets almost anywhere in North Vietnam. That was not new, however, for most of the targets listed in the directive had been attacked prior to the 1968 bombing halt. The main departure from previous operations was that, for the first time, it allowed the mining of the approaches to North Vietnamese ports.

U.S. intelligence agencies had estimated that North Vietnam's average daily import requirement was about 6,300 tons. About five-sixths of this came in by sea, most of it through Haiphong. So a priority aim for Linebacker would be to mine the approaches to prevent ships entering the port, to hit supplies recently unloaded and to destroy rail links from the city.

For the purposes of U.S. air attack planning, North Vietnam was divided into six so-called Route Packages (see map) shared between the Air Force and the Navy. General Vogt's Seventh Air Force was responsible for attacks on targets in Route Package 1 in the extreme south, and 5 and 6A (which included Hanoi). Navy Task Force 77, commanded by Admiral Damon Cooper, was responsible for attacks on targets in Route Packages 2, 3, 4 and 6B (which included Haiphong).

IN ANY attack on the internal transport system of North Vietnam, bridges would be prime targets. The country's single most important bridge was the Paul Doumer road and rail bridge, which lay astride the Red River on the east side of Hanoi. Situated at a strategic point for both the road and the rail networks, the bridge

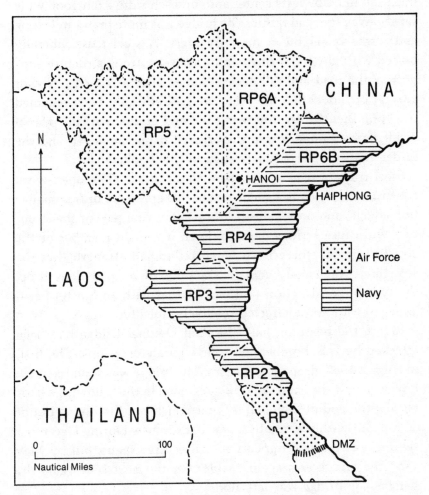

For the purposes of U.S. air attack planning, North Vietnam was divided into seven Route Packages. The Air Force was primarily responsible for attacks in Route Packages 1, 5 and 6A, the Navy for attacks in Route Packages 2, 3, 4, and 6B.

carried the only rail link and the main highway from the port of Haiphong to the capital.

Completed in 1902, the Paul Doumer Bridge carried a single track rail line down its center and, on each side, a ten-foot-wide carriageway for road traffic. The bridge was more than a mile long and rested on eighteen masonry piers. A steel truss, liberally braced with girders, formed an immensely strong structure supporting the road and rail decks. Named after a French governor general of Indochina, the structure had officially been renamed the Long Bien Bridge following the end of colonial rule. Hanoi residents continued to use the original name, however, and the bridge will be referred to as such in this book.

Steel truss bridges are resilient to air attack. The open-work construction presents a small area to blast pressure or fragmentation effects, and only a direct hit on some vital part of the structure will cause serious damage. Even if a main member of the structure is cut, there is so much redundant strength that the structure will usually remain standing. If a span does drop, the type of construction—rather like that with an Erector Set—allows repairs to be effected relatively quickly.

Before the bombing halt, the Paul Doumer Bridge had been attacked by U.S. bombers on four separate occasions. The first, in August 1967, dropped one span. The bridge was soon repaired, however, and road and rail traffic resumed in the following October. At the end of October another attack put the bridge out of action, but within a month it was back in use. During December two heavy attacks dropped five consecutive spans, but by May 1968 the bridge was again usable. For the next four years the patched-up bridge was left alone.

With a resumption of large-scale attacks on North Vietnam imminent, the Paul Doumer Bridge was at the top of General Vogt's target list. Weather permitting, it was to be attacked on the first day of the new campaign.

DURING PREVIOUS attacks on the Paul Doumer Bridge the Air Force planes had employed regular free-fall bombs. To get the accuracy necessary to hit vital points, crews had to release them in 45-degree dives from altitudes around 8,000 feet. And that meant flying into a veritable inferno of flak from the batteries positioned to defend this most important of targets.

Now, in the spring of 1972, the Air Force had two new weapons in the operational test stage that promised to be far more effective against bridges than any previously used: the electro-optically guided bomb and the laser-guided bomb. These so-called smart weapons were 2,000-pound free-fall bombs, fitted with "strap-on" guidance systems to increase their accuracy.

The electro-optical guided bomb (EOGB) was fitted with a TV guidance system that homed on the image contrast of the target against its background. The guidance system was autonomous, and after release the bomb required no further direction from the launching aircraft.

The other weapon, the laser-guided bomb (LGB), was fitted with a laser seeker nose. Phantoms attacking with LGBs operated in pairs, one of which carried a Pave Knife laser designator pod. Throughout the fall of both planes' bombs, a laser beam had to be kept pointed at the target and the LGBs homed on the laser energy reflected off the target.

Both types of "smart" bomb had been tested in Laos and South Vietnam, where they proved accurate to within twenty to thirty feet. They were effective against small targets, such as trucks, artillery positions and bridges. Neither weapon had yet been used against a heavily defended target in North Vietnam, but the portents were good. The planes would attack in the dive as with unguided bombs, but would release the new bombs from above 12,000 feet and pull out, keeping beyond the reach of the worst of the flak. Thus the new types of bomb promised far greater accuracy, for far less risk, than the attack weapons previously used over North Vietnam.

SINCE THE halt to operations over North Vietnam in 1968, the U.S. Navy had introduced an important new combat training program for its fighter pilots. Following an inquiry into ways of improving its fighters' kill-to-loss ratio against MiGs, the Navy had established the Post-graduate Course in Fighter Weapons, Tactics and Doctrine. That title, too wordy to survive in common usage, was soon changed to "Top Gun" (the course would be dramatized and immortalized in the 1986 film of the same name).

At Top Gun, run at Miramar Naval Air Station, near San Diego, Navy fighter crews learned the correct offensive and defensive tactics to employ, and those to avoid, when engaging each type of Soviet-built fighter. They learned to fight in loose but coordinated pairs, with each plane covering its partner. They learned how best to engage a more maneuverable adversary, and when and how to break out of a fight if they found themselves at a disadvantage. The course included mock combats with "MiG surrogates," A-4, T-38, F-8 and F-106 aircraft flown by pilots employing Soviet-style tactics. Although fighter crews were enthusiastic about the course, Top Gun was not without detractors. The elaborate training was expensive, both in dollars and in planes lost in accidents during the high-speed maneuvering of planes in close proximity with one another.

By the spring of 1972 a high proportion of Navy fighter crews had been through Top Gun. A similar program run by the Air Force was slower in taking effect, and few fighter crews in Southeast Asia had received this form of training. Until air-to-air fighting resumed on a large scale, however, there was no way of knowing whether the money and effort invested in air combat training gave fighter crews any clear advantage in action.

ANOTHER INNOVATION aimed at improving the effectiveness of U.S. fighters against the MiGs was an electronic device code-named Combat Tree. Fitted in a few Air Force Phantoms as an addition to the airborne intercept radar, Combat Tree received and displayed signals from the MiGs' radar identification friend or foe (IFF) equipment.

During previous operations over North Vietnam, there were usually many more U.S. planes in the area than MiGs. So before a U.S. fighter crew could let fly with air-to-air missiles, it had first

LULL BEFORE THE STORM

Constellation's flight deck on May 9, 1972. All seven Phantoms shown would go into action on the following day. That nearest the camera, 106, was mount for Matt Connelly and Thomas Blonski when they shot down two MiG-17s. The next, 207, was damaged beyond repair by flak. Plane 110 was flown by Brian Grant, Randy Cunningham's wingman during the Hai Duong action. Plane 5797 (nose number 212), top left, was shot down by flak and Steve Rudloff was taken prisoner. Plane 112 was flown by Dwight Timm and was fortunate to escape destruction by MiGs. Plane 210 was flown by Austin Hawkins during the combat near Kep airfield. Plane 211, nose-on to the camera, was flown by Curtis Dosé when he shot down a MiG-21.

WRIGHT

HANOI

Above and below, bustling street scenes in Hanoi, photographed by Joe Wright, the British consul-general in Hanoi, early in 1972. Note the almost complete lack of motor vehicles. Above right, Pat Wright pictured in one of the ubiquitous "pipe shelters" that dotted the city. Below, Joe Wright (right), with his deputy David Simmons.

WRIGHT

WRIGHT

WRIGHT

PAUL DOUMER BRIDGE

The Paul Doumer Bridge, photographed in 1987. Above and above right, general views of the bridge. The lighter parts were those repaired following air attacks. Far right, the immensely strong steel framework around the rail line, forming the central core of the bridge. Near right, the roadway on the south side of the bridge carrying westbound traffic; a similar roadway on the north side carried traffic in the opposite direction.

NORTH VIETNAMESE GROUND DEFENSES

Above, an SA-2 firing unit in North Vietnam with six missiles on their launchers under covers. At the left of the row of vehicles is the Fansong missile guidance radar. Top right, a launch crew preparing an SA-2 missile for action. Center right, 57-mm gun in a typical revetted position, pictured during a visit by President Ho Chi Minh. Bottom right, a 37-mm gun with firing crew.

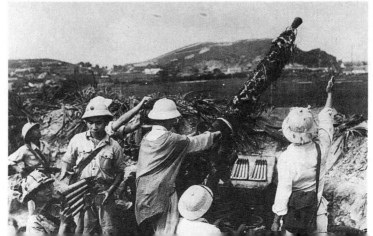

MIGS

Above, a MiG-19, the type that shot down both Phantoms lost in air-to-air combat on May 10, 1972. Above right, the MiG-21 MF whose performance at low altitude came as an unpleasant surprise for U.S. pilots. Below, North Vietnamese pilots run to their MiG-17s. Below right, Soviet-made P-35 radar provided control for the MiGs.

COMBAT NEAR YEN BAI

Above, Major Bob Lodge and Captain Roger Locher, who shot down a MiG-21 on May 10 but immediately afterward were shot down by a MiG-19. Above right, Lieutenant Le Thanh Dao of the 3rd Company PAVNAF, believed to have piloted the MiG-19 that shot down Lodge and Locher. Below, Yen Bai airfield beside the Red River. Roger Locher landed by parachute on the high ground at the top of the photo.

DRVN

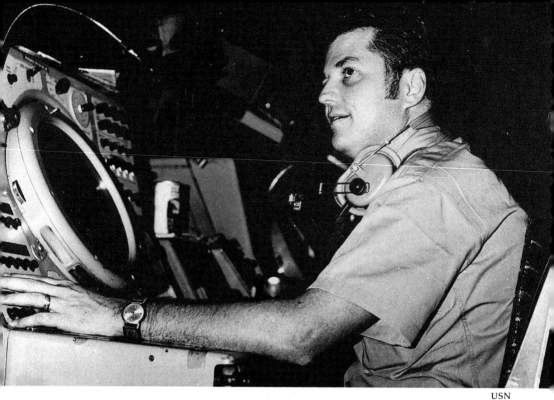

MIG HUNTERS

Above, the voice of Red Crown: Senior Chief Radarman Larry Nowell directed Oyster Flight from the Combat Information Center of USS *Chicago*. Below, MiG killers of Oyster Flight pictured after their return from action on May 10. Left to right: Lieutenant John Markle and his WSO Captain Stephen Eaves (Oyster 2), and WSO Captain Chuck DeBellevue and Captain Steve Ritchie (Oyster 3). Each crew destroyed one MiG-21. Right, Captain Bill Ridge of Balter Flight tussled with MiG-19s and MiG-21s.

RIDGE

PAUL DOUMER BRIDGE ATTACKERS

Above, an F-4D Phantom of the 8th Tactical Fighter Wing carrying a pair of 2,000-pound laser-guided bombs. Below, a laser-marking Phantom of the 8th TFW. This plane, 680, flew on the May 10 mission as part of Biloxi Flight. Note the asymmetric loading of the plane, which carried, from left to right: a drop tank, a 2,000-pound LGB, a centerline tank, a Pave Knife laser-marking pod and a 2,000-pound LGB.

Below, close-up of the Pave Knife pod. Above, an F-4D Phantom of the 8th Tactical Fighter Wing carrying a pair of 2,000-pound electro-optically guided bombs. During the attack on May 10 the weapon performed poorly, and all seven released missed the target.

MEN WHO BOMBED THE PAUL DOUMER BRIDGE

Some of those who attacked the Paul Doumer Bridge: above left, Colonel Carl Miller, commander of the 8th Tactical Fighter Wing, led the attack at the head of Goatee Flight. Above right, Major Bill Driggers piloted Jingle 4. Below, left and right, Captain Mike Messett (Napkin 3) and Captain Mike Van Wagenen (Napkin 4) were in the final element to attack.

to maneuver to within a mile or so of the target aircraft and visually identify it as hostile. The radar-guided Sparrow missile could destroy planes at distances far beyond visual range, but the need for prior visual identification had prevented this capability from being exploited. Now, provided they had clearance that no U.S. planes were in the area, the crew of a Phantom fitted with Combat Tree could engage a plane emitting hostile IFF signals, without having first to identify it visually. At a stroke the new device would more than double the effective range of Sparrow.

THE NORTH VIETNAMESE air defenses had also improved since the bombing halt. The respite had allowed better training of ground fighter controllers and most, probably all, were now North Vietnamese (during the earlier campaign there had been hints that Soviet "advisers" were doing much of the controlling). Also during the intervening period the system for directing fighters into action had been tightened, as had coordination between gun, surface-to-air missile (SAM) and fighter defenses.

Whereas in earlier years there was evidence of Soviet and North Korean pilots flying combat missions over North Vietnam, by 1972 it is believed that only North Vietnamese pilots flew the MiGs in combat.

Since 1968 there had been improvements both in the quantity and the quality of fighters operated by the People's Army of Viet Nam Air Force (PAVNAF). Now it possessed about eighty-five MiG-15s and MiG-17s (the former for operational training). It had thirty-two examples of the MiG-19, a first-generation supersonic fighter but a superb low-altitude dogfighter. Of its seventy-five MiG-21s, some were of the latest MF version (NATO code-name Fishbed J), which was faster than earlier versions particularly at low altitude. Previously U.S. fighters had had few encounters with the MiG-19 or the MiG-21MF, and their capabilities would cause some unpleasant surprises.

The Soviet-made Dvina (NATO code-name SA-2), the only type of SAM system operational in North Vietnam at this time, was well known to U.S. intelligence. In the spring of 1972 there were about two hundred sites in North Vietnam from which the missiles could be fired, but only about thirty-five operational Dvina firing units. To make life as difficult as possible for U.S. planes the firing units moved position from day to day, ready to play a lethal version of the shell game with Air Force and Navy planes when the attacks resumed. At the beginning of May 1972 the densest concentrations of active SAM sites were around Hanoi (thirteen) and Haiphong (ten).

In May 1972 it was estimated that defending North Vietnam were thirty-three hundred antiaircraft guns of all calibers (23 mm, 37 mm, 57 mm, 85 mm and 100 mm), most of them positioned in the areas around Hanoi, Haiphong and surrounding towns. Like the SAM firing units, the antiaircraft gun batteries shifted position from day to day to increase their effectiveness against attacking planes. In addition to the dedicated antiaircraft weapons, there were numerous smaller-caliber automatic weapons positioned around targets which could also engage low-flying aircraft. (For more detail on the North Vietnamese air defense system, see Appendix D.)

ON MAY 4 Admiral Thomas H. Moorer, chairman of the Joint Chiefs of Staff, briefed the President on the Navy plan to mine the North Vietnamese ports. The following day a signal went to CinC (Commander in Chief) Pacific to prepare for the operation, to be launched on receipt of an executive order from the Pentagon.

At "Blue Chip," Seventh Air Force's operational headquarters at Tan Son Nhut near Saigon, plans for the renewed attack on North Vietnam were also well advanced. General Vogt had good intelligence on the numerical strengths of the various parts of the North Vietnamese air defense system. But until air fighting resumed he could not know by how much and in what areas its combat proficiency had improved during the previous thirty months. The general told the authors: "I was concerned about the tactics, whether or not we could operate and survive in the new and very difficult environment. If we suffered heavy losses it would be a serious setback and might cause morale problems. We had to get our feet wet, demonstrate we could get to the target and get back without undue losses. So I was very heavy on defense suppression, jamming, chaff dispensing and MIGCAP [anti-MiG combat air patrols]; for every airplane going to the target carrying bombs would be two or three others backing it up, to get in and out."

ALSO ON May 4, National Security Adviser Henry Kissinger returned from Paris after the breakdown of yet another attempt to negotiate an end to the war in Southeast Asia. Following their successful spring invasion, the North Vietnamese were unwilling to make concessions. President Nixon believed that Operation Linebacker would cause them to reconsider, but he saw the timing of the operation as crucial. In two weeks he was to visit Moscow for a long-planned summit meeting with General Secretary Brezhnev on which he had placed high hopes. A resumption of large-scale air attacks on North Vietnam might wreck that summit. The President agonized on whether to order the bombing and put the summit talks at risk or to withhold permission until the talks were over. Later he wrote:

> The arguments on both sides seemed persuasive. It was hard to see how I could go to the summit and be clinking glasses with Brezhnev while Soviet tanks were rumbling through Hué or Quang Tri. That would show callousness, or weakness, or both. For us to cancel the summit, however, would inevitably be criticized as an impulsive action that dashed the hopes for progress toward a more peaceful world.

On May 8 the President summoned the National Security Council and announced his decision: Operation Linebacker was to proceed. At 1:40 P.M. that day, Washington time, the executive order to mine North Vietnamese ports was transmitted down the chain of command to Task Force 77 in the Gulf of Tonkin.

· · ·

OFF HAIPHONG, 8:00 A.M. local time, May 9. Six hours and twenty minutes after the executive order left the Pentagon, A-6 and A-7 planes from the USS *Coral Sea* released mines into the waterways leading to the port. Soon afterward other mines splashed into the sea off Cam Pha, Hon Gai, Vinh and Thanh Hoa.

At its first step Operation Linebacker came close to sparking an international incident. Off Haiphong the Soviet merchant ships *Pevek* and *Babouchkine* came under fire and suffered damage and casualties. It is not clear whether the rounds came from U.S. planes or from North Vietnamese antiaircraft guns engaging those planes.

AT 9:00 P.M. on May 8, Washington time, one hour after the first mines were dropped, President Nixon went on television to deliver a major speech to the nation on developments in the conflict in Southeast Asia. His face stern, the President spoke slowly to emphasize the gravity of his words. After a brief review of the war situation, he said he believed the nation had now to choose one of three courses of action: immediate withdrawal of all American forces from Southeast Asia; continued attempts at negotiation; decisive military action to force the North Vietnamese to soften their hard line. After expressing his firm belief that acceptance of either of the first two would result only in increased bloodshed in the area, the President said he had reluctantly decided to adopt the third option: "I have ordered the following measures, which are being implemented as I am speaking to you. All entrances to North Vietnamese ports will be mined to prevent access to these ports and North Vietnamese naval operations from these ports. United States forces have been directed to take appropriate measures within the internal and claimed territorial waters of North Vietnam to interdict the delivery of supplies. Rail and all other communications will be cut off to the maximum extent possible. Air and naval strikes against military targets in North Vietnam will continue."

To allow foreign ships to leave North Vietnamese ports safely, the mines were set to become "live" at 6:00 P.M. Hanoi time on

May 11. Any ship passing through North Vietnamese waters after that time would do so at its own risk.

Forty-seven minutes after the President began his speech, the Pentagon issued the executive order to launch the next phase of Operation Linebacker. The onslaught against land targets was to begin on the next full day in North Vietnam: May 10, 1972.

PRINCIPAL U.S. AIR BASES IN SOUTHEAST ASIA

MORNING, MAY 10

Midnight–7:00 a.m.

After stratagem has failed, let the sword decide.
—Arab proverb

12:01 A.M., GULF OF TONKIN. As May 10 began its eventful course in North Vietnam, six darkened ships of a U.S. Navy Task Group moved northwest at speed, each trailing a luminous off-white wake. Commanded by Vice Admiral William Mack, the force comprised the cruisers *Oklahoma City, Providence* and *Newport News* and the destroyers *Fox, Hanson* and *Buchanan. Newport News* was to bombard targets near Haiphong; the other ships were to provide covering fire should North Vietnamese forces retaliate.

At 2:00 A.M. the ships arrived off the coast and their crews went to General Quarters. Forty-five minutes later the eight-inch guns of *Newport News* barked out her first shells, each weighing 335 pounds, at targets up to fourteen miles away. North Vietnamese coastal batteries returned the fire and the other warships joined in the exchange. The artillery duel lasted about twenty minutes, during which *Newport News* fired 77 eight-inch shells and 40 five-inch shells. Then, unscathed, the warships broke off the action and headed out to sea.

YANKEE STATION. As the early morning stillness returned to Haiphong the scene moved two hundred miles south. At Yankee Station, at sea off the border that was supposed to separate North Vietnam from the South, the attack carriers *Constellation, Kitty Hawk* (both 74,000 tons) and the older and smaller *Coral Sea* (49,000 tons) cruised slowly with their attendant destroyers.* Ahead lay a heavy day of operations and the rows of planes, many loaded with ordnance, sat with wings neatly folded. For now the angular F-4s, the benign-looking A-6s, the dumpy A-7s and the big RA-5Cs and EKA-3Bs were silent—quiescent metal forms awaiting the human catalyst that would bring them to life.

THAILAND. At Ubon, Udorn, Takhli, Korat and U-Tapao, the U.S. Air Force bases whose planes were to mount the attacks on North Vietnam, ground crews were hard at work in the early morning darkness preparing the planes and loading ordnance.

Around 3:30 A.M. the aircrews assigned to the mission were awakened and started to dress. Shortly before four the men began arriving at their respective officers' clubs for breakfast. To Captain James Allen, an F-4 pilot at Ubon, this was a giveaway that a major mission was in the offing. "It was obviously no secret. There was too much excitement, too many people eating. Everybody was talking about it. If the enemy had spies among the staff at the officers' club, and I think they did, they must have realized."

Ubon was home to the F-4 bombers of the 8th Tactical Fighter Wing, which formed the kernel of the strike forces to attack targets in North Vietnam. From Udorn would come more F-4s, those of the 432nd Tactical Reconnaissance Wing, to provide reconnaissance and fighter support for raids. From Korat, home of the 388th Tactical Fighter Wing, would come the F-105s and

*For a full list of U.S. warships in the Gulf of Tonkin, see Appendix C.

EB-66s providing defense suppression and electronic counter-measures support. From U-Tapao would come the high-flying U-2 reconnaissance aircraft. Also from U-Tapao, and from Takhli, would come the KC-135 tankers providing the fuel necessary for fighter-bombers to reach targets deep in North Vietnam.

The first plane to take off as part of the force raiding North Vietnam that day, however, came from outside the Southeast Asian operational theater.

OKINAWA, 6:00 A.M. local time (4:00 A.M. Hanoi time). At Kadena Air Force Base a single Boeing RC-135M of the 82nd Strategic Reconnaissance Squadron, 376th Strategic Wing, lifted noisily off the runway. After takeoff the plane turned southeast and climbed slowly to cruising altitude. Based on the design of the Boeing 707 airliner, the RC-135M carried a 35-man crew and a fuselage packed with sensitive electronic receiving equipment. Ahead lay a three-hour flight to the Gulf of Tonkin.

4:00 A.M., HANOI. Beside the Thong Nhat Hotel, near the center of the capital, a party of sleepy foreign journalists began boarding the official cars and jeeps sent to pick them up. The correspondents were to attend a news conference later that morning in the port of Haiphong, to hear official reaction on the U.S. mining operation the day before. Most of the newspapermen came from Communist-bloc countries, though there were a few Westerners, including Théodore Ronco and Claude Julien representing the French newspapers *L'Humanité* and *Le Monde*.

The cars set out in trail, headlights illuminating the near-deserted streets as they snaked their way to the northeast edge of the city. Slowly the vehicles trundled across the Paul Doumer Bridge over the Red River, its structure bearing the scars of air attacks in the past. For most of the correspondents it would be their last crossing of the famous bridge.

Once east of the Red River, the vehicles gathered speed. Although on maps it appeared as a major arterial road, the old French Colonial Route 5 from Hanoi to Haiphong was not in the league of the Pennsylvania Turnpike. The Vietnamese road was a simple asphalt surface just wide enough for two vehicles to pass. In poor repair, it had so many potholes that it was dangerous to exceed twenty-five mph.

Dawn came shortly after 5:00 A.M., the first trace of watery pink that pulled from sight the patterns of stars to the east. During the minutes that followed, the sky brightened rapidly as the sun's disk rose above the horizon. It promised to be another fine day.

DAWN came to Thailand a few minutes later. The second plane to take off in support of the attack was a lone Lockheed U-2 of the 99th Strategic Reconnaissance Squadron based at U-Tapao. Shortly after first light the spindly all-black plane lifted off the ground, raised its snout to the heavens and rose steeply like a kite borne upward on a strong wind. It leveled out at around 70,000 feet and made its silent way toward North Vietnam. This plane was to act as a communications intelligence relay: to pick up enemy radio traffic and relay it to the collection center in Thailand.

Following the U-2, a single RF-4C of the 14th Tactical Reconnaissance Squadron took off from Udorn. Its task was to conduct a weather reconnaissance over North Vietnam and to check that the designated target areas were clear of cloud.

At Ubon Lieutenant Colonel Rick Hilton, an F-4 pilot of the 433rd Tactical Fighter Squadron, was donning flight gear before the mission. While he did so he recorded his thoughts on a tape to send his wife, Ann:

> It's early and we're going on a special mission on this morning. Because of security I can't tell you, yet, where we're going in case we don't go and the tape would be available for somebody to listen to. But after the President's speech you've a good idea of what kind of missions we're going on these days and the sort of targets. . . .
>
> It's starting to get light outside, and it really looks good. The clouds are very high. The sun is not up yet, but it's light outside.

The sun is coming up and it's shining on the clouds. I don't know how this one is going to go this morning. . . .

I'm guilty on this tape of what I was on the others—you said I didn't have any words for you and it was just a matter-of-fact conversation and we weren't communicating. But we will, love, soon. I love you.

Also at Ubon Lieutenant Colonel Brad Sharp, operations officer of the 25th Tactical Fighter Squadron, went to the ramp to see how his maintenance crews were doing: "I would go down and walk the flight line and tell the guys what was going on. I figured that if they knew, they might tighten up those bolts a little better. They would be watching out for me and had some coffee ready. They called me 'the old man,' though half of those grizzly sergeants were old enough to be my dad."

Soon after 6:00 A.M. crews began arriving at the intelligence center at Ubon for the briefing, to learn of the targets for the day and their place in the operations. The 8th Wing was assigned two main targets: the Paul Doumer Bridge at Hanoi and the Yen Vien railroad sorting yard to the northeast of the city. If bad weather prevented these attacks, the Wing's alternate targets were the Thanh Hoa bridge and Bai Thong airfield in the center of the country. On this day Air Force and Navy strike forces would not operate simultaneously over North Vietnam, thus ensuring that planes from one service did not get in the way of those from the other.

Attack forces were to approach their targets at altitudes around 15,000 feet, where they would be low enough to make difficult targets for the SAMs while remaining beyond the reach of most types of antiaircraft fire. The planes would rely on their self-protection jamming equipment to shield them from radar-directed missiles and heavy-caliber guns. They would attack in a dive, releasing their bombs as high as possible commensurate with accurate delivery—about 12,000 feet for "smart" bombs against the bridge, about 9,000 feet for unguided bombs against the rail yard. Unless absolutely necessary for the mission, planes were to avoid flying below 3,500 feet over defended areas, where optically aimed small-caliber automatic fire could be lethal.

Lieutenant Lanny Toups, an F-4 back-seater, knew it was going to be a big mission the moment he stepped into the briefing room. On his previous missions there had never been more than ten crews present; there were forty crews at this briefing.

Captain Mike Messett had a personal score to settle with the Paul Doumer Bridge. As a back-seater he had flown on the very first attack against the bridge, in August 1967. During the action an 85-mm shell exploded beside his F-4, causing severe damage and wounding the pilot. Messett took control from the backseat, jettisoned the bombs and brought the crippled plane home, an act for which he was later awarded the Silver Star. Now he was to lead a pair of F-4s attacking the bridge with laser-guided bombs.

Lieutenant Brewster Shaw, one of the F-4 pilots assigned to attack the Yen Vien rail yard, summed up the general mood when crews learned of their targets: "Everybody thought that attacking North Vietnam would bring the end of the war closer, everyone was excited about doing that. But there was an element of fear about going North because that was where all the bad stuff was. So most people had mixed emotions."

Brad Sharp particularly remembered the intelligence briefing: "We had this big map of North Vietnam, with all the high-threat areas marked in red. Well, almost the whole damn map was red, I don't know why the intelligence people bothered! They would show a little corridor we could squeeze through where there was a medium-threat area, but we might have to go two hundred miles out of our way to do that. It got to be a joke, because either you joke or you cry about a thing like that."

Lieutenants Barry Morgan and Jim Dunn, F-4 pilots with the 433rd Tactical Fighter Squadron, never made it to the main briefing at Ubon. The first Morgan knew of the mission was when he was rudely awakened soon after 5:00 A.M. "Somebody banged on our door. He said there was a big briefing at the squadron and we were to get down there. When we showed up, the mass briefing was over, everybody was going out. Only then did we see our names were listed on the board, to fly with a chaff flight." New arrivals on the squadron straight from training, Morgan and Dunn received hasty briefings for their first-ever mission over North Vietnam.

After the main briefing there was an unofficial alteration to the Paul Doumer Bridge attack plan. Instead of taking the briefed egress route around the north of Hanoi, the crews agreed to run over the center of the city accelerating to Mach 1.2 at 7,000 feet. The sonic booms created, it was hoped, would tell Americans incarcerated in the "Hanoi Hilton" that they had not been forgotten and give a fillip to morale.

The briefing at Korat for crews assigned to the Wild Weasel and radar-jamming missions had its usual canine observer, Roscoe. A mongrel with a trace of German Shepherd in his ancestry, Roscoe had come to Korat in the cockpit of an F-105 some years earlier. When his master was shot down over North Vietnam the dog became mascot of the 388th Tactical Fighter Wing. "Roscoe had the run of the base," remembered Major Don Kilgus, an F-105 Wild Weasel pilot with the 561st Tactical Fighter Squadron. "He would sit by the road, and you had to stop and let him get in your vehicle. His seat was in front on the passenger's side—if anyone was sitting there he had to climb in the back so the dog could get in.

"Roscoe always attended the strike briefings. It was said that if he slept through the briefing it was going to be a good mission; but if he was alert it was going to be a bad day." The authors have found no record of whether Roscoe slept through the briefing on this occasion.

TAN SON NHUT, SAIGON. Shortly after dawn General John Vogt walked the few hundred yards from the bungalow where he lived to his headquarters. On arrival he went straight to his Command Center, "Blue Chip." The Center, a room the size of a small theater within the main headquarters building, had been a hive of activity since he left it the previous evening. Against a background of subdued chatter, the staff of about fifty officers and enlisted personnel sitting in rows facing the commander's dais made last-minute adjustments or confirmed points of detail with the operational units in Thailand. Vogt received an update on the latest developments and was shown signals that had come in during the night and required immediate attention. Then, satisfied that the operation was proceeding along the lines he wished, he walked to his office to attend to other aspects of running his command.

AT YANKEE Station signalman Greg Slavonic was on watch as a lookout on *Constellation*'s signal bridge: "The sunrise that morning was really beautiful. There was little activity on the flight deck, the day hadn't really got started. It was real quiet and there was a lot of time to reflect on what might happen."

Although his post was on *Constellation*'s deck as dawn broke, Lieutenant Steve Rudloff's duty demanded little. While in the war zone each carrier maintained a pair of fighters and a pair of attack planes on deck alert, with crews in the cockpits. He was radar intercept officer in one of the F-4s. Sometimes the planes were scrambled in response to enemy activity, but it did not happen on this morning. Rudloff managed to snatch a little sleep before his two-hour stint ended and the relief crew arrived at 6:00 A.M.

Slowly the ship came to life. While the planes received final preparations, the ship's own systems had also to be checked to ensure they worked properly. Airman Loren Bidwell helped with the daily check-out of one of *Constellation*'s bow catapults: the men carefully examined the long rubber seals running the length of the tracks, then made three or four "dry" shots to confirm that the mechanism functioned as it should. There were similar checks at the ship's three other catapults. At the stern the cables and gear of the all-important arrester wires received their daily check too.

Soon after 6:00 A.M. the flyers assigned to the day's first attack mission began receiving their final briefings. There the briefings were much shorter than at the land bases, for the Navy crews had been told their targets the previous evening and had already completed most of their flight planning. Each of the three carriers on Yankee Station was to launch an Alpha Strike (a maximum-effort attack) on Haiphong. *Constellation*'s target was the petro-leum-storage area west of the city, *Coral Sea*'s aircraft were to bomb the railroad yard, and *Kitty Hawk*'s aircraft were to attack the main rail and highway bridge leading out of the port.

Phantom pilot Lieutenant Randy Cunningham was not assigned to the first mission, and had time on his hands. He walked to the catwalk beside *Constellation*'s flight deck and gazed at the low, wispy clouds turned a beautiful orange by the rising sun. Yet the sight could not keep his thoughts from problems brewing half a world away. "My mind would wander back to home, my wife and child and the possibility that I might never see them again. I fought back tears and a lump in my throat often. This brooding had come over me on the morning of the tenth, only more consuming. A few days earlier I had received a 'Dear John letter' from my wife. She wanted out of the marriage. . . ."

7:00 A.M., NORTHERN LAOS AND THE GULF OF TONKIN. By now most of the planes and the ship forming the electronic surveillance force were at their assigned stations off North Vietnam, or would soon reach them. The planes involved in this part of the operation were an odd assortment. In addition to the Boeing RC-135M from Okinawa and the U-2 from Thailand, there was an elderly EC-121D Constellation radar picket plane of the 552nd Airborne Warning and Control Wing from Korat in Thailand. From Da Nang in South Vietnam came an EP-3B Orion Sigint plane of Navy Squadron VQ-1. Completing the force, though for the time being they remained on their carriers *Kitty Hawk* and *Constellation*, were a couple of E-2B Hawkeye radar picket planes.

Except for the high-flying U-2, which flew alone, the planes were to work as a team with the cruiser *Chicago* in the Gulf of Tonkin. *Chicago* was designated as PIRAZ (Positive Identification Radar Advisory Zone) ship and her combat information center was to keep track of enemy movements using data from all sources. The ship's own radars and those on the radar picket planes would provide some of the plots, but due to ground clutter these radars had limited ability to track planes flying low over land. To assist with such tracking the electronic surveillance force relied on secret signals intelligence (Sigint) techniques, which even now, more than fifteen years later, cannot be described in detail.

During the 1960s progress in miniaturized electronic systems had led to a quantum leap in capability, and the new supersensitive receivers could pick up and analyze signals that previously had been too feeble to use. Sigint made use of the latest equipment to exploit electromagnetic radiations by the enemy. A MiG-21 fighter, for example, radiated signals from its airborne intercept radar, its radar identification equipment (IFF), its radio altimeter, its VHF radio and its radio navigational system. By taking a running bearing on any one of these signals, the plane's movements could be tracked. In a separate application, Sigint could warn when a SAM battery was about to launch, from the distinctive signals radiated.

By the 1970s Sigint analysis had become so rapid that information could be passed out in real time to assist U.S. forces in contact with the enemy. *Chicago* carried a small team for this purpose, commanded by Lieutenant Guy Thomas. To safeguard the confidentiality of the source, all Sigint information passed out over normal communications channels was to sound as if it had been learned from *Chicago*'s own radars.

On the morning of May 10, as the U.S. attack units girded themselves for action the electronic snoopers prepared for a busy day's eavesdropping.

7:00 A.M., HAIPHONG. Three hours after leaving Hanoi the convoy of vehicles carrying the foreign journalists reached Haiphong. Passing through the port, Henri Joel of the Agence France Presse noted the nationalities of the eleven freighters tied up at the dockside: five were Soviet, two Chinese, two Polish, one was British and one North Vietnamese. Several other cargo ships were moored to buoys in the harbor.

The journalists' first stop was at the city hospital, to interview Soviet sailors wounded when their ship was hit the previous day. From there the party went to a nearby hotel for the press conference. The harbor director stated briefly that American planes had dropped mines in the channels leading to the port, and clearance operations were about to begin. Ships that had unloaded would leave Haiphong before 6:00 P.M. the following day, when the U.S. government had said the mines would become live. The rest of the ships would remain in port to finish unloading. The journalists were told that earlier that morning American "destroyers" had come within eight miles of the coast to bombard Do Son and other villages south of Haiphong. Coastal batteries had returned the fire and claimed hits on two of the warships. After the U.S. president's speech, nobody doubted that these operations were only a start. The full-scale resumption of attacks on North Vietnam might take place any day.

TARGET HAIPHONG

6:45–9:15 a.m.

Fierce fiery warriors fought upon the clouds,
In ranks and squadrons and right form of war.
            —Shakespeare, *Julius Caesar*

6:45 A.M., YANKEE STATION. On USS *Constellation* the aircrews assigned to the first mission of the day strode purposefully out on deck carrying helmets and flight bags and weighed down by survival gear. When they reached their planes the crews began the essential ritual of the preflight checks. They pushed against missiles, bombs and tanks to assure themselves they had been rigidly attached. Eyes scanned the array of panels for any left open or unlocked, peered into intakes for anything loose waiting to be sucked into the gaping maw and wreck the engine's delicate innards, glanced at the deck for the patch of wet that might betray a fuel or hydraulic leak. The aircrew check was a backstop: all of these things should already have been done by the planes' captains. But once a pilot accepted a plane he alone was responsible for the costly piece of machinery and would be held accountable for its fate. All humans are fallible, and the penalties of failure were too severe for normal considerations of politeness or trust to hold sway.

The external rites completed, the flyers climbed into the confines of cockpits permeated by the indefinable, slightly acrid odor that goes with a military jet. Surrounded by the familiar galaxy of dials, switches, buttons and levers, each man strapped himself tightly to the ejection seat on which his life might depend. Then in each plane there began the private ceremony of bringing it to life. Within minutes similar scenes were being enacted on the decks of *Coral Sea* and *Kitty Hawk*. Shortly afterward the sense of quiet bustle on each ship was shattered by a series of loud *pooofs*, followed by loudening whines, as engines started.

At 7:15, as the crews assigned to the attack forces went through their well-practiced routine, *Constellation* turned south into the wind and her planeguard destroyer USS *Badger* slid dutifully into position two miles behind. A single E-2B Hawkeye aircraft sped off one of the bow catapults, then *Constellation* resumed her northerly heading, downwind, to position herself for the launch of the main force. Burdened by a powerful long-range search radar, the slow propeller-driven plane needed a long start if it was to be in position near the target area when the attack began.

Fifteen minutes later, *Constellation* turned into the wind once again, this time to launch her strike force. During a massed launch danger lurked almost everywhere on a carrier's deck. The slightest act of carelessness could have terrible consequences for the perpetrator or those nearby. Garrett Olinde, one of the "green-shirts" assigned to hook planes to the ship's port bow catapult, wrote graphically on the scene of barely controlled violence:

> Planes, men and tractors constantly flowed in a surrealistic dance of moving aircraft and potential death. One became adept at running under rapidly taxying aircraft, simultaneously dodging intakes, wheels and exhausts, all of which could kill very quickly. You learned to keep an eye on your work and the other on the

lookout for a half-witted plane director about to make an aircraft either run over someone, or blow him off the deck.

I wore a plastic and canvas helmet designed to protect the wearer from small flying objects and to deaden the sound (an F-4 in afterburner is painful at 100 feet; we routinely stood 10 to 15 feet from them). Other items of equipment included goggles, leather gloves, steel-toed shoes, and a life preserver in case one was blown overboard. The launchings had looked impressive from the island; however, at a few feet their power was tremendous.

Constellation was farthest south of the carriers on Yankee Station, so she was first to launch her strike. Twenty minutes later the process began on *Coral Sea*, ten minutes after that on *Kitty Hawk*. To shoot off the thirty or so aircraft for an Alpha Strike took a well-drilled deck crew about ten minutes, using all four catapults. As the last machine left each carrier the noise and the bustle and the danger of the preceding minutes suddenly evaporated. It was as if an orchestra had completed the crescendo at the close of a complex musical passage, just before the intermission. No round of applause greeted the end of this performance, however; during the launch of an Alpha Strike the players far outnumbered the audience.

The first of the main force to launch had been the tanker planes, the EKA-3Bs and KA-6s, which now climbed to fifteen thousand feet and circled their mother ships. These planes served as markers on which the rest assembled into formation, and also they passed fuel to the F-4s, which needed to top off their tanks before setting out on the mission. In ones and twos, the rest of the planes spiraled up to join the carousel over their ship.

Half an hour elapsed between the first launch and the time the last plane joined the formation. *Constellation*'s thirty-three-plane strike force for the attack on Haiphong—those from the other two carriers were similar—comprised sixteen bombers and seventeen supporters:

Six A-6 Intruders, each carrying sixteen 500-pound bombs,
Ten A-7 Corsairs, each carrying twelve 500-pound bombs,

U.S. NAVY AIR SQUADRONS ON YANKEE STATION, MAY 10, 1972

(Unit radio call signs that day, where known, in parentheses)

USS *Coral Sea* (CVA-43)
Carrier Air Wing 15

VF-51	12 F-4B (Screaming Eagle)
VF-111	11 F-4B (Old Nick)
VA-22	10 A-7E (Beefeater)
VA-94	12 A-7E (Hoboken)
VMA (AW)-224	13 A-6A and B; 3 KA-6D (Bengal)
VAQ-135 (Det)	3 EKA-3B (Lightning Bolt)
VFP-63	2 RF-8G
HC-1	4 SH-3G

USS *Kitty Hawk* (CVA-63)
Carrier Air Wing 11

VF-114	12 F-4J (Linfield)
VF-213	10 F-4J (Black)
VA-192	10 A-7E (Jury)
VA-195	11 A-7E (Chippie)
VA-52	12 A-6A and B; 3 KA-6D (Viceroy)
RVAH-7	4 RA-5C
VAW-114	4 E-2B (Hormel)
VAQ-135 (Det)	2 EKA-3B
HC-1	4 SH-3G
HC-7	5 HH-3A

USS *Constellation* (CVA-64)
Carrier Air Wing 9

VF-92	12 F-4J (Silverkite)
VF-96	12 F-4J (Showtime)
VA-146	10 A-7E (Busybee)
VA-147	12 A-7E (Jason)
VA-165	12 A-6A, 4 KA-6D (Boomer)
RVAH-11	4 RA-5C (Glenrock)
VAQ-130 (Det)	2 EKA-3B (Gunpowder)
VAW-116	4 E-2B (Sun King)
HC-1	3 SH-3G

USS *Okinawa* (LPH-3)

HC-7	3 HH-3A (Big Mother) Search and Rescue
HMM-164	14 CH-46D, 6 CH-53D and 3 UH-1E

Nine F-4 Phantom escorts, each carrying four Sparrow and four Sidewinder air-to-air missiles,

Four F-4s configured for flak suppression and escort, each carrying six Rockeye cluster bombs and two Sparrow and four Sidewinder air-to-air missiles,

Two A-7s configured for the Iron Hand missile suppression role, each carrying two Shrike radar-homing missiles and six cluster bombs,

One RA-5C Vigilante reconnaissance aircraft,

One EKA-3B Skywarrior tanker and electronic counter-measures aircraft.

At 8:00 A.M. *Constellation*'s Air Wing set course for Haiphong, heading up the Gulf of Tonkin. The formations from the other two carriers swung into line behind at ten-minute—sixty-mile—intervals. Soon the entire force was assembled, some ninety planes heading majestically north-northwest at fifteen thousand feet, like troops on parade advancing in review order. Lieutenant Mike Bolier, flying a flak suppression F-4, was one of several impressed by the show of force: "As we went in I looked at the strike force—I remember thinking, God, this is like the old movies, all these planes! There were about thirty airplanes spread out over a three-mile area. And the radar pings heard on the warning gear meant the North Vietnamese knew we were coming."

THE NORTH VIETNAMESE certainly knew the planes were coming. The assembly of *Coral Sea*'s and *Kitty Hawk*'s formations and the flight to Haiphong took place in full view of early warning radars along the coast. Moreover, the Soviet intelligence ship *Kursograf,* cruising in the Gulf of Tonkin, was well placed to observe the movements of American ships and aircraft in the area.

USS *Constellation*'s Air Wing leads the attack, with those from *Coral Sea* and *Kitty Hawk* following at 10-minute (60-mile) intervals. On their way to the target the air wings fly past the Soviet intelligence ship *Kursograf* monitoring activity in the Gulf of Tonkin, then past the Red Crown control ship USS *Chicago*. The limit of the North Vietnamese early warning radar cover is shown (A), as is the approximate boundary of the SAM zone (B). The ships continually changed positions and those shown are approximate.

THE RAIDERS APPROACH HAIPHONG, 8:32 A.M. ON MAY 10, 1972

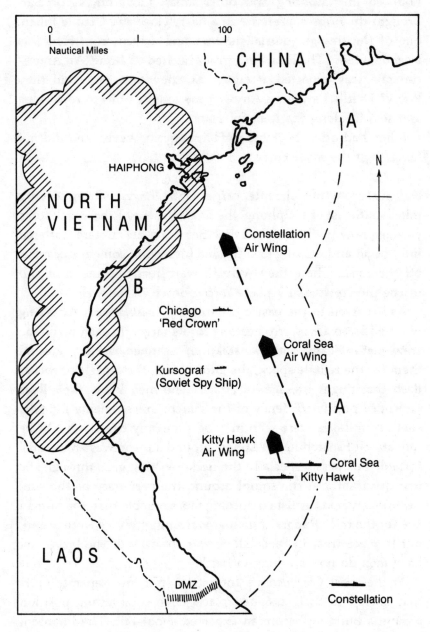

Soon after 7:30 A.M. an early warning of the attack was announced in Haiphong and other areas. Government officials brought the press conference to a hasty close and Claude Julien, one of the foreign journalists who had driven from Hanoi to attend, noted: "The local authorities hurried us along. An American raid was expected at eight A.M. they said. How did they know? That is a mystery. Anyway the convoy of jeeps re-formed and set out along the road for Hanoi."

Julien had other business in Haiphong, however, and did not leave with the main party.

8:39 A.M. From the helicopter carrier USS *Okinawa*, sitting seventy miles southeast of Haiphong, the final element of the attack force package now got airborne. Three Sea King helicopters clattered into the air and, staying low, headed for a point some thirty miles off the coast. There they were to wait, ready to move in and rescue the crew of any plane forced down in the area.

As it passed to the east of Haiphong, *Constellation*'s Air Wing wheeled on to a westerly heading for its target. In each plane the crew methodically and painstakingly scanned the sky around them for the telltale speck, the glint of sun, the muzzle or rocket flash that might presage an attack. The men knew their lives depended on the efficiency of the search: unless enemy fighters, shells or missiles were seen in good time, any evasion might be too late. But searching the sphere around a plane was an uncomfortable business, especially the neck-twisting gaze through the rear quadrant and the squint around the periphery of the sun. Technology had furnished nothing more reliable than the human eye for the task. Radars and radar warning receivers were useful, but to place trust in those alone was the way of the lazy man. Lazy men do not live long in battle.

At the coast *Constellation*'s formation split into separate units that moved to their assigned places, like cops taking position around a building before an expected shoot-out. The Phantom escorts made for their patrol areas to the north, west and south of Haiphong, ready to ward off incoming MiGs. The Iron Hand A-7s dropped back and began flying "S" turns, waiting for SAM radars to turn on so they could home in and attack them. The EKA-3B electronic warfare plane climbed to twenty thousand feet and orbited southeast of the port, from which position it jammed enemy air defense radars in the area. The bombers and the attendant flak suppression Phantoms made straight for the petroleum-storage area.

Passing just north of Haiphong in a flak suppression Phantom, Mike Bolier observed several merchant ships anchored in the waterway waiting to unload. They were off limits for attack, and the sight angered him: "We couldn't touch those ships, but we would often risk thirty planes at a time to go and bomb what turned out to be piss-poor targets."

Immediately afterward the first shots of the action boomed out. Antiaircraft batteries opened fire at the A-6 flight and clusters of black and white smoke puffs surrounded the planes. But the gun-control radars had been effectively jammed and the bursts were too far away to inflict damage. In reply, four Phantoms dived through a crosshatch of tracer to lay their cluster bombs across the gun positions. Mike Bolier recalled: "I remember seeing tracers coming up. If you try to concentrate on a target and that stuff comes by your head, the initial reaction is to duck to the left or the right. In the end I thought, Jeez, that's pretty stupid. If it's going to hit me it's going to hit me! I released my CBUs and pulled up." Although they came under vigorous return fire, the Phantoms escaped damage.

IN HAIPHONG Claude Julien had remained behind after the main party of journalists left the city. At first it seemed the report of an impending American attack was a false alarm, for 8:00 A.M. passed without incident. Then, nearly three-quarters of an hour later, the hotel shook as a nearby antiaircraft battery opened fire. The port's sirens sounded their long-drawn-out note of warning and the French reporter was hustled to an underground shelter.

> I was pushed into the shelter 2.50 meters [9 feet] under the ground. I measured it: 7.50 m [24 feet] long, 1.50 m [5 feet] wide and hardly 1.70 [5½ feet] high and in that confined space crouched

some 30 people. Most of my companions were workmen who had been repairing trucks and military vehicles in the square nearby. The young woman opposite me was calm at first but ended up by stopping her ears with her hands, elbows on her knees. Her neighbor, who was older, put an arm around her shoulder.

AROUND HAIPHONG the SAM radar beams began sweeping the sky as batteries prepared to engage the raiders. One of the Iron Hand A-7s curved in to deliver an attack on one launching site, and as it did so a missile rose off the ground in a huge cloud of smoke and headed for the bombers. The A-7 loosed off a Shrike homing missile at the enemy radar, forcing the North Vietnamese operators to shut down. During the next few minutes the other Iron Hand A-7 engaged a couple of missile sites active west of Haiphong, and forced their radars to shut down also.

The Iron Hand operations were having the usual effect. The Shrike homing missiles forced the Fansong radars to shut down, thus depriving the air-launched missile of guidance. But any SAMs airborne under control of that Fansong received no further guidance either, and the ground-launched missiles arced aimlessly across the sky until they reached the end of their trajectories and blew themselves up. Patrolling to the south of Haiphong, two Phantom crews observed this sequence of events: On the radar warning receiver they heard the distinctive rattle as a Fansong radar tracked them and they saw a SAM heading in their direction. Then, probably following a Shrike launch, the radar signals ceased abruptly. The missile lost interest, missed them by a wide margin and exploded in the distance.

With the supporting planes taking on the defenses, the bombers were able to reach the target unscathed. Two by two the aircraft peeled into their 45-degree attack dives, released their bombs at 7,000 feet, pulled up steeply to keep above 3,500 feet, and sped out of the area. Trains of bombs stitched across the petroleum-storage tanks, starting several fires.

As a parting shot, after launching their Shrikes at SAM sites, the two Iron Hand A-7s dropped their cluster bombs on Kien An airfield west of Haiphong.

"THIS IS Teaball on Guard. SAM, SAM, Haiphong . . ."

"Teaball" was the RC-135 Sigint plane from Okinawa, now orbiting over the Gulf of Tonkin; "Guard" was the 243 megahertz emergency frequency that most crews monitored in addition to the main communications channel. The plane's operators had picked up telltale emissions from a SAM site preparing to launch missiles and broadcast a warning to the force.

The last of *Constellation's* aircraft through the target area was an RA-5C Vigilante taking the poststrike photos, and its escorting Phantom, flown by Lieutenant John Olsen. Heading toward Haiphong from the east at 4,000 feet, the pair closed on their target at 600 knots. At low altitude the clean-lined Vigilante was faster than an F-4 carrying tanks and missiles and Olsen had difficulty keeping up. "I was dropping further and further behind the Vigie; I remember being concerned about that. I decided that when he turned over the city I would cut the turn and catch up. I was not particularly concerned about MiGs; I was more worried about ground fire. I had never been over Haiphong; it's a big place and it's scary to be over a major city— there's nowhere to hide. My radar warning receiver was going crazy with rattles and groans!"

The SAMs were not long in coming, launched simultaneously from two separate sites. Olsen continued: "My RIO [Lt. Al Kraut] yelled that SAMs were coming in from three o'clock [from the right]. I glanced over there and I saw something, but as I turned my head I caught sight of something in front of the airplane: two dots with fire around them. I couldn't see the sides of the missiles, only dots. They were coming straight for me! I yelled to the Vigie to pull up, and I pulled up." Seconds later the missile nearest Olsen exploded, tossing his plane upside down like a flapjack. "The concussion knocked our Phantom on its back, one of the generators went out and a bunch of circuit breakers popped." Olsen righted the plane and reset the generator and the circuit

THE CLOCK CODE

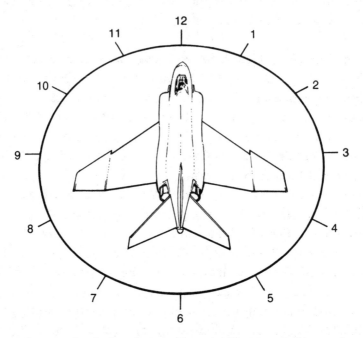

12
11   1
10   2
9   3
8   4
7   5
6

Fighter pilots use the clock code to indicate the direction of objects relative to their plane, as if it were in the center of a clock face; the nose points to 12 o'clock and the rear to 6 o'clock. Thus a call "SAM coming in from 3 o'clock" means there is a missile coming from right.

breakers. The Phantom and its crew were lucky to escape with only a shaking.

Commander Al Neuman, piloting an F-4 on patrol in the area, watched the other missile streaking up toward the Vigilante: "The Vigie was out in front of us, down below. I watched the SAM come up, everybody was calling it. It went off right under him, then a cloud of smoke and the plane disappeared. I thought that was the end of it. But the Vigie came out the other side and pressed on to the target." Splinters from the warhead rammed into the reconnaissance plane, though without causing serious damage and without the crew realizing it. Throughout it all the Vigilante's cameras had been running and one of them had photographed the missile as it detonated. The reconnaissance

plane completed its run, then darted back for the coast, Olsen's
F-4 trailing behind.

TEN miles west of Haiphong at 14,000 feet, Lieutenant Austin
Hawkins led a pair of Phantoms of VF-92 on patrol. The planes'
radars swept the sky ahead for enemy fighters, but it seemed the
MiGs were not coming up to fight. From time to time Lieutenant
Curtis Dosé, flying on Hawkins's wing, glanced toward the harbor. He could not see the bombers, they were too far away; but
there were several signs of a raid in progress: flashes from exploding bombs, smoke rising from the blazing fuel tanks, puffs from
the antiaircraft shell bursts and orangy-white trails from SAMs
arcing across the sky.

As *Constellation*'s bombers left the coast each element transmitted a brief "Feet wet!" radio call with the plane's side numbers;
this enabled the crew of "Sun King," the Hawkeye radar plane
orbiting off the coast, to keep tally of the planes leaving enemy
territory. After several such calls, a quite different one seized the
attention of fighter crews:

"This is Red Crown on Guard. Bandits. Bullseye zero-three-
five for twenty-three, altitude unknown, time four-six. Out."

"Red Crown" was the call sign of the cruiser *Chicago,* the control ship in the Gulf of Tonkin. "Bandits" were enemy fighters.
"Bullseye" was the code word for Hanoi, the reference point for
such messages, and the bearing of 035 degrees at twenty-three
miles put the enemy fighters near Kep airfield. Kep lay forty miles
northwest of Haiphong—about five minutes' flying time for a
MiG.

Austin Hawkins was nearing the end of his tour without a
successful MiG engagement. The previous evening he had
briefed Lieutenant Charles Tinker, his back-seater, on his inten-
tions if he got the chance. Tinker recalled: "He told me there were
MiGs at Kep airfield, and once our attack guys were on their way
out we were going to take a look at Kep." Such unauthorized
probes were strictly forbidden, and Tinker had to promise not to
divulge the plan to anyone. Following the MiG call, Hawkins

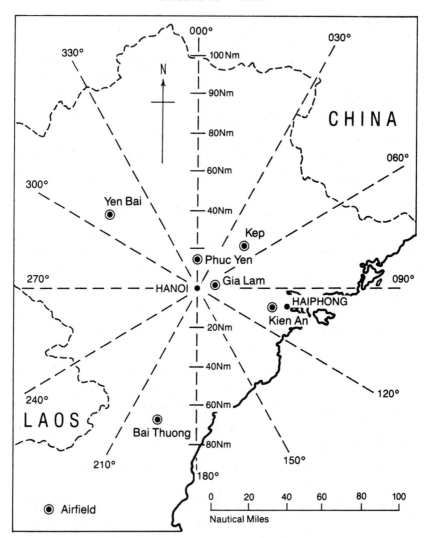

Broadcasts from U.S. surveillance ships or planes gave the position of MiGs as a bearing and distance relative to "Bullseye," the city of Hanoi.

started to execute his plan. He curved to the northwest, accelerated to 600 knots and headed inland. Curt Dosé followed.

The two Phantoms arrived over Kep at 10,000 feet seemingly unnoticed by those on the ground; the antiaircraft defenses remained silent. Dosé was on the left, nearer the runway, and on glancing down he noticed two silver MiG-21s on a taxiway beside the runway. He scanned the sky to make sure none of their comrades were already airborne, and pondered what to do next—air-to-air missiles were useless against planes on the ground. Then Jim McDevitt, Dosé's radar intercept officer, called that the MiGs were accelerating down the runway in the opposite direction. They were taking off—the North Vietnamese pilots were about to solve Dosé's problem for him!

Dosé took charge. "I called, 'MiGs on the roll, I've got the lead—Silverkites [the call sign of VF-92] in-place, turn port now, burner!' We went supersonic in the descent as we turned through a semicircle, and ended up just to the right of the runway. I was trying to position myself to be behind the MiGs when they broke ground, as we came barreling down the runway at about Mach 1.1." Out of the corner of his eye Dosé glimpsed frenzied activity around MiGs in camouflaged blast pens to his right, as maintenance men scurried for cover or threw themselves flat. The Phantom pilot returned his attention to the front and saw the MiGs lift off the ground and shed their external tanks. Obviously the control tower had warned them of the Phantoms closing rapidly from behind.

Holding formation, the MiGs banked steeply to the left and pulled into a tight turn, keeping close to the ground. The Phantoms swung after them, bleeding off speed in the turn but still gaining rapidly. Dosé led the pursuit with the other F-4 slightly behind and to his left. "I said I would take the MiG on the right, the wingman. Hawkins acknowledged and said he would take the leader. At this point the MiGs were in a hard left turn, going between hills and down valleys. We were closing rapidly and literally dodging trees, real low. I told Hawkins I was pulling for a shot at the wingman."

Dosé squeezed the trigger, and a Sidewinder streaked away from the Phantom leaving a trail of white smoke. "It looked great until it got up to the MiG, then it flew right through the jet plume and detonated on the other side. I could see the dust kicked up on the ground by the exploding warhead." The MiG had been turning too sharply for the missile's proximity fuse to detonate at the right time for a kill.

Undaunted, Dosé moved closer and launched another missile. Charlie Tinker watched the missile cut across the center of the circle, then turn back toward the target: "Curt's second AIM-9 went up the tail of the MiG-21, the plane exploded." The flaming wreckage slammed into the ground.

Now both Phantom crews concentrated on the surviving MiG. They were going faster than their quarry but were turning through a wider circle; from above they looked like a couple of water-skiers swinging fast and wide as their towboat made a tight turn. Dosé tried to fire yet another Sidewinder, but the missile he selected was a dud and remained on its launcher. Hawkins then fired three missiles in succession at the MiG, but all missed. By holding his tight turn close to the ground the enemy pilot managed to keep just outside the reach of the Sidewinders.

The chase continued through three-quarters of a circle, until the trio was heading back for Kep airfield. Dosé launched his last Sidewinder: "At first it looked as if it was going fine, then about halfway to the MiG it hit the top of a hill. There was a big red flash and a cloud of dust, and that was the end of it. By then I was getting a little frustrated with my Sidewinders—though when you've just shot down a MiG with one it's hard to have any big complaint."

Dosé now had no usable Sidewinder left. In the cockpit behind him Jim McDevitt tried to lock his radar on the MiG for a Sparrow shot, but they were too low and the clutter of ground returns made it impossible; moreover, the tight turn prevented a straight boresight shot at the enemy fighter. It seemed the Phantom's four Sparrow missiles were unusable. Dosé studied the enemy fighter just 400 feet in front of him. "The MiG was shiny silver with stars on the wings and fuselage. It was very pretty, it looked like an air-show plane. I could see the guy's stabilizer moving, I was real close." The Phantoms were in an ideal position to attack with guns, but neither fighter carried them.

Hawkins widened his turn, trying to get in position for another Sidewinder launch. But still the MiG held its turn, giving few opportunities for a shot. Then Dosé had an idea. If he pulled into a barrel roll and fired an unguided Sparrow past the MiG, perhaps that would force the North Vietnamese pilot to straighten out long enough for Hawkins to get off a good shot. "I pitched up and ruddered over at the top of the roll to lob a Sparrow at the MiG. But as I glanced over my shoulder I saw two MiG-21s at five hundred feet coming in from our four o'clock [right quarter]. I called, 'Silverkites, two MiGs, four o'clock high, break right!' We broke right and flew through the MiGs head-on."

As the Phantoms broke away Tinker suddenly realized they were in more danger than he had thought: "As I cleared our six [rear] I realized the sky was dark with AAA [antiaircraft artillery] bursts—the enemy had been shooting at us the whole time! We also had a SAM launched at us, but it missed and went off in a cloud of orange smoke about two thousand yards away." Having survived five actual or attempted Sidewinder shots, the MiG they had been chasing made good its escape.

The events just described occurred far quicker than they have taken to tell; it was only about 50 seconds from the time Curt Dosé first noticed the MiG-21s beside the runway at Kep until he and Hawkins abandoned the chase.

Nearly out of missiles and starting to run short of fuel, the Phantoms went supersonic and sped toward the coast. "At that time we had strong intelligence that the MiG-21 could not do more than Mach 1.05 below five thousand feet. We were doing Mach 1.15 in combat spread, feeling cocksure as we headed towards the coast," Dosé recalled. "Then a MiG-21 came up behind, overtaking fast. He made it look effortless. When I saw the MiG it was about three-quarters of a mile behind Hawkins. I called for an in-place turn, and as we began turning the MiG fired an Atoll missile at Hawkins. Initially it guided, but it couldn't handle the Gs and it wasn't ever a real threat." After attacking, the MiG broke away to the right. Instinctively Dosé turned after it, until McDevitt demanded incredulously, "What are you doing!" The back-seater's tone reminded Dosé that they had neither the missiles nor the fuel for another engagement. Chastened, the pilot reversed his turn and headed for the coast.

Almost certainly the MiG-21 that had caught up with the Phantoms was the new MF sub-type. It was the first time American crews had encountered this version, and its much improved low-altitude performance came as an unpleasant surprise.

While Curt Dosé and Austin Hawkins had been jousting with the MiGs, the strike forces from *Coral Sea* and *Kitty Hawk* attacked their targets around Haiphong. The ten-minute separation between air wings gave each time to carry out its attack and get clear of the target area before the next one arrived. *Coral Sea*'s aircraft cratered the railroad yard; those from *Kitty Hawk* dropped one span of the main rail and highway bridge out of the city. The raiders then withdrew without loss and without interference from enemy fighters.

FROM the underground shelter in downtown Haiphong Claude Julien had listened to the sounds of exploding bombs and antiaircraft shells, and the less frequent whoosh of SAMs rising from their launchers. Between each successive wave of attackers there was a lengthy pause. Then, following the third raid, the explosions ceased and people started to drift outside. The dank and uncomfortable cavern had emptied long before the all-clear sounded.

ONCE clear of the Vietnamese coast Dosé and Hawkins took fuel from the waiting EKA-3B tanker, then set course for *Constellation*. Their services not needed, the three Sea King rescue helicopters made their way back to *Okinawa*.

As the main body of each air group regained its carrier the formations split and the different types of aircraft orbited at their separate altitudes. The F-4s, usually the shortest on fuel, circled at 2,000 feet and landed first. The A-7s circled at 3,000 feet, the A-6s at 4,000 feet and the other types above that. When the last F-4 left the stack to enter the landing pattern, the other aircraft types dropped 1,000 feet in the stack and landed in turn. And despite the pressures of war the Navy did not relax its normal operating standards. "You had to get yourself together and make a good landing; every one was graded and posted on the board at the ready room as if there was no war. It was all part of the program, because you could kill yourself just as quickly hitting the back of a ship as you could over North Vietnam," recalled John Olsen.

Dosé and Hawkins reached *Constellation* after her other fighters and attack planes had landed. To the delight of those on deck, Dosé performed a victory roll, then made a wide orbit and landed. A few minutes later the EKA-3B tanker that had given him fuel also landed. Shortly after an arrester wire drew the "Electric Whale" to a halt, the carrier reduced speed and turned downwind. The morning strike was over.

Curt Dosé taxied his F-4 to the deck park and shut down the engines, watched by a crowd of waving onlookers. Acknowledging their applause, Dosé and McDevitt climbed out and strode proudly back to their squadron's ready room. Already the most eventful of their lives, the day would have further adventures in store for the pair. We shall return to them later.

After the mission Lieutenant Mike Stansel went to look at the Vigilante reconnaissance plane that had taken SAM damage. "The Vigie was a phenomenal plane, but it had all kinds of fuel and hydraulic lines running the length of the aircraft. I stood underneath it and there were about five places where you could look up and see right through the plane. The maintenance guys opened the panels and you could see where SAM fragments had missed lines by inches and gone on out the top of the plane. They didn't hit a single line or anything. Those recon guys had God as their copilot that day!"

. . .

PASSING through the outskirts of Haiphong on his way back to Hanoi, Claude Julien's jeep took him along Route 5 within 400 yards of the oil depot attacked by *Constellation*'s planes. The journalist saw several storage tanks well ablaze, with columns of billowing black smoke towering high into the sky.

The vehicle soon left the port behind it, and in the countryside normality had returned. Julien later wrote:

> All is calm again. The indescribable landscape with its very pale sky, sumptuous green paddy fields in full sunlight and slender darker lines of trees. Children paddle in the stretches of water. They raise their arms and shout a greeting to the white man going past who, they think, must be a Russian. The smaller children play on the backs of buffaloes, the older ones fish with rods and nets. The thatched huts and little shops are poor, but perfectly serene. Peasants are digging ditches and reinforcing dikes.

AT YANKEE Station deck crews on the three carriers toiled to rearm, refuel and reposition aircraft for the next massed launch, scheduled in just over two and a half hours. Meanwhile the scene shifts to the skies over northern Thailand, where the Air Force planes assigned to the second large attack of the day were airborne and about to move into enemy territory.

THE ACTION AROUND HANOI, THE OPENING PHASE

8:00–9:50 a.m.

You can squeeze a bee in your hand until it suffocates;
but it will not suffocate without having stung you.
—Jean Paulhan

7:00 A.M., THAILAND. A major strike by Air Force
planes from Thailand followed rules different
from those that governed the Navy planes' tactics.
An aircraft carrier could launch heavily laden
fixed-wing planes only when heading into the
wind, and often geography or the enemy limited
the time she could steam in one direction. So for
an Alpha Strike a carrier would launch her planes
in rapid succession over a ten-minute period.
They would then assemble in formation and head
for the target together and at the same speed. Air
Force attack planes flew from land bases and did
not face such constraints. They would take off in
ones, twos or larger units over a much longer period and converge on the target from different
directions and speeds.

The equipment philosophy of the Navy and Air
Force wings was different, too. A carrier air wing
was a self-contained attack force with its own

U.S. AIR FORCE AIRCRAFT INVOLVED IN ATTACKS ON NORTH VIETNAM, MAY 10, 1972

Weather Reconnaissance

1 RF-4C from the 14 TRS, 432 TRW Udorn.

Prestrike Support in Target Areas, Time on Target from 9:45 A.M.

4 F-4D from the 555TFS, 432TRW Udorn, Oyster Flight. MIGCAP.

4 F-4D from the 13 TFS, 432 TRW Udorn, Balter Flight. MIGCAP.

4 EB-66E from the 42 TEWS, 388 TFW Korat, Cowsip and Valent Flights. To provide stand-off jamming support.

5 F-105G from the 17 TFS (Wild Weasel), 388 TFW Korat. Fletch Flight. Iron Hand defense suppression (5th plane airborne reserve, to return to base when flight left tanker on ingress route).

4 F-4 from 433 TFS, 8TFW Ubon, Dingus Flight, to lay chaff trail to targets.

4 F-4, 435 TFS, 8TFW Ubon, Hitest Flight, mission as above.

Paul Doumer Bridge Attack Force, Time on Target 10:00 A.M.

4 F-4D/E of the 435 TFS, 8TFW Ubon. Goatee Flight, to attack with 2,000-lb. EOGBs.

12 F-4D/E of 25, 433 and 435 TFSs, 8TFW, Ubon. Jingle, Biloxi and Napkin flights, to attack with 2,000-lb. LGBs.

4 F-4E from the 336 TFS, 432 TFS Udorn, Harlow Flight. Strike Escort.

5 F-105G from the 17 TFS, 388 TFW Korat, Galore Flight. Iron Hand defense suppression (5th plane airborne reserve).

Yen Vien Rail Yard Attack Force, Time on Target 10:05 A.M.

16 F-4 of 25, 334, 336 TFSs, 8TFW. Bertha, Gigolo, Icebag and Gopher flights. To attack with Mark 82 (500-lb.) bombs.

4 F-4E from the 432 TFW Udorn, Arroyo Flight. Strike Escort for Bertha and Gigolo flights.

4 F-4E from the 432 TFW Udorn, Bowleg Flight. Strike Escort for Icebag and Gopher flights.

5 F-105G from the 561 TFS, 388 TFW Korat, Calgon Flight. Iron Hand defense suppression (5th plane airborne reserve).

Poststrike Reconnaissance, Time on Target 10:06 A.M.

2 RF-4C, from the 14 TRS, 432 TRW Udorn, Cousin Flight.

U.S. AIR FORCE AIRCRAFT INVOLVED IN ATTACKS ON TARGETS NEAR HANOI
MAY 10, 1972

Search and Rescue

1 HC-130 from the 3rd Air Rescue and Recovery Group, 56th Special Operations Wing, Nakhon Phanom, call sign King 21. SAR coordination and helicopter refueling.

2 HH-53B from the 40th Aerospace Rescue and Recovery Squadron, 56 SOW, Nakhon Phanom, Jolly Green Flight.

4 A-1, 1st Special Operations Squadron, 56 SOW, Nakhon Phanom, Sandy Flight.

4 F-4 from the 432 TRW, Udorn, Brenda Flight. Search and rescue escort.

Air-to-Air Refueling Support

20 KC-135 of various units based at U-Tapao and Takhli.

4 F-4 from the 432 TRW, Udorn, Dogear Flight. Tanker escort.

USAF AIRCRAFT INVOLVED IN THE ACTION ON MAY 10, 1972, BY ROLE

Bombers

32 F-4s, carrying 65 tons of bombs

Supporters

28 F-4s armed for air-to-air combat

8 F-4s carrying chaff

15 F-105s defense suppression (including 3 reserves)

4 EB-66s stand-off jamming support

1 U-2R weather reconnaissance and Comint

1 RF-4C prestrike weather reconnaissance aircraft

2 RF-4C poststrike reconnaissance aircraft

1 RC-135M Sigint support aircraft

1 EC-121D Airborne Command and Control Center

1 HC-130 rescue control aircraft

2 HH-3B rescue helicopters

4 A-1 rescue support aircraft

20 KC-135 tanker aircraft

88 supporters

120 aircraft involved, total

fighters, bombers and tankers, reconnaissance, defense suppression and radar jamming planes. In contrast the wing at each Air Force base concentrated on a few roles. Ubon would provide bombers; Udorn, air-to-air fighter and reconnaissance planes; Korat, radar jamming, defense suppression and airborne command and control planes; Nakhon Phanom, search-and-rescue planes; and U-Tapao and Don Muang, tankers.

At 7:30 A.M. the initial wave of seven KC-135 tankers began taking off from U-Tapao in the south of Thailand. Each plane carried seventy-five tons of fuel, half of which could be transferred to other aircraft in flight. Altogether twenty tankers would support the operation.

Next off was the search-and-rescue force from Nakhom Phanom. This comprised an HC-130 Hercules airborne command post, two HH-53B "Jolly Green Giant" helicopters and four A-1 rescue support planes, and its task was to pick up U.S. airmen shot down. Its speed governed by that of the slow and ungainly helicopters, the force needed a long start to reach its waiting area over Laos before the attack opened.

Shortly after 8:00 A.M. the weather reconnaissance RF-4C reported on high-frequency radio that the skies were clear in the Hanoi area. The attack could go ahead against the primary targets.

The vanguard of the attack force comprised eight Phantoms armed for air-to-air combat, Oyster and Balter flights. These left Udorn at 8:05 A.M. and headed north. Four more flights followed—Harlow, Arroyo, Dogear and Brenda, each with four Phantoms, assigned to escort different parts of the attack force. Last off from Udorn were a pair of RF-4Cs, Cousin Flight, to take poststrike photographs of the targets for damage assessment.

From Korat, 170 miles south of Udorn, four EB-66s took off to provide stand-off radar jamming cover—Cowsip and Valent flights. Three flights of five Wild Weasel F-105s (four plus an airborne reserve) followed to provide defense suppression cover for the force—Fletch, Galore and Calgon flights.

From Ubon, 170 miles east of Korat, ten flights of Phantoms

took off: Hitest and Dingus flights carrying chaff bombs; Goatee, Napkin, Biloxi and Jingle flights to attack the Paul Doumer Bridge; and Gopher, Icebag, Gigolo and Bertha flights to attack the Yen Vien rail yard.

Some of the crews had not known until the last moment whether they were to go on the mission. Captain Douglas Nix and Lieutenant Johnny Wyatt of the 25th Tactical Fighter Squadron had been assigned to a "running spare" F-4 at Ubon. They had briefed for several different parts of the mission, taxied out first and sat beside the runway in a fully armed plane, engines running, ready to take the place of anyone forced to abort the mission. Nix recalled: "There I was sitting across the runway, watching each four-ship take off and logging them off my list. I had mixed emotions; I wanted to be a part of it, but I wasn't exactly tickled about jumping into the middle of some flight where I didn't know the leader or, if it was from a different squadron, the members of the flight. Then someone aborted in the arming area and they called for a spare." Nix took off as Gigolo 4.

By 8:50 A.M. the entire armada was airborne and on its way north. Of the total of 120 aircraft, eighty-eight were scheduled to penetrate enemy territory.

TAN SON NHUT, SAIGON. General Vogt returned to the Command Center, "Blue Chip," as units reported their planes airborne and the information was flashed on the electronic wall displays. On the far wall a huge situation map covered the whole of North and South Vietnam, Cambodia, Laos and Thailand, with the planned routes of the various attacking and supporting forces marked by different-colored twines. Markers showed the latest information on each force and whether it was in its planned position.

With the force airborne and the pieces of the intricately planned operation coming together, there was little Vogt could do to influence events. Alterations to the briefed plan could have disastrous consequences and, like many a commander before him, he felt he had to let the battle take its course. "It had taken hours with a lot of computerization to get the operation going. Everybody was in his little niche in the sky. The tankers were in place. The fighters and the bombers were on their way, the Wild Weasels were heading for the SAM sites and the EB-66s for their jamming positions. It was like a grand ballet," he commented. And, like a grand ballet, the performance of it had to be left to those onstage.

The general retained one option of control for use as a last resort, the recall code words India Zulu that would have brought back all or part of the force. But, as he explained, the chances of his using that option were minimal: "There was no situation I could imagine that might lead to the recall, short of unexpectedly severe weather. If the enemy sent up a lot of fighters, my disposition was to let the guys fight it out."

Again Vogt left the Command Center. He would return when the raiders reached their targets or if they encountered unexpected problems. Now he joined another part of his staff, that drawing up plans for the attacks scheduled for the following day.

OVER northern Thailand six KC-135s waited at the rendezvous area. The planes flew in line astern, stepped up in altitude from 24,000 feet, fat sows waiting to suckle their litters. The refueling operation had begun at 8:35 A.M. and, as with the Navy attack, it took place in full view of the North Vietnamese early warning radars. A Phantom or Thunderchief required about five and a half tons of fuel to top off its tanks, and a KC-135 took about fifteen minutes to refuel the four planes in a flight.

Already, the cutting edge of the initial fighter sweep had been blunted. Balter 2 had electrical problems, Balter 3 was unable to refuel; both had to return to Udorn. Oyster 4 suffered a radar failure but its crew decided to continue the mission. Balter 1 and 4 joined up as an element and continued northeast, as did the four aircraft of Oyster Flight. The fighter sweep had been devised by Major Bob Lodge, Oyster Flight leader, an experienced air fighting tactician with two MiG kills to his credit. The Phantoms were to establish a barrier patrol northwest of Hanoi, Oyster Flight at

OYSTER FLIGHT

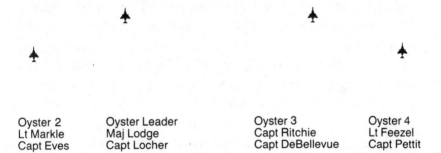

Oyster 2	Oyster Leader	Oyster 3	Oyster 4
Lt Markle	Maj Lodge	Capt Ritchie	Lt Feezel
Capt Eves	Capt Locher	Capt DeBellevue	Capt Pettit

low altitude and Balter Flight behind it at 22,000 feet in full view of the enemy. Any MiG moving against Balter Flight would fly over the Oyster Flight planes waiting in ambush.

Oyster Flight crossed into North Vietnam at 9:20 A.M., followed shortly afterward by the remnant of Balter Flight. In each Phantom the crew searched the sky around, both visually and with radar. Captain Chuck DeBellevue, weapon systems officer in Oyster 3, recalled: "We were all hyper for going into combat. We were scared, but it was the sort of fear that makes you extremely alert, not the sort of fear that makes you incapable of anything."

At 8:23 the EC-121 Constellation radar picket plane over northern Laos warned Lodge that enemy fighters had taken off. This and subsequent transmissions were tape-recorded.

"Oyster, Disco. Activity bearing zero-five-zero [degrees] ninety-six [miles] your position."

The enemy aircraft were in the vicinity of Kep airfield, far to the northeast and representing no immediate threat. When Oyster and Balter flights reached their patrol areas they began flying figure-eight orbits, waiting for the MiGs to come to them.

Two minutes after the call from Disco, Red Crown (USS *Chicago*) informed Lodge of MiGs seventy-five miles to the northeast. During the next seven minutes Chief Radarman Larry Nowell, senior intercept controller on the cruiser, passed a succession of reports of enemy fighters closing in. At 9:31 A.M. the nearest MiGs were within twenty-one miles, then they turned around and the distance opened. At 9:33 Nowell reported four separate forces of MiGs airborne: "You got one at three-four-five at fifty. You got a bandit at zero-one-five forty-five, a bandit at zero-five-seven fifty-seven, another bandit at zero-eight-one at ninety. . . . [the rest garbled]."

One minute later Nowell reported: "OK. Heads up for the bandits coming back in. The nearest one to you there, he's on the zero-three-zero at twenty miles."

Again the MiGs came south but, like insects partaking in some elaborate courtship rite, they again turned away at the last moment. By now the American bomber force had completed its refueling and was heading over Laos. The North Vietnamese fighter controller would probably have received reports of these formations moving in and it is likely he did not want to commit his fighters prematurely.

At 9:42 A.M., nineteen minutes after the shadowboxing began, the North Vietnamese controller finally ordered his fighters into action. Yet once more the MiGs headed south and Nowell informed Lodge: "Multiple bandits in your area. I hold a Bandit at three-four-zero at twenty-four. The closest bandit I hold is zero-two-two at sixteen." Running in at fifteen thousand feet, the MiGs were suddenly much more aggressive. Balter Flight edged toward Oyster to provide top cover.

Nowell's timely warning enabled Lodge to turn his flight to meet the MiGs nearly nose-on. As they leveled at 2,000 feet, Oyster 1, 2 and 3 jettisoned their external tanks, cut in afterburner and accelerated to fighting speed. The flight's members had flown together many times and Lodge did not think a radio call necessary before such a maneuver. But in Oyster 4, Tommy Feezel and Larry Pettit had been carefully searching the sky behind the flight. When Feezel next looked to the front, he was shocked to see the other three Phantoms a mile in front and pulling away rapidly. Aware of his vulnerability if he was pounced on by MiGs, Feezel dumped his tanks and accelerated after his colleagues.

In air combat, victory usually goes to the side that is first to see its opponent. Lodge kept low to remain out of sight for as long as possible while the four MiGs ran obliquely past his nose at 15,000 feet. Although the two forces were not meeting head-on, their combined closing speed was more than 900 knots—one mile every four seconds. Suddenly the MiGs appeared on the Phantoms' radars:

"Oyster Two has contact!"

"Oyster One has a contact zero-five-zero for fifteen!"

"Oyster Three is contact, Bob!"

"Right, we got 'em!"

"Oyster One on the nose, twelve miles, fifteen [degrees] high, overtake nine hundred [knots] plus!"

In Oyster 3 Chuck DeBellevue picked up MiG IFF transmissions on his Combat Tree equipment and informed his pilot that he had a positive hostile identification on the planes in front: "He's squawking MiG! . . . He's squawking MiG! . . . Stand by to shoot!"

There were similar clipped instructions in Oyster 1 and 2 as the back-seaters locked on their radars and made the final switching for a head-on attack with Sparrow missiles. With the nearest MiG ahead, above and almost in missile range, Bob Lodge eased his Phantom into a shallow climb. The Phantoms on either side followed. Meanwhile Tommy Feezel in Oyster 4, still some distance behind, was catching up fast. With his radar locked on the target eight miles in front, beyond visual range, Lodge squeezed the trigger and a Sparrow surged out in front trailing smoke. The missile, twelve feet long and weighing about 450 pounds, accelerated from its launch speed of 600 knots to 1,800 knots in 2.3 seconds. Then the motor exhausted its fuel and cut out. The missile should have coasted the rest of the way to the target, but it was a dud and for some reason it exploded when the motor cut. Lodge squeezed his trigger again and a second Sparrow roared toward the same target.

Lieutenant John Markle in Oyster 2, slightly behind Lodge and 600 yards to his right, also fired a pair of Sparrows and had one fail: "Our first missile apparently did not get rocket motor ignition. The second missile came off the aircraft and turned slightly right as it climbed. We continued to maintain position on Oyster One in an easy right turn, slightly nose up. As I checked the missile's progress, the trail showed a slight left turn toward the radar target."

Captain Steve Ritchie in Oyster 3, 3,000 yards to the left of Lodge, also launched a Sparrow but its motor failed to ignite. Tommy Feezel, coming up from behind, saw the missile fall away from the Phantom "like a bomb."

Of the five Sparrows launched, only two functioned as advertised. But when everything worked, the missile's 66-pound warhead was devastating. The recorder in Markle's plane captured his reaction as he saw his second missile strike home: "Oh right! . . . Now! . . . Good! . . . Woooohooo!"

Then, on the radio:

"Oyster Two's a hit!"

Lodge replied:

"I got one!"

Steve Eaves, Markle's back-seater, confirmed the leader's kill.

"Roger, he's burning and he's going down one o'clock!"

Captain Roger Locher, Lodge's back-seater, saw two explosions a long way in front, and as he got closer he caught sight of two North Vietnamese fighters tumbling from the sky. "The MiG-21 Markle had shot down was the closer, it did a cartwheel and went underneath us about half a mile in front, in a ten-degree dive. A few seconds later I saw the one we had hit going down in a sixty- or seventy-degree dive. Its left wing was shot off, it was in a pretty fast roll to the left, on fire and trailing smoke. The guy had already ejected."

The two surviving MiGs continued their headlong charge and flashed close over the Phantoms as the latter swung right to get on their opponents' tails. One MiG pilot misjudged the rate of closure or Lodge's turn, and narrowly missed colliding with Oyster Leader. When Lodge rolled out of the turn he was only 200 feet behind the MiG, and from the rear seat Locher had a close-up view. "We were in his jet wash. There he was, burner plume sticking out, the shiniest airplane you've ever seen. He was going up in a chandelle to the right, we were right behind him." The MiG in front of Lodge was too close for a missile attack, but the Phantom pilot had eased off his turn and the enemy fighter's range was opening. Soon it would be in position for a missile shot.

The combat was going well for Oyster Flight when, suddenly, the tables were turned. Zooming up from below to gate-crash the fight came a pair of MiG-19s, probably flown by Lieutenants Le Thanh Dao and Vu Van Hop of the 3rd Company. They curved after Lodge's F-4 as Markle, to his left and in no position to engage them, shouted a warning. "OK, there's a bandit. . . . you got a bandit in your ten o'clock, Bob, level!"

In a sweeping left turn the MiG-19s passed behind Oyster Leader, then began closing in from his right.

"Bob, reverse right, reverse right, Bob. Reverse right!"

"The bandit's behind you. . . . [the rest blotted out]."

Lodge thought the MiG-21 in front had opened the range sufficiently for a close-in shot. Locher remembered: "We were ready to blow this guy away when I heard John telling us to reverse right. Then I saw another MiG-21 overshoot to the left, about one thousand feet away.

"Oyster One padlocked!"

"Padlocked" meant Lodge was concentrating on the MiG in front, and immediately afterward he launched a Sparrow.

From the leading MiG-19 a string of fiery grapefruits bridged the gap between it and Lodge's Phantom. Again Markle's voice came over the radio: "He's firing, he's firing at you!"

Locher described what happened next: "One or two seconds later, wham! we were hit. I looked up and saw the MiG [the MiG-21 in front] separating away. I thought we had mid-aired because that was exactly my interpretation of how a collision would feel. We both said 'Oh shit!' but my 'Oh shit!' was because the guy in front was getting away from us."

Initially the Phantom's crew thought their plane had escaped with minor "fender bending," but the notion was dispelled shortly afterward. More 30-mm shells slammed into the plane and Locher realized what had happened. "The next thing I knew we were decelerating—I think the right engine had exploded. We ended up doing some really hard yaws to the right." From that moment the Phantom was doomed, though this had yet to dawn on its crew. "Bob complained that the airplane was not flying properly, so I said, 'Let's set two-one-zero and get out of here, egress back to the southwest.' He didn't respond, so I said, 'Hey, you know if we put it on autopilot we can probably get it a little further.' That was a technique in the F-4 to minimize loss of hydraulic fluid if there was a leak. He said, 'Rog, you don't understand. We don't have any hydraulics.'"

The pilot's measured words brought home to Locher the harsh reality of their situation; the fighter was not going to get them home. A big rugged airplane, the Phantom could fly with many systems inoperative. But not the hydraulics. The hydraulics were indispensable; when the last of the pressure bled away, the main flying controls would cease to work and the plane would fall out of the sky. The back-seater was still pondering the implications of what he had heard when a yet more immediate danger manifested itself: the blaze started in the rear fuselage had begun to eat its way forward and, roasted by the heat, the transparent plastic of the canopy over Locher's head was slowly turning an opaque orange. Smoke started to seep into the cockpit.

Locher selected full oxygen to keep the fumes out of his mask. "I looked at the altimeter, we were passing eight thousand feet. I said 'Hey, Bob, we're passing eight thousand feet. It's getting awful hot back here, I'm going to have to get out.' He looked over his right shoulder and said, 'Why don't you eject, then?'"

As Locher prepared to leave the Phantom the air battle continued. The MiG Lodge had been chasing escaped the Sparrow aimed at it. But the remaining MiG-21 from the original formation was less fortunate. Steve Ritchie in Oyster 3 rolled out 6,000 feet behind it with a radar lock-on. He squeezed off two Sparrows and watched the first pass wide of the enemy plane. But the second guided accurately, detonated close under the target and blew pieces off it. As the Phantom swept past its victim Chuck

DeBellevue in the rear saw a black shape flash past less than 100 feet away to his left; it was the MiG's pilot, trailing from a parachute in the process of opening. DeBellevue gave a jubilant shout: "Oyster Three's a splash!"

DeBellevue's victory call was the last thing Locher heard before he ejected. By then the Phantom was upside down and falling fast. "We were under negative G at the time. My ass was off the seat, I was pinned against the top of the canopy." Locher reached for the handle between his legs, grabbed it with both hands and pulled hard. "I saw the canopy go, then I went out under negative G. There was a lot of wind blast, I started to see again. Then *thwack!* the parachute opened. And *zoooom!* past me went two MiG-19s."

The other members of Oyster Flight watched in dread fascination as Lodge's plane went down, silently praying for the sight of parachutes. Tommy Feezel recalled: "We watched it go down and hit the ground, but all we could see was a black pall of smoke. We kept looking for chutes but we didn't see any." None of the watchers above saw Locher eject or his parachute open. The back-seater was fired downward, and probably smoke from the burning aircraft screened him. It appears the pilot was still in his cockpit when the Phantom dived into the ground.

Flying at 20,000 feet, much higher than the combatants, Balter Flight arrived in time to see the final moments of the Phantom's meteoric plunge. Neither crew saw Locher's escape either. Dean White did see two parachutes at about 10,000 feet, several miles apart, but their canopies were the distinctive light tan color used by MiG pilots (American parachutes had orange, white and green panels). "There was smoke in the vicinity of the two Vietnamese 'chutes, you could tell that something had burned there. But apart from Bob's aircraft I didn't see any wreckage burning on the ground."

Shaken by the sudden loss of their leader, the survivors of Oyster Flight sped southwest away from the area. "We had been sandwiched! We were lucky to come out of that engagement with only one loss," Ritchie commented later. "We figured we had better get out, there were probably more MiGs behind us. The standard exit procedure in a situation like that was to get on the deck and go as fast as we could."

As the survivors of Oyster Flight sped out of North Vietnam at low altitude, a MiG-21 MF arrived to cause consternation for the second time that day. Oyster 2 ran out alone, 3 and 4 stayed together. Chuck DeBellevue, in Oyster 3, watched with disbelief as the Soviet-made fighter closing from behind seemed to join formation on the pair. "We were running out at seven hundred to seven hundred fifty knots [Mach 1.06 to 1.13], the F-4 wouldn't go any faster that low. And we had a MiG-21 chasing us and keeping up—that surprised the hell out of us!" To DeBellevue, the MiG's ability to keep up was disconcerting; to Captain Larry Pettit in Oyster 4 it was terrifying: "He was at our eight-thirty position [left quarter], one hundred feet above and about three hundred feet out to the side. He caught up with us and was staying with us! I don't know if he saw us, but he had a gun and he could have strafed the shit out of us." Larry Pettit's next move did nothing to lessen the danger but was understandable in the circumstances: "I lowered my seat to the floor, to hide from him! He banked towards us and I thought, Oh no, he's going to let us have it with cannon. . . . But he turned and went off in the opposite direction. Tommy [Feezel] and I thanked our lucky stars and got the hell out of there."

ROGER LOCHER was in the final stages of his parachute descent into North Vietnam when the MiG turned away from his colleagues. He landed among forty-foot-high trees on a wooded ridge line and took some knocks as he crashed through the upper branches. Once on the ground he undid the quick-release and stepped out of his harness, then he tried to pull the rest of the parachute down from the trees. The canopy was draped over several branches, however, and resisted all attempts to jerk it clear. Next the airman tried to disconnect the survival pack from the parachute harness. But his fingers simply refused to obey his brain's commands to undo the connecting strap (he thought his spine had been injured, but in fact it was a symptom of shock following ejection and would soon wear off). There was no alternative—the parachute and the precious pack had to be left behind to betray his point of arrival.

Next Locher took out a beeper radio. He did not think rescue possible that deep in enemy territory but wanted to inform his colleagues that he had reached the ground safely. He switched on the radio and made a brief call: "This is Oyster zero one Bravo. I'm on the ground. I'm OK." Then, fearful the transmissions might betray his position to the enemy, he switched off. He discarded his flying helmet and body harness, and set out at a brisk trot to distance himself from the parachute. He had covered about half a mile when he heard a babble of voices coming from the direction of where his plane had crashed. It was the posse sent to bring him in. Dead or alive.

THE ACTION AROUND HANOI, SOFTENING THE DEFENSES

9:40–10:00 a.m.

I think and work with all my power to bring the troops to the right place at the right time; then I have done my duty. As soon as I order them forward into battle, I leave my army in the hands of God."

—General Robert E. Lee

9:40 A.M., HANOI. As the Air Force raiders closed in, the capital's sirens began their warning wail. The streets emptied rapidly. At the time Joe Wright, the British consul general, was in his office reviewing papers with his deputy, David Simmons. Wright left Simmons to lock away the documents and strode briskly to the British Residence, a few hundred yards away, to join his wife, Pat. He arrived to find all the windows in the building open, a routine precaution to reduce the risk of panes being shattered by blast. The Residence lacked a proper air raid shelter, so the Wrights made for the safest part of the building, the alcove under the stairs, and waited. With luck it might be yet another false alarm.

. . .

THE PURPOSE of the second phase of the action was to blunt the cutting edge of Hanoi's SAM and antiaircraft gun defenses to prepare the way for the bombers. Four EB-66E stand-off jamming aircraft, four Wild Weasel F-105Gs and eight F-4 chaff bombers were assigned to this task; their role could be likened to that of blockers in a football game—to open a path through the defense so the running back could sprint for the goal line.

The first "blockers" to make their presence felt were four EB-66s of the 42nd Electronic Warfare Squadron, Valent and Cowsip flights. At 9:45 A.M. the planes, each carrying a battery of eighteen jammers, arrived at their assigned orbit positions at 30,000 feet just outside the western edge of the Hanoi SAM zone and began jamming the enemy air defense radars.

Meanwhile four Wild Weasel F-105Gs of Fletch Flight, 17th Tactical Fighter Squadron, had slipped into the defended area at low altitude looking for active SAM sites. Each plane carried three anti-radar missiles: two short-range Shrikes and one long-range Standard ARM, which could home on the signals from enemy radars. The Wild Weasel operation has been described as "a kind of high-speed three-dimensional football game, with more than one ball and no rules." Major Don Kilgus described some of the methods used during this period: "A Weasel flight of four aircraft would usually split into pairs and bracket the target area; the basic fighting unit was the element of two. Our tactics varied from day to day. Often we would go in low, hoping to catch the radars looking at the strikers up above. If the enemy radar was tracking somebody else, it was not looking at us; that was great, that was the optimum.

"Once we had found an active site we would go into afterburner and increase speed to between four hundred fifty and five hundred twenty knots. Speed gave us survivability and maneuver potential, because when we started pulling G the plane would slow down. The Thud [F-105] was a super plane but it was not the tightest turner in the world, and you had to plan ahead if you wanted to make violent maneuvers. So we would light the burner, pull up and turn at the same time to establish the firing parameters for the missile. Needles showed where the Shrike was looking and gave an indication of range plus or minus about twenty percent. If a loft attack was necessary, for maximum range, we would launch in a thirty-degree climb from fifteen thousand feet. Or if we were close to the site we would pitch over and push the missile down his throat."

Nearing Hanoi, Lieutenant Colonel James O'Neil, Fletch Flight leader, received a radio warning of MiGs in the area. But unless they came in his direction the SAM sites remained his primary concern. His electronic warfare officer, Lieutenant Colonel Jim Waller, picked out the signals from an enemy Fansong missile control radar and programmed the plane's Standard missile to go after it. O'Neil eased into a climb and launched the missile, then pulled into a defensive turn to look for MiGs. He saw none, and returned to low altitude to resume his hunt for SAM sites. Once launched, the Standard missile was on its own; O'Neil did not see where it impacted.

While the Wild Weasels played their deadly game with the MiGs and the SAM batteries, the next part of the action opened. Dingus and Hitest flights, each with four Phantoms, closed on Hanoi from the southwest. Each plane carried nine M-129 chaff bombs, and their task was to lay a line of chaff—millions of thin metallized strips each about the length of a man's little finger—to confuse North Vietnamese gun and SAM control radars in the area.

Dingus and Hitest flights had been briefed to release their chaff bombs from 26,000 feet. Nine minutes later the main attack force was to follow the same route at 15,000 feet, and during the intervening period the chaff was to spread out as it fell to the lower altitude. But as he neared Hanoi the chaff force leader, Major Bob Blake, could see the plan was not workable. A bank of haze at 26,000 feet would make it difficult to see upcoming SAMs. Blake called Colonel Carl Miller, the attack force commander and Goatee Flight leader, asking permission to release the chaff bombs 3,000 feet lower than planned. That would mean that the bombers would have to run in lower, too. Blake chose his words carefully, for almost certainly the enemy was listening.

"Goatee, Dingus."

"Roger, Dingus."

"Roger, you might go in a couple of thou [thousand feet] below what you programmed, because it looks like the viz is substantially better a little lower. We're going to drop about three thou lower than we planned."

JAMMING POD FORMATION

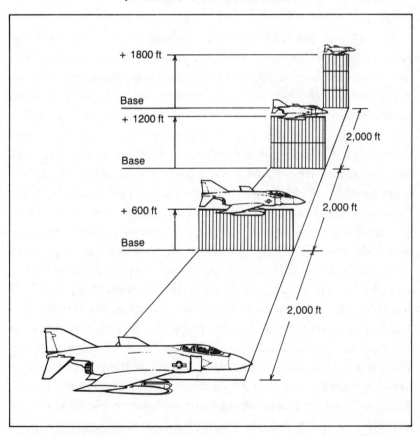

Aircraft flying in line abreast, separated 2,000 feet laterally, stepped up with 600 feet vertical separation.

"Roger."

One minute before the chaff bombers entered the Hanoi SAM zone, Blake ordered the crews to switch on their radar jamming pods. The latter acknowledged in turn, in the clipped tones and minimum of chatter that is the mark of a well-disciplined force:

"Dingus and Hitest, pods on."

"Two."

"Three."

"Four."

"Hitest."

"Two."

"Three."

"Four."

At 9:47 A.M. the chaff bombers charged into the Hanoi SAM zone, each flight flying in "jamming pod formation": four aircraft in line abreast, with 2,000 feet horizontal separation and 600 feet vertical separation between adjacent Phantoms. Close formation is relatively easy to fly; this wide-spaced formation was tough to fly and even more difficult to maneuver. But if it was flown properly, the jamming pod formation promised a high degree of invulnerability from SAM attack. Each plane radiated jamming from an ALQ-87 electronic countermeasures pod under the fuselage, and the jamming from the four planes correctly spaced produced a thick wedge of overlapping strobes on the enemy gun and SAM control radars. The North Vietnamese radar operators could track the formation as a whole but they could not pick out an individual plane accurately enough to engage it effectively. If a SAM guided on one member of the formation, the whole flight would begin a moderate descent. If the missile changed course to follow the descent, the flight would pull into a moderate climb. Only if a SAM continued homing on one of the planes would it break formation and pull into a more violent evasive maneuver. These tactics had proved effective over Hanoi in 1968, before the bombing pause; if the city's defenses had been improved since then to negate the tactic, the members of Dingus and Hitest flights would be the first to know. . . .

At 9:49 A.M. the chaff bombers reached a point eighteen miles south of Hanoi and started their turn toward the capital. In Dingus 2 Lieutenant James Dunn, on his first mission over North Vietnam, remembered things starting to get hot. "Shortly before we turned on the northbound track I started seeing lots of strobes on my radar warning gear. It was the first time I really heard anything on the warning gear. It made noises, and the noises were not good! Later I would learn which noises were important, but at that point it was all a blur." Dunn gave up trying to sort out the unfamiliar sounds and concentrated on holding his place in formation. "I wasn't afraid, because I didn't know what was trying to kill me!"

This account from a missile battery near Hanoi, which appeared later in the North Vietnamese newspaper *Nhan Dan,* is believed to describe an engagement on the morning of May 10:

> The order from headquarters was repeated: "Unit 1, destroy target coming from the south!" Unit Chief Tan instructed the missile crew to locate the target. Nguyen Kim Ho, the missile radar operator, reported that he had the target on his screen. . . .
>
> A group of aircraft appeared in the sky. Self-assuredly the commanding officer, Thang, shouted: "Stand by!" Rapidly the missile crew locked on to their targets. Unit Chief Tan's voice resounded: "Fire!" Two missiles shot forward heading straight toward the target, guided by missile men Ho, Trung and Ton. . . .

The Phantoms' crews watched the missiles blast away from their launchers, leaving great clouds of orange and white smoke. At the end of the boost phase the smoke ceased and for a while there was nothing to see. Then missiles hove into view, looking like telephone poles strangely out of place.

The two flights of F-4s continued their turn, pivoting on the inside plane. Lieutenant Barry Morgan, piloting Dingus 4 on the outside of the turn, could not hold position and started to drop back. At this point he should have crossed to the inside of the formation and cut the corner, but was glad he didn't. "During the turn a SAM came up and detonated close under the lead aircraft, Bob Blake's, and it took some damage. If I had cut the corner as I was supposed to, I would have been under him when the SAM went off. . . ." Morgan used full afterburner to regain position in formation after the turn.

"OK, continue left, Hitest."

"Hitest is left."

"Dingus and Hitest, ready . . . Pickle!"

Bob Blake's call to "pickle" meant to "release ordnance," and each Phantom dropped a single chaff bomb. Fifteen seconds later each dropped another; fifteen seconds after that, yet another. The process continued throughout the two minutes it took Dingus and Hitest flights to cover the eighteen miles from the turning point to Hanoi. After a short fall the casing of each bomb split open, to disgorge its load of metallized strips into the sky.

Meanwhile, far below, the Wild Weasels' battle with the ground defenses continued.

"SAM high three, Fletch [SAM control radar transmitting at high pulse rate, strength three, site probably about to launch]!"

"SAM at two o'clock low, Hitest!"

"No problem!"

"You got it too, Fletch Two?"

"Say again?"

"You got a SAM low?"

"Don't see one."

"Fletch Three's Winchester."

"Two is Winchester!"

"Winchester" meant "out of ordnance"; Fletch 2 and 3 had fired off their anti-radar missiles and were now effectively out of the fight.

As Dingus 3 bore Captain Larry Honeycutt and Lieutenant Charles Crisp over the target, the drama of their intercom chatter was recorded on tape. The clipped phrases were set against a background of heavy breathing, as men under extreme stress gulped oxygen, and almost continual squeaks and rattles from the radar warning receiver:

"OK, there's another launch light. . . . [indicating a SAM launch]."

"Say, they're coming from the right, we must keep an eye over there."

"There's the airfield, there's Hanoi! Want to see it better. . . ."

"They're coming from the right, somewhere. . . ."

"Look at the Triple-A [antiaircraft artillery fire]!"

"There's another SAM. . . . Holy shit!"

"Keep your eyeballs peeled to the right!"

"Look at it go!"

Hitest Flight was heavily engaged at this time, too. William Byrns, piloting Hitest 2, was another who survived because he did the unconventional. "A SAM came for us and someone yelled 'Look out!' I turned my head and my reaction was to pull back on the stick. That was not the normal reaction, I should have gone down. But I believe God took my hand and made me go the other way. The missile went underneath my plane, underneath the F-4 across the way and exploded on the far side of him. If I had gone down it would have hit us and we would probably not have got out. . . . I said to my back-seater, 'Praise the Lord!' He said, 'You can say that again!' "

Lieutenant Ron Moore, piloting Hitest 3 to the right of Byrns, also had cause to remember that particular missile. "Normally if a SAM appeared to move across your canopy, if there was gross movement, you knew it was going for somebody else. That one came from twelve o'clock and there was so much apparent movement I thought it was going for the other flight. But then it came for us and went off between Four and me. It was fused late—if it had gone off five hundred feet in front of us the fragments would have hit us. It went off right off our wingtip, within three hundred feet. The concussion rolled our airplane to ninety degrees—it was the closest I ever had a SAM go off."

In Hitest 4, to the right of Moore, back-seater Lieutenant Lanny Toups was yet another who remembered that SAM. "All of a sudden I saw the RHAW [radar warning] gear light up. I told

Mike [Suhy, his pilot] I had a SAM at ten o'clock. He said, 'Oh shit, take it down!' And just about the time we started down, the missile detonated. It went off between us and three, and the blast turned us upside down."

Though shaken by the explosion, both Phantoms escaped damage. Following this pummeling the chaff formation became ragged, but the planes pressed on toward the target, releasing their bombs at regular intervals.

FOR THE AMERICANS incarcerated in the Hoa Lo prison, alias the "Hanoi Hilton," the sight or sound of U.S. planes over the city always provided a welcome boost to morale. It showed they had not been forgotten. Those questioned found it difficult to recall individual actions, however, for during captivity the days tended to merge together in the collective memory. Whenever there was a raid the procedure was the same. Captain Jim Mulligan, USN, recalled: "I was in a cell with three guys, there were three guys in the next cell and we could walk between them. The windows of my cell looked north, west and east. Those from the next cell looked south, west and a bit to the east. When there was a raid each guy would go to his assigned corner to track what was going on. But if a guard came during the raid, we had to get back on our bunks or we could be in trouble." Between them the prisoners were usually able to assemble an accurate picture of what had taken place. Captain Eugene McDaniel, USN, another inmate, recalled the main source of discomfort was not bombs but the Hanoi defenses: when the heavy antiaircraft gun battery nearby opened fire, the concussion shook chunks of plaster from the ceiling that fell on anyone below.

The British Residence, one mile southeast of the prison, lay almost directly under the Phantoms' flight path. Pat Wright, sitting with husband Joe beneath the stairs, remembered the "tremendous din" as the city's antiaircraft guns barked their hatred at the raiders.

DINGUS FLIGHT, almost over the Paul Doumer Bridge at the end of the chaff bombing run, was singled out by the gunners. Barry

Morgan in aircraft 4 recalled: "Just prior to our outbound turn, all of a sudden shells burst between me and Three. We were about one thousand feet apart and he was blotted out, they burst at exactly the right altitude but between us. I had heard of flak so thick you could walk on it—this stuff looked like you really could!"

As the last chaff bombs fell clear, Dingus and Hitest flights curved on to a westerly heading pursued by flak bursts.

"Triple-A, keep it up! Triple-A, Dingus!"

"Roger, got it. We're going left."

"Hitest egress heading, hard left!"

"Hitest."

"Dingus gone."

"OK, Hitest leads, heading two-four-zero [west-southwest]."

TWO miles east of the Wrights in their improvised shelter, Théodore Ronco and Henri Joel were returning by car from the morning press conference at Haiphong. Suddenly they heard the unmistakable banging of antiaircraft fire; the Vietnamese driver swung off the road and stopped under a line of trees. Everyone got out and Ronco noticed that also drawn up under the trees were the guns and vehicles of a field artillery unit, probably on their way to the South.

Shortly afterward the chaff bombers swept past the watchers from left to right, high in the sky and wreathed in flak bursts, like leaden ducks sliding across a fairground shooting booth. The reporters watched the Phantoms turn west over Hanoi but afterward there were none of the expected bomb explosions. Ignorant of the purpose of the operation, the observers thought it odd that the Americans should hazard planes for so little result (several hours would pass before the chaff reached the ground). The Frenchmen speculated that perhaps the planes were on a reconnaissance to plot the positions of antiaircraft gun and SAM batteries in the area before another force delivered an attack.

Despite the fierce cannonade the chaff bombers emerged from Hanoi virtually unscathed. Only the leader's Phantom suffered minor damage when a SAM exploded nearby. The jamming from planes flying in the special formation, supported by more jam-ming from EB-66s and lethal harassment from Wild Weasel F-105s, effectively prevented accurate engagements by SAMs and radar-controlled guns.

Having exhausted their anti-radar missiles, the F-105s of Fletch Flight also withdrew. James O'Neil remembered May 10 as one of his quieter Wild Weasel actions. "We [the Wild Weasel aircraft] didn't have any SAMs fired at us that day. Sometimes we seemed to be the prime target, other times they ignored us. That day there were MiGs in the area, so we would not normally get missiles fired at us. It was either one or the other."

As the chaff bombers and the Wild Weasels left the target area, the EB-66s remained on their orbit lines jamming the enemy radars; these planes would stay there for another ten minutes until the main attack forces were clear of their targets.

IN THE Yen Bai area northwest of Hanoi, scene of Oyster Flight's combat, the only American fighters present were Balter Flight's two F-4s. Dean White's back-seater picked up a contact on radar that, because no other friendly fighters were in the area, was almost certainly hostile. The Phantoms began stalking it, and three minutes later White caught sight of a MiG-21 slightly higher in a climbing turn, crossing his nose from left to right. The Phantom pilot tried to get into a firing position, but the MiG held its turn and he ended up closing from the side and far too rapidly. White loosed off a couple of Sparrows, but the geometry of the attack was all wrong and neither guided properly.

White continued after the MiG, trying to get into position to attack with Sidewinders. But first he had to look in the cockpit to switch to the infrared missile, and when he next looked out, the MiG had disappeared.

Meanwhile Captain Bill Ridge, White's wingman, was about to engage a MiG-21 he had found. "He must have been about half a mile ahead of me—I pulled the trigger and saw the Sparrow go after him. But the MiG out-turned the missile. We passed canopy to canopy, about two hundred feet separating us; he was looking up at me and I was looking up at him. I kept the turn going, trying to get him in front of me. When I finally got him in front I happened to look over my left wing, and there was a MiG-21 sitting about half a mile behind Dean." Almost immediately afterward the North Vietnamese fighter launched a pair of missiles. Ridge blurted a warning over the radio: "Hard, Dean, break, break, Dean! . . . Break hard, Dean!" In that situation most fighter pilots would instinctively have pulled to the left. For some reason he still cannot explain, Dean White pulled hard right. Moments later the Atolls scorched past the left of his tail. The MiG that had fired them also broke away and was not seen again. Fearful that other MiGs might be moving into position to deliver similar snap attacks, White called Red Crown for help.

"You got some in our six [o'clock], Red Crown?"

"Contacts all around you, Balter, some at about two-three-zero at ten."

"OK, Balter, let's get the shit outa here!"

"All right, let's go!"

The two fighters accelerated to supersonic speed and headed west at 5,000 feet. But still they were not out of danger. Near the Laotian border the Phantoms stumbled into a trio of MiG-19s. Bill Ridge noticed flashes about three miles ahead, the sun glinting off the enemy fighters turning toward him. He pulled right to line up for a head-on missile shot closing at 1,200 knots— twenty miles per minute. There was no time for finesse, however, and the Sparrow launched on boresight at a range of half a mile passed over the MiG without detonating. Ridge and his intended victim both turned steeply and climbed to reengage each other. But the MiG-19 proved the more agile plane; it swung in behind the heavier Phantom and opened fire. Ridge used full afterburner to accelerate out of the fight as the cockpit recorder captured his snap assessment of the MiG-19's maneuverability: "Boy . . . those cocksuckers can turn!"

IN THEMSELVES the skirmishes around Yen Bai were indecisive, but they produced the desired effect—they held most of the MiGs

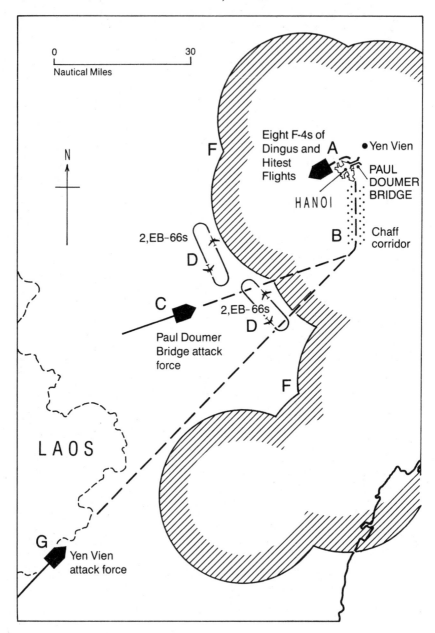

0   30
Nautical Miles

N

Eight F-4s of
Dingus and   A   • Yen Vien
Hitest
Flights   PAUL
                    DOUMER
                    BRIDGE
HANOI

2, EB-66s   B   Chaff
                                   corridor
D

C   2, EB-66s
                 D
Paul Doumer
Bridge attack
force
                        F

LAOS

G
Yen Vien
attack force

F

Air situation west of Hanoi at 9:54 A.M., as forces move in to attack the Paul Doumer Bridge and the Yen Vien Rail Yard. The 8 F-4s of Dingus and Hitest Flights (A), having laid their chaff corridor (B), are egressing the target area. The Paul Doumer Bridge attack force (C), comprising 16 F-4 bombers, 4 F-4 escorts and 4 F-105 Wild Weasel aircraft, are about to pass the 4 EB-66s of Cowsip and Valent Flights (D) before entering the SAM zone (E, approximate boundary). Four minutes behind is the Yen Vien attack force (F), comprising 16 F-4 bombers, 8 F-4 escorts and 4 F-105 Wild Weasels.

---

airborne in the area northwest of Hanoi. As a result the F-4 bombers now closing on the capital from the southwest had clear runs to their targets.

Several minutes elapsed before the chaff laid by Dingus and Hitest flights took effect. Slowly the clouds of sinking, spinning, tumbling strips expanded—as drops of ink falling on blotting paper diffuse to give expanding circles of color—spread out along a corridor two miles wide, more than a mile deep and eighteen miles long leading up to Hanoi. The "blockers" had done their job, now the "running back" could sprint for the goal line.

THE ACTION AROUND HANOI, THE PAUL DOUMER BRIDGE STRIKE

9:55–11:30 a.m.

Don't send me to Hanoi,
Don't put my name down.
The shooting is bad there.
Don't send me downtown.
    —"Don't Send Me to Hanoi"
      (to the tune of "Winchester Cathedral")

9:55 A.M., THIRTY MILES SOUTHWEST OF HANOI. Following the same route as the chaff bombers, the Paul Doumer Bridge attack force stormed into the western edge of the SAM defended zone, flying at 540 knots at 13,000 feet. Goatee, Napkin, Biloxi and Jingle flights, each with four Phantoms in jamming pod formation, flew in a gridlike pattern with two miles between flights.

Eighteen miles south of Hanoi the raiders turned onto a northerly heading for their target. The trail of chaff laid earlier showed clearly on the planes' radars, and Colonel Carl Miller, commander of the 8th Tactical Fighter Wing and leader of Goatee Flight, had no difficulty following it to Hanoi.

Far below the Phantoms, four Wild Weasel

F-105Gs of Galore Flight fanned out ahead of the force. Yet despite their harassment, the cacophony of jamming from the EB-66s and the F-4s of the main attack force, and the smoke-screen effect of the chaff corridor, the defending SAM batteries were still able to lay on an impressive display of wrath. Carl Miller recalled their efforts. "Visibility was good and you could see the SAMs for miles. That is the main thing I remember about that mission, the vast number of SAMs going over us, under us, in front of us, behind us. It was quite a sight to behold. If you had one go by you fairly close, it was pretty exciting. . . ."

In Napkin Flight, following Miller's, Major Bill Driggers was on his first mission over North Vietnam. "It was a beautiful clear morning; there were a few puffy clouds to the west of Hanoi but they didn't hinder us. I saw the Paul Doumer Bridge right after we turned in, sitting there dark brown at the northeast end of town," he recalled. "About thirty seconds after the roll out I saw my first SAM. Someone called a SAM a ten o'clock, I looked up and thought, Well, I'll be damned, that's what they look like! It looked like a cigar, about a mile away; it was coming in our direction, but it didn't bother me because I could see the side of it." If the side of the missile was visible, it was going somewhere else.

Flying straight and level in jamming pod formation while under attack from SAMs was like the first time one snuffed out a candle with one's fingers—an unnatural act needing courage to overcome instinct. Captain Lynn High, Biloxi Flight leader, commented: "We had to sit in formation and grit our teeth when the SAMs came through the formation. It took nerves of steel to watch a SAM come straight at you, even though you knew that in all probability it would not hit you and if it detonated it would detonate too soon or too late. I watched about six SAMs do exactly that."

In Jingle 4 at the rear of the formation, Captain Mike Van Wagenen described the indications in the cockpit when the SAM batteries prepared to engage: "The length of the strobe on the screen of the radar warning gear told how close you were to the

Goatee Flight, EOGBs
2,000 ft between aircratt
in Jamming Pod formation.

Napkin Flight, LGBs
2 miles behind Goatee Flt.

Biloxi Flight, LGBs
2 miles behind Napkin Flt.

Jingle Flight, LGBs
2 miles behind Biloxi Flt.

missile radar. You didn't pay much attention to one-ringers or two-ringers. But a three-ringer, the longest, strongest signal, that one said 'Hey! he's tracking you, better start looking out. . . .' "

As the flight neared Hanoi the missiles started coming up. Van Wagenen continued: "Rick [Lieutenant Colonel Rick Hilton, Jingle Flight leader] picked up the first one, down on our left at ten o'clock. I'll never forget that call, Rick's voice was so calm. I remember him say, 'OK, take it down two [thousand feet] and bring it up. . . . Go.' Everybody in the flight started nosing over. With our spacing you could tell which airplane the SAM was tracking, and this one was tracking Rick. As we went down the SAM started to come down with us. It came down for a few seconds looking as if it was tracking, then it went ballistic [ceased to guide]. It was as if our electronic countermeasures were getting into it. It whistled over the top of our heads and went off a mile or two down range. As soon as it went over we stopped worrying about it, it wasn't a threat. We started worrying about the next one. . . ."

During the run-in a recorder in Jingle 1 taped the almost incessant chatter on the radio and intercom conversations between Rick Hilton and Captain Bill Wideman. Then came the threatening rattle from the warning receiver—again a Fansong radar was tracking the plane.

"Got us again!"

"Launch light, Jingle Two!"

"I don't see it, coming out of that haze somewhere."

Fansong signals ceased.

"This is Red Crown on Guard. Bandits, Bullseye two-two-five thirty-one, angels unknown, heading one-nine-zero. Time five-seven, out!"

"Harlow Flight, go MIGCAP primary [primary MiG-hunting frequency]."

"Fletch Three, do you read, Fletch Four?"

"Jingle has indication ten o'clock!"

"There's the airfield, Gia Lam."

"Keep moving around, Goatee."

"Jingle's got a strobe at ten [o'clock]!"

"God damn's got to be the longest river in the world!"

"Yeah, there's the bridge, I can see it."

"You got it? Like me to set the outbound point on?"

"Roger."

"OK, got my head in the cockpit."

Yet more Fansong signals.

"That's a SAM, I'll look out."

"Missile launch, ten o'clock!"

"Can you see it?"

"Well, I don't see the missile."

"I don't see it either."

"Have you got it?"

"Negative."

"I know they're shooting at us but I sure don't see it!"

Fansong signals ceased.

While all this was happening the leading flight, Goatee, completed the inbound turn south of Hanoi and entered its bomb run. Each Phantom carried two 2,000-pound electrooptical guided bombs, weapons designed to home on the image contrast of the target against its background. Heading almost due north and following the Red River, the raiders approached the bridge at 90 degrees to its length. The sun on their backs put the shadows on the far side of the target, where they would not interfere with the bomb's TV guidance system. Each back-seater operated a hand controller to position the bridge under the sighting reticle on his TV screen, then pressed a button to lock the first bomb on the target. He then repeated the process for the second bomb.

---

1. Turn-in point for the force, south of Hanoi.

2. Aircraft with electro-optical guided bombs attacked the bridge across its width from almost due south, out of the sun. This was to put shadows behind the target, lest they distracted the bombs' guidance system.

3. Turn-in point for aircraft with laser-guided bombs, which attacked the bridge down its length.

4. After releasing their bombs, planes that had been carrying laser-guided weapons made supersonic runs over Hanoi to boost the morale of U.S. prisoners incarcerated in the city.

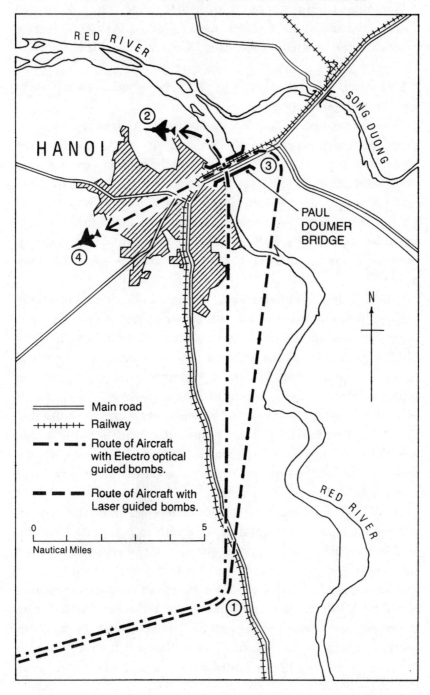

RED RIVER

SONG DUONG

② ④

HANOI

③

PAUL
DOUMER
BRIDGE

N

RED RIVER

——————— Main road

+++++++ Railway

—·—·— Route of Aircraft
with Electro optical
guided bombs.

— — — Route of Aircraft with
Laser guided bombs.

0   5

Nautical Miles

①

Five miles from the target Carl Miller nosed into a 30-degree descent and the rest of Goatee Flight followed. At 12,000 feet he broadcast the bomb-release call: "Goatee . . . Pickle! Pickle! Pickle!"

One bomb refused to leave its rack, the other seven fell away and rapidly gathered speed.

The electro-optical guided bombs seldom lived up to their supporters' extravagant promises, and on this occasion they performed miserably. Carl Miller watched in exasperation as they went their various ways. "I pickled off my EOGBs. One made a ninety-degree turn and went for downtown Hanoi— I think it impacted near the train station. I don't know where the other went. The EOGB was a launch-and-leave weapon, they were supposed to stay locked on after release. But they didn't."

While Goatee Flight attacked, the three following flights made for a point a couple of miles to the east of the bridge. This put them into position to attack the structure along its length. Thus Bill Driggers in Napkin 4 was in an ideal position to observe the results of Goatee Flight's attack. He fully expected to see the bridge collapse under a torrent of high explosive. "As we rolled in to attack the bridge I saw big waterspouts rising from the Red River. The first EOGBs fell short, those that made it to the bridge went through the gaps between the pylons. I saw two, maybe three, of the bombs explode in the water on the other side." Not a single EOGB found its target.

On the way to the target Napkin Flight leader suffered an equipment failure, so Captain D.L. Smith in Napkin 3 took the lead of the flight. As he passed abeam the bridge Smith applied full power and made a climbing turn to the left, which took his Phantom up to 21,000 feet. Then he rolled into the 45-degree attack dive. Bill Driggers in Napkin 4 stuck close to Smith during the maneuver: "I went under him and came out the other side in position. I was really tucked in, a few feet off his right wing. I thought to myself, If the Thunderbirds ever looked this good, they'd be proud!"

The second pair of Phantoms of Napkin Flight followed the first pair into the attack dive.

STANDING on the ground about two miles east of the bridge, journalist Théodore Ronco suddenly took a more personal interest in the events taking place in the sky above. Wheeling almost directly over the Frenchman, the leading pair of Phantoms peeled into their attack dives, and for a time it seemed as if they were about to attack the artillery unit drawn up under the trees beside him. Ronco glanced around for cover and suddenly the magnitude of the danger struck him; the nearest truck was laden with shells! Then he looked back at the Phantoms and was relieved to see they were aligned on a target some distance to the west.

AS if descending on successive steps of an escalator, the leading Phantoms dived at their target. Now the 37-mm and 57-mm guns defending the bridge opened up; lines of moving tracer, punctuated by stationary puffs from exploded shells, crisscrossed the sky over the eastern side of Hanoi. A report on the action, which later appeared in the newspaper *Nhan Dan,* stated:

> The battle positions in Hanoi were ready and active, including the floating ones on the Red River. They worked together closely to put up a curtain of fire to all levels, to encircle and destroy the enemy. During the action Bui Hien Dang, the company's observer, continuously followed the targets and instructed the gunners where to aim.

Huddled under the stairs at the British Residence, Joe and Pat Wright had their hands over their ears, but nothing could keep out the fearsome noise from the guns around them.

At 12,000 feet each Phantom let go its two 2,000-pounders and began pulling out of the dive. Lieutenant Wayne King, Smith's back-seater, switched on his laser designator and held the beam on a point at the east end of the bridge. In the nose of each bomb the laser seeker head guided the weapon toward the point thus marked. **During** the bombs' seventeen-second flight Smith could make only **gentle** turns to avoid antiaircraft fire, lest he pull the laser beam off the target.

The salvo of bombs exploded on the Paul Doumer Bridge or in the river beneath, hurling a column of smoke, spray and debris hundreds of feet into the air. As he saw them impact, King switched off the laser designator, and the two Phantoms, no longer constrained, pulled into steep turns and accelerated out of the area. Behind them, the other two planes in Napkin Flight were already established in their attack dives.

Théodore Ronco had a grandstand view as, two by two, the Phantoms dived to attack. "We could see their bombs fall, but there was no danger to us—we were about three kilometers [2 miles] from the bridge. Nor were we in danger from shell splinters—the guns around Gia Lam airfield were firing away from us."

Leading Biloxi Flight, the next to attack, Lynn High suddenly realized that the enemy antiaircraft barrage was concentrated in the wrong part of the sky. "The Vietnamese gunners obviously expected us to release from a lower altitude, they coned their fire on a point seventy-five hundred to nine thousand feet above the target. It looked like an Indian tepee sitting over downtown Hanoi. But we released our bombs at a higher altitude, we kept out of it." Biloxi Flight's eight 2,000-pounders burst around the bridge and threw up further columns of debris, smoke and spray.

Following Biloxi came Jingle Flight. Captain Mike Messett, the pilot with the personal grudge against the Paul Doumer Bridge, piloted Jingle 3 and led the final pair of F-4s. Mike Van Wagenen in 4 was last to attack:

"I expected that when I got to the bridge there would be nothing left to bomb. In that case we were briefed to go for any pylons that were left. I rolled in, flying formation on Mike, started tracking the bridge and made sure my dive angle was right.

"Then all of a sudden I realized, the bridge was still standing! There was a lot of smoke around it from other bombs but that sucker was still standing!

"There was so much going on it was impossible to comprehend everything. The human mind cannot take that many inputs, so it rules out a lot of them. The radio seemed to go quiet, the radar warning gear went quiet, everything appeared to go quiet as I tracked the Doumer Bridge underneath my sighting pipper. We just stopped thinking about the other things going on around us. My back-seater was calling off the altitudes: fifteen . . . fourteen . . . thirteen [thousand feet] . . . The pipper was tracking up the bridge, I had the parameters like I wanted to see them and released both bombs."

Van Wagenen hauled on the stick and watched the horizon sink rapidly past his windscreen as the G forces pushed him into his seat.

"As we came off the target it was like plugging in the stereo— slowly one's senses came back and one could hear the radar warning gear, the radio transmissions, everything else. The human computer was working again. I jinked hard left and right, picked up Mike and joined up on him. Then I rolled back to the right to see where my bombs had gone. It appeared all four, Mike's and mine, had hit the first span on the east side of the river. I took one more look to see if the span was standing, but I couldn't tell—there was a lot of smoke around."

As Van Wagenen left the bridge all its spans were in place, though the laser-guided bombs had caused severe damage. Two spans at the eastern end had broken apart and the section between the breaks was some feet lower at its western end. Though the Paul Doumer Bridge was still standing, it was impassable to wheeled vehicles.

FROM THE garden at the British consulate David Simmons and the Vietnamese houseboy watched the Phantoms thunder over the city from the direction of the bridge, curving to avoid the antiaircraft fire. The planes were flying supersonic and the resultant booms should have shaken the city. Perhaps they did. But Simmons does not remember hearing them. Nor do Joe and Pat Wright. Nor do American prisoners questioned by the authors.

The sonic booms, so disruptive when heard in isolation, were submerged in the general uproar of battle.

AS IT CAME off target Goatee Flight had a brush with MiGs. One of its planes launched a Sparrow at a MiG chasing an F-105, which forced the enemy fighter to break away. Then, Carl Miller recalled: "Somebody in my flight called other MiGs coming in, two MiG-19s. We broke into them. One fired a missile but we evaded it. Then they took off, they didn't stick around to fight. Neither did we. Once we had got rid of them we pushed forward the throttles and got the hell out of there."

As he thundered away from Hanoi in Napkin 4, Rick Bates also noticed the MiGs. "As we came off the target we passed a Thud [an F-105] followed by a MiG followed by a Thud. Then I saw a MiG-21 that looked as if it was trying to turn on us. But we were going so goddarn fast he had no chance. . . . Those three or four minutes was absolute and total chaos as far as I was concerned, my pulse rate was going at about eight million a minute. . . ."

Leaving the target area, Biloxi 2 suffered a partial electrical failure, which cut off power to some of the plane's equipment. Captain Mike Pomphrey remembered a "terse in-flight emergency," but the engines and flying controls kept going and he was able to keep up with the rest of his flight.

AS THE Paul Doumer Bridge attack force left Hanoi going west, the Yen Vien attack force came in from the southwest. Just short of the SAM defended zone the eight F-4 escorts (Arroyo and Bowleg flights) curved away to mount anti-MiG barrier patrols south and east of the target. The sixteen F-4 bombers (Gopher, Icebag, Gigolo and Bertha flights), loaded with 500-pound bombs, took the same route as previous attackers and followed the chaff corridor to the city. Major Kelly Irving, leading Gigolo Flight, particularly remembered the chaff. "I was impressed at how well it showed up on my air intercept radar. That was how we made sure we were positioned in it. That was a godsend, we drove up that thing like it was a highway."

As the new wave of attackers crossed high over the Paul Doumer Bridge, Captain Jim Shaw in Gopher 4 noticed something odd. "As we passed the bridge I saw all these flashes, it looked exactly like CBUs [cluster bombs] going off all over the approaches to the north and south ends. I thought, I don't remember any flak suppression being briefed, who's got the CBUs? Then I realized—the flashes were from the muzzles of guns shooting at us!"

Supporting the Yen Vien raiders were the four F-105 Wild Weasels of Calgon Flight. Captain Robert King, electronic warfare officer in Calgon 2, directed his pilot to attack a SAM site northwest of Hanoi. The Shrike missile was launched, but a few seconds later the enemy radar shut down. During the earlier actions most of the SAMs ready for launching in the Hanoi area had been fired. The missile-site crews had had insufficient time to reload their launchers, with the result that the Yen Vien raiders had a relatively clear run. King did not see a single SAM airborne that day.

The bombers ran toward the Yen Vien railway sorting yard at 15,000 feet. One after another the flights pulled up to 20,000, swung into echelon right and peeled left into their 45-degree attack dives. Jim Shaw, in the leading flight, recalled: "We followed the other three down the chute and Bud Pratt [his pilot] pickled bombs. When we pulled off I looked back, and saw somebody's bombs do a pretty good job across the south choke point. While in the target area we tried to change something—heading, altitude or speed—every ten seconds to defeat the radar aimed fire."

It was a necessary precaution, for as Gopher Flight came off the target it suddenly came under heavy fire. Shaw recalled: "Lead got away with it, Two flew through some of it, Three could not avoid it. We broke left and came very sharply back to the right. I got an eyeful of all the standard colors of smoke puffs, the larger the caliber the darker the smoke: white puffs were 23 mm, light gray puffs were 37mm, gray were 57 mm and black puffs were 85 mm." Running out fast trying to dodge the flak bursts, Gopher Flight had difficulty rejoining formation.

Shaw continued: "Beforehand every flight leader briefs that he will fly a wide arc coming off the target so those behind can cut off the turn and join up for mutual support. But when they are being shot at, very few leaders do it to the degree their wingmen would like. We went out scalded-ass fast and it took a while to get the flight back in order. Everybody had a distinct interest in getting away from the people they had just been nasty to!"

Lieutenant Laird Johnson in Gopher 2 came out fast, but he saw someone else come out faster. "As we were going out I checked our six and saw something very low coming at me fast. I wondered what it was, I thought it might be a missile. My front-seater [Lt. James McCarty] rolled the plane over so we could look at it. It was an F-105 Wild Weasel, exiting the target area at an incredible speed. . . ."

Icebag Flight attacked second and pulled away from the target area. Then Kelly Irving rolled in to attack, at the head of Gigolo Flight. He was struck by the small size of the railroad yard at Yen Vien. "I grew up around railroads, I used to live next to a real big yard at El Reno, Oklahoma. I remember the switching yards in the States, which were significant things. As I looked at the target, I remember thinking this looked a very puny little railroad yard. I aimed at the center of the yard and let the spread of dumb bombs take care of the area. It was a perfect target for dumb bombs." The recorder in Gigolo 3 captured the conversations between Major Dan Nesbett and back-seater Lieutenant Henry Goddard:

"OK, where's the railroad yard?"

"OK, there's the fuckin' railroad."

"OK, activity . . . blinking launch."

"I don't see a missile. . . . I don't see a missile!"

"Fuckit!"

"Come on, Goddamnit!"

The missile passed safely clear, then the flight pulled up and the Phantoms arced over into their attack dives. While Nesbett concentrated on holding his fighter-bomber at the correct dive angle and speed, Goddard called off the altitudes and kept watch outside the cockpit.

"Are you tally [in visual contact] on the railroad yet?"

"That's affirm!"

"Eighty-seven-hundred-foot Pickle [8,700-foot bomb release altitude]."

"That's an eighteen-seven [18,700 foot altitude of plane] . . . have ten thousand feet to go! I don't see anything coming up so far."

"OK, there's fifteen-seven . . . fourteen-seven . . . thirteen-seven . . . twelve-seven, a little fast, eleven-seven . . . ten . . . nine, ready, Pickle!"

"It's over for now, let's move it!"

Piloting the "running spare" F-4 that had been impressed into the mission as Gigolo 4, Doug Nix had a nasty moment when the four 500-pounders on one of his outboard racks failed to release despite all his efforts to make them go. Restrained by the extra drag, the Phantom fell farther and farther behind the others in the flight leaving the target. "Can't think of much worse than being alone over Hanoi," he later commented. The defenders ignored him, however, and by using full power he was able to rejoin the flight.

Lieutenants Brewster Shaw and Garry Reed, in Gigolo 2 and 3, respectively, recalled the attack as straightforward and with little interference from the defenses. Bertha Flight then rounded off the attack. None of the Phantoms sent against the rail yard suffered damage.

TAN SON NHUT, SAIGON. General Vogt had returned to his Command Center, "Blue Chip," when the raiding forces reached their targets. He had guided the enterprise to this point, but now his role was merely that of spectator. On leaving the target each formation leader transmitted the code words Echo Tango to indicate an apparently successful attack. Relayed via a KC-135 over Laos, the arrival of the poststrike messages at the Command Center broke the tension and drew spontaneous outbursts of approval. Vogt

appreciated the calls—they meant that nothing had gone seriously wrong over the North. But he was too experienced a commander to be overoptimistic about information from this source
on the damage inflicted: "The guys knew they had hit the Paul
Doumer Bridge and they thought they had dropped it. But previously in war I had had so many reports of successes that were
later disproved. I had learned to wait for proof from the poststrike
reconnaissance."

NORTH OF Hanoi the two RF-4Cs of Cousin Flight, 14th Tactical
Reconnaissance Squadron, were assigned to get that proof. Now
they moved into position ready to begin their photo runs as soon
as the Yen Vien raiders were clear of the target. Near the start
point the RF-4Cs came under SAM attack, but they easily out-
maneuvered the missiles. Major Sid Rogers, flying lead, gave the
order to jettison the drop tanks. Captain Don Pickard in the
second aircraft pressed the button to release his and felt the plane
yaw violently—the left tank had not released. "The airplane
pulled hard left, as if I had stomped the rudder. It started to roll
on its back. I regained control and the tank separated." The reason for the Phantom's antics soon became clear. Pickard checked
the fuel gauges and found that instead of the expected 12,400
pounds he had only 9,500 pounds, one quarter less. The left tank
had not been feeding fuel; probably it was still full when he
released it. A full tank weighed about 3,000 pounds, and the
asymmetric load under outboard pylon on the left wing had made
the plane lurch to that side before the tank fell clear.

Pickard decided to continue the mission; if he husbanded his
remaining fuel, he should have sufficient to get home with a small
reserve. At the start line twenty-five miles north of Hanoi the two
Phantoms accelerated to 650 knots, then, varying altitude between 4,000 and 6,000 feet, described a huge elongated "S" in the
sky as they charged past the MiG base at Phuc Yen, the rail yard
at Yen Vien and the Paul Doumer Bridge. Automatic cameras in
the nose of each plane captured on film the scene ahead and on
either side. Sweeping past the rail yard, Pickard saw it had been

hit, but the smoke from several fires made it impossible to make any detailed assessment of damage.

During their photo run the Phantom pilots had to make a conscious effort not to let their planes go supersonic because that would have deprived them of the maneuverability necessary to line up on targets. Flying in loose pair, the Phantoms headed for the Paul Doumer Bridge, Pickard slightly behind and about 1,000 feet to the right of his leader. By then the defending gunners were beginning to zero in on the planes and they laid on an awe-inspiring fireworks display. Pickard recalled: "After we passed the rail yard we got everything in the world shot at us. We started jinking, and as we approached Hanoi there was a trail of black puffs from bursting shells behind Sid. I said to my back-seater, Chuck Irwin, 'Good God, look at that stuff behind lead!' Chuck replied, 'It's a good thing you can't see the stuff behind us!' "

As the Paul Doumer Bridge swept past him half a mile to the east, Pickard glanced at the structure; all its spans seemed in place. Then Gia Lam airfield passed below and suddenly Pickard noticed a MiG-17 about 500 yards behind and to the left trying to get into a firing position; his panoramic camera snapped the North Vietnamese fighter. The RF-4Cs dropped their noses and easily outdistanced the slower MiG.

South of Hanoi a SAM battery joined the unequal contest and loosed off a missile. Although his camera photographed the SAM approaching from below, Pickard saw nothing of it before the warhead detonated. The first he knew of its presence was the Phantom bucking under its blast: "I didn't see the SAM but I saw a whole bunch of red things, like tracer rounds but fanning out, come past my nose. I ducked, it looked like we were going to hit them." Miraculously the missile fragments all missed the plane.

Immediately afterward, Pickard recalled, there was another MiG scare. "As we headed away from Hanoi, Red Crown called to say we had a bandit behind us. At that time I was trying to conserve fuel, I was down to fifty-three hundred pounds. But we started accelerating to the southwest in burner. We were at low altitude and really using gas, it was beginning to hurt."

Once they were clear of the reported MiGs the Phantoms slowed down, but even at the lower rate of consumption Pickard knew his remaining fuel would not get him home. He needed to go high, to the rarefied air above 40,000 feet, where the aerodynamic drag was only one-third that at sea level and each pound of fuel would carry the plane more than twice as far. Although it would cost fuel to get to altitude, the improved consumption once there far outweighed this disadvantage. Swiftly the two Phantoms rose to 43,000 feet, throttled back and leveled out.

The MiGs had forced the reconnaissance birds well east of their planned egress route and clear of the KC-135 tanker rendezvous area. Pickard recalculated his fuel. If he headed straight for Udorn, if there were no further problems, he would reach his base. Sid Rogers had plenty of fuel and flew in the covering position.

10:14 A.M. East of Hanoi the rest of the raiders were running out, going southeast. Four flights of F-4s covered the withdrawal: Harlow Flight was northwest of the capital, Bowleg Flight was south-southwest and Arroyo Flight was south-southeast of the city; and to the southwest, near the Laotian border and astride the withdrawal route, sat Dogear Flight, which had moved forward after "riding shotgun" for the KC-135 tankers.

The earlier MiG activity had tapered off and for the past few minutes there had been little sign of the defending fighters. Tempted by the relative inactivity, Harlow Flight edged past Yen Bai airfield at 8,000 feet, flaunting itself to lure North Vietnamese fighters into battle. The move succeeded all too well. With appalling suddenness the would-be predators became the prey. Seemingly from nowhere a MiG-19 appeared 500 feet behind Harlow Flight's second element; there is evidence the pilot was Dang Ngoc Ngu of the 3rd Company. The radio warning, when it came, was both late and misleading:

"Harlow Three, Harlow Three, you got a MiG on your ass!"

"Harlow Three, you got a MiG back there, take it down!"

Desperately the crews of Harlow 3 and 4 searched behind the

former. They failed to see the MiG that was then closing fast on Harlow 4, flown by Captain J. Harris and Captain D. Wilkinson. Either the threatened Phantom was wrongly identified or someone had made a slip of the tongue. In almost any other situation so simple an error would have passed unnoticed, but in air-to-air combat mistakes are rarely forgiven. Cannon shells tore away part of the Phantom's left wing and the plane rolled into an uncontrolled dive. Seemingly in slow motion the shattered plane went into a long steep dive and plunged into the ground, leaving a trail of smoke to mark its epitaph. Those watching in stunned horror saw no parachutes and heard no beeper signals to indicate that either crewman had survived.

Lieutenant Colonel Rollins, Harlow Flight leader, curved after the assailant and launched a retaliatory Sidewinder, then two Sparrows. The missiles, fired at their engagement limits, all missed. The MiG pilot did not push his luck; he dived away and disappeared as suddenly as he had come.

OVER northern Thailand the first to reach a tanker on the home-bound flight were the three survivors of Oyster Flight, desperately short of fuel after their battle with MiGs followed by the supersonic low-altitude dash from North Vietnam. When they reached the tanker, the Phantoms were down to about ten minutes' worth of fuel each. John Markle, the lowest on fuel, hooked up first and took just enough for his immediate needs. Then he disconnected, the other two Phantoms moved up in turn, each took just enough before disconnecting. Then in succession the three hooked up again and each took enough fuel to get to Udorn.

For security reasons the crews of the tanker aircraft were told no more than what was strictly necessary about the missions they supported. Notwithstanding this, the crews of the "flying gas stations" maintained a strong affinity with those flying fighter-bombers and felt the loss keenly when one failed to return. Lieutenant Warren Weaver, a KC-135 copilot, explained: "You can't imagine how terrible it was for a tanker crew to refuel a flight of four aircraft on the way in, and only three on the way out. And you *never* asked what had happened to the other aircraft—that was a strict rule."

IN HANOI, as the Phantoms of Cousin Flight receded into the distance and the city's defenders ceased fire an unnatural silence descended on the city. Then, haltingly at first, the shrill note of the cicadas gradually resumed its usual intensity. The all-clear sounded, people emerged from shelters and the air of bustle and activity returned to the streets.

After the attack the inhabitants tried to check that their families and friends were unharmed, and inspected their homes for damage. At the British Residence a skylight set into the roof had shattered into a thousand jagged splinters, which crunched underfoot in the hallway. Whether the damage was caused by bomb blast, splinters from a shell or missile or a sonic boom, the Wrights never discovered.

Leaving Pat to supervise the cleaning-up operation, Joe Wright returned to the consulate. On arrival he learned that pieces from an exploded SAM had fallen around the building, and some lay embedded in the woodwork. The consul general's next task was to discover the extent of the damage caused by the attack.

"I asked the Vietnamese staff to try to find out where the bombs had fallen. They were Party members, they had their grapevine. One told me the Paul Doumer Bridge had been hit, so I summoned my car and asked the Vietnamese driver to take me there. He was as keen to see the damage as I was. We took the road along the Red River and approached the bridge as slowly as we dared—we did not want to attract attention by appearing too interested. I could just make out a span at the far side of the bridge tilted up at one end. From the lack of traffic, it was clear the bridge was out of action."

As the elderly Peugeot neared the bridge Wright noticed police and soldiers manning a roadblock ahead. Rather than face a lot of awkward questions he told the driver to turn down a side street, and they returned to the consulate.

• • •

OVER central Laos at 43,000 feet and short of fuel, Don Pickard called the tower at Udorn and asked for priority for a straight-in approach and landing. The tower controller replied that a few minutes earlier a plane had run into the airfield's crash barrier, and until it was towed clear the runway was blocked. It was not Pickard's day.

Quickly the Phantom pilot recalculated his remaining fuel. If he throttled back and descended slowly for the next one hundred miles, he would have just enough to reach the airfield at Nam Phong about forty-five miles south of Udorn. That was the fall-back position—if possible Pickard still wanted to land at Udorn. He asked the controller to tell him when the runway was clear. "I had passed Udorn heading for Nam Phong when the controller called: 'The runway is clear. You're cleared to land right now, we can hold the runway for you.' I was high, over twenty thousand feet; Udorn was closer than Nam Phong, so I turned back. I pulled one engine back and at twelve thousand feet I threw the gear and flaps out and started a steep turning descent to the runway."

Pickard had no margin for error. After a missed approach a Phantom needed 500 pounds of fuel to fly a closed pattern and land. As he lined up the pilot knew he had less than 300 pounds. "I told Chuck Irwin to rotate the handle so that if he ejected we would both go. I told him that if we did not land first time I was going to climb and head south. As soon as the first engine quit he was to pull the handle and eject us both. There was no way we could make it back to the runway."

The steep visual approach went perfectly until, just short of touchdown, Pickard pushed on power to halt the plane's fierce rate of descent. With so much on his mind he had overlooked a vital switch, and the omission was about to jeopardize both the plane and its crew. During the return flight through the stratosphere the outside air temperature had been minus 56 degrees centigrade, colder than the coldest deep freeze, and the inside of the canopy was chilled below freezing point. Now the Phantom's engines wound up and the air-conditioning system blew moist warm air over the frozen surfaces. In no time a layer of opaque white frost formed on the inside of the canopy.

Pickard shut off the air-conditioning system to prevent things from getting worse, tore off his oxygen mask and pulled off his left glove with his teeth. Then he desperately scratched the frost away from a small area at the side of the canopy, using his fingernails. Through the clear patch Pickard could just make out the runway coming up to meet him; fortunately he was used to making landings with little forward visibility. "As an instructor I had spent a lot of time landing or teaching landings from the back seat. I banged the Phantom down on the runway, we rolled to the end and turned off. We had under two hundred pounds of fuel left. . . ."

Lacking sufficient fuel even to reach his squadron's dispersal area, Pickard taxied off the runway and shut down. It had not been the sort of flight he wanted to have to repeat in a hurry.

BY 11:15 A.M. the raiding force was back on the ground at its bases in Thailand. The 8th Tactical Fighter Wing at Ubon had sent out forty F-4s to lay the chaff corridor, and to attack the Paul Doumer Bridge and the Yen Vien railway yard; all returned safely, though one had minor damage. The 388th Tactical Fighter Wing at Korat sent twelve F-105s, four EB-66s and an EC-121 to support the operation; all returned safely. The 432nd Tactical Reconnaissance Wing at Udorn had sent thirty F-4s and RF-4Cs to support the operation; only twenty-eight returned, and the two Phantoms shot down by MiGs were the only Air Force planes lost during the mission.

James Allen described the mood of the crews on their return. His description applied to the Ubon Wing, but similar scenes were repeated at Udorn and Korat: "On the crew truck everybody was excited, everybody talked about the mission. At the maintenance debriefing everybody was talking but very little of it was about the aircraft. It was hard to get the aircraft debrief done. Back in the crew truck everybody still talked and some played tapes recorded during the mission. At the intelligence debrief everybody talked about the mission yet again. People were still excited, they talked about every missile, every round of triple-A, every MiG they had seen. Finally we got back to the squadrons, got a cold beer and an iced towel—boy, they were nice. But now it was real hard to debrief the flights—people had got tired of talking!"

After the various debriefings Charlie Crisp went to look at the damage to the Chaff Formation leader's Phantom, caused when the SAM exploded a few hundred feet away: "The plane had little bitty chunks out, all over. Nothing big, like paint chipped off the tanks in several places and fibrous material hanging off the radome where the fragments had poked holes in it."

AT UDORN the film magazines were removed from the RF-4Cs Pickard and Rogers had flown, and rushed to the analysis center for developing. Poring over the negatives with a photo inter- preter, Colonel Charles Gabriel, commanding the 432nd Tactical Reconnaissance Fighter Wing, had to make a rapid initial assess- ment of the bomb damage. The pictures of the Paul Doumer told a disappointing story: the bridge was still standing, all its spans in place. Those of the Yen Vien rail yard showed the through lines blocked and numerous craters in the classification yard. Gabriel called General Vogt on the secure radio link and passed on the news. Nobody liked to bear bad tidings, but Gabriel had no alternative.

That task complete, the interpreters began work on a more detailed report on the photographs. During their hectic dash past Hanoi the Phantoms' automatic cameras had been running con- tinuously. In addition to the Paul Doumer Bridge and the Yen Vien rail yard, the films covered three airfields, three SAM sites and five operational antiaircraft gun sites, one of which was firing at the planes when it was photographed.

THE RETURN of the raiding force marked the end of the Seventh Air Force's involvement over North Vietnam for the day, though it would continue to provide support for the land battle in South

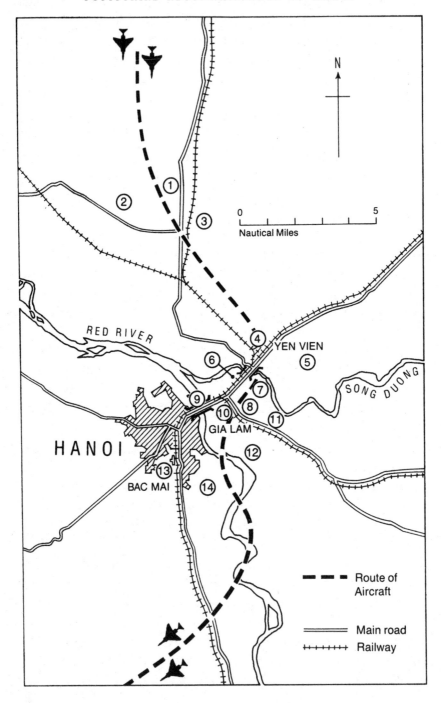

N

0   Nautical Miles   5

RED RIVER

YEN VIEN

SONG DUONG

HANOI

GIA LAM

BAC MAI

- - - Route of Aircraft

———— Main road

+++++++ Railway

Analysis of photos taken during the poststrike reconnaissance by Major Sid Rogers and Captain Don Pickard, 14th Tactical Recon Squadron.

1. Three field guns, 7 howitzers parked off the road, trails in traveling position.
2. Phuc Yen airfield, partial coverage: two MiG-21s, one MiG-17 and three Il-28 bombers, all parked.
3. AAA site, 8 guns probably 37 mm, part of airfield defenses.
4. Yen Vien railroad yard. Smoke limited interpretation. Cratering of through lines, nine of twelve tracks in classification yard appeared cut. Several craters and secondary fires noted in immediate area. About a hundred assorted items of rolling stock remained, apparently undamaged, in the classification yard.
5. SAM site VN 347: three SA-2 missiles on launchers, three empty launchers, one Fansong radar. Two SA-2s on transporters and four possible SA-2s on transporters nearby. Numerous support vans.
6. AAA site: four guns, probably 85 mm, firing at aircraft.
7. AAA site: six 85 mm guns in revetments, one Firecan radar.
8. AAA site: six 57 mm guns, possible Firecan radar.
9. Paul Doumer railroad and highway bridge. All spans in place, the impact point of the bombs could not be determined. There were 27 vehicles on the bridge. On the photographs the bridge appeared operational, though we know a break at the eastern end prevented wheeled traffic.
10. Gia Lam airfield: two Il-12 and two Il-14 (twin-engined transports), three Li-2s (Soviet built Douglas DC-3s), six An-2 (single-engined biplane transports), two Mi-1 (helicopters).
11. AAA site: eight guns, probably 85 mm, in revetments.
12. SAM site VN 009: site unoccupied, no missiles or radar observed. Mi-4 helicopter observed.
13. Bac Mai airfield: no aircraft observed (airfield out of use).
14. SAM site VN 243: five SA-2 missiles on launchers, one empty launcher, one Fansong radar.

Vietnam. During the twenty-four-hour period the Seventh Air Force would fly 347 sorties against targets there, including sixty-six by B-52s. Now we return to the Gulf of Tonkin, where the planes lining the decks of the three American carriers were ready to launch for the next attack on the North.

THE ACTION OVER HAI DUONG

11:00 a.m.–2:15 p.m.

Killing a man is murder, unless you do it to the blare of trumpets.

—Voltaire

11:00 A.M., YANKEE STATION. For the second time that morning *Constellation*'s intelligence center was a hive of activity as crews received their final briefings. The next attack was scheduled to open in two hours; the target was the rail yard at Hai Duong, a small provincial town midway between Hanoi and Haiphong.

Lieutenant Steve Rudloff, an F-4 radar intercept officer of VF-92, was assigned to the TARCAP (TARget Combat Air Patrol) mission. Later he wrote:

> Because of the complexity of the mission and the fact that it was the wing's first deep thrust into enemy territory on this cruise, our brief was unusually long. The assignment given to our two-plane section was to fly in the forward echelon of the strike force until we reached the target area, then to accelerate out in front and fly counter-

clockwise around the target while the actual bombing was in progress. When we saw the final attack aircraft pull out of its bombing run we were to follow the strike force out until all aircraft were over the water.

When the formal briefing was over the Air Wing commander [Commander Gus Eggert] added a postscript directed solely at the fighter community. First he stated that there would be no "trolling for MiGs" as had occurred on the morning flight to Haiphong. His second and last comment, however, concerned only the TARCAP and permitted me, in effect, to seal my own fate. His orders were for the TARCAP to remain with the strike force from the time it reached the coast-in point until it was safely out over the water, with two exceptions. We could remain in the target area after the strike if an actual MiG engagement involving our MIGCAP [anti-MIG Combat Air Patrols] was in progress, or if enemy aircraft were in the vicinity of the target but had not yet taken an offensive posture.

The reference to "no trolling for MiGs" was significant. The violation of standing orders by Austin Hawkins during the first Alpha Strike, in leading the unauthorized sweep to Kep airfield looking for MiGs, could not be shrugged off by his superiors. If others followed this example it could lead to near chaos. Charlie Tinker, Hawkins's back-seater, recalled: "Everyone was excited about Curt's MiG kill, but Hawk was in deep shit for leaving the strike to go trolling. The 'elephants' were still deciding our fate when we manned up for the strike on Hai Duong. We were punished by tying us to an Iron Hand A-7 as escort. Hawk was told, . . . If you don't come back with him, don't come back at all!' "

According to their squadron's original schedule, Lieutenants Randy Cunningham and Willie Driscoll of VF-96 should not have flown on the mission. But at the last moment their names were added, to fly one of the four F-4 flak suppressor aircraft; each of these planes was loaded with four cluster bombs, but retained an air-to-air armament of four Sidewinders and two Sparrows. The chance decision to include this crew would have an important bearing on the action that followed.

Before and after the briefing, the talk among fighter crews had been of the unprecedented MiG activity that morning. As he strode to his Phantom, flown by VF-92's executive officer, Commander Harry Blackburn, Steve Rudloff felt "high as a kite" at the prospect of getting his first shot at an enemy fighter that very day.

The sense of anticipation felt by the fighter crews was not shared by those assigned to fly *Constellation*'s attack planes during the mission. On previous operations each A-7 had carried a Sidewinder missile for self-protection. But following the expenditure of seven of these weapons during the morning engagement, it was necessary to remove them from the A-7s so that each F-4 would have its full complement. A-7 pilot Lieutenant Norman Birzer recalled: "We had carried a 'winder' on every mission during the entire cruise, with almost no prospect of ever needing it. When I found clean AIM-9 [Sidewinder] rails on my Corsair I was dumbfounded. I stormed over to the 'gunner' and asked where my Sidewinder was. He said the fighters had used up so many that morning and CAG [commander air group] wanted all fighters to have four 'winders' each, so there weren't any left for the A-7s," he continued. "It was the one time in our entire combat experience when we were most likely to need a Sidewinder and they were taken from us. I was furious!" In fairness it should be pointed out that CAG, Commander Eggert, was to lead the mission in an A-7 that had also had its Sidewinder removed.

11:48 A.M. *Constellation*'s steam turbines ran up to maximum power and she turned into the wind. To Airman Loren Bidwell, a "green-shirt" whose task was to attach planes to the catapult, this brought welcome relief. Previously the carrier had been cruising slowly downwind with scarcely any wind over her deck. Those in the open sweltered under the oppressive noonday heat. "It was very hot, with temperatures up to one hundred twenty degrees. When the ship turned into the wind for the launch, it was a real blessing—a cool summer breeze that went all the way down to one hundred degrees."

The carriers launched their planes in the same order as for the previous strike, and the form-up took place without incident. For this mission *Constellation*'s Air Wing comprised thirty-two aircraft—one fewer F-4 escort than during the morning strike. Her planes set out from Yankee Station at 12:19 P.M., followed at intervals by those from the other two carriers. As before, the operation was closely watched by the North Vietnamese early warning radars.

12:54 P.M. *Constellation*'s Air Wing crossed the coast of North Vietnam near the mouth of the Red River at 15,000 feet, and turned north-northeast for Hai Duong. As the formation entered the SAM defended zone the EKA-3B dropped back, climbed and started jamming the ground radars.

As he came over the coast Steve Rudloff ran an eye over his flying map to check the positions of defended areas. Then he refolded the map and put it in its usual place beside his right foot. Only in his worst nightmare could he have imagined the circumstances in which he would next see that map, and the trauma its reappearance would cause. With the cockpit squared for combat he made a careful radar search for enemy fighters. He found none.

Southeast of Hai Duong the two Iron Hand A-7s and their escorting F-4s eased out the formation and moved to their assigned stations on each side of the target. Norm Birzer was piloting the A-7 covering the east flank. "Because Shrikes had been successful against SAM radars," Birzer said, "the North Vietnamese were more interested in survival than high kill rates. They had been firing their SAMs at aircraft, and not sending radar signals until it was too late for us to respond with our antiradiation missiles. So we cooked up a counterstrategy: twenty-five miles from the target each Iron Hand plane turned about twenty degrees from the strike group track, towards the probable SAM launch sites. At twenty miles we each 'Nav-lofted' a Shrike towards these sites."

"Nav-lofting" meant firing the missile into an area of likely SAM activity, before the missile control radar began transmitting. The idea was that when the SAM radar did come on, the Shrike would be well placed to make a quick kill.

Birzer loosed off the Shrike, but in his area the North Vietnamese were not interested in playing his game. He heard no SAM radar signals on which his missile could have homed. Throughout the maneuver Austin Hawkins, in the escorting F-4, chastened by his dressing down following the morning action, remained dutifully in position off Birzer's wing.

When it came, the initial SAM threat was from the west of the strike force. A quick call from one of the A-6 crews alerted the force.

"Boomer [A-6 of VA-165] SAM strobe at seven o'clock!"

"SAM high, strobe at seven o'clock!"

Lieutenant Tom Gravely, flying the other Iron Hand A-7, launched a Shrike at the source of the signals and shortly afterward the radar transmissions ceased.

A-6 pilot Lieutenant Randy Foltz recalled his feelings as he neared Hai Duong. "I'd seen a lot of John Wayne movies about World War Two, with planes flying over Germany and the flak coming up. As we moved towards the target there were black and white flak puffs all over the place. I remember thinking that perhaps my canopy was a motion picture screen and I was watching something that wasn't real. It was like Hollywood was all around me."

South of the target *Constellation*'s Air Wing split into its component parts. As before, the MiG-hunting F-4s accelerated in front and moved north of the rail yard to protect the strike group from that direction. The A-6s made for a point to the northeast of the target; they were to roll in and attack first. Simultaneously the A-7s made for a point northwest of the target, they were to go in after the A-6s to deliver a pincer attack.

From his A-6, Lieutenant Ron Pearson began to realize that the

---

Constellation's Air Wing is closing on the rail yard at Hai Duong and its attack aircraft are about to begin their bomb runs. *Coral Sea*'s Air Wing follows 60 miles behind, bound for the bridge over the Binh River near Hai Duong. The cruiser *Chicago*, Red Crown, lies about 85 miles southeast of the target. Already several MiGs are airborne and converging on Hai Duong; the most intensive air action fought over Vietnam will begin in less than a minute.

THE RAIDERS APPROACH HAI DUONG, 12:59 P.M. MAY 10, 1972

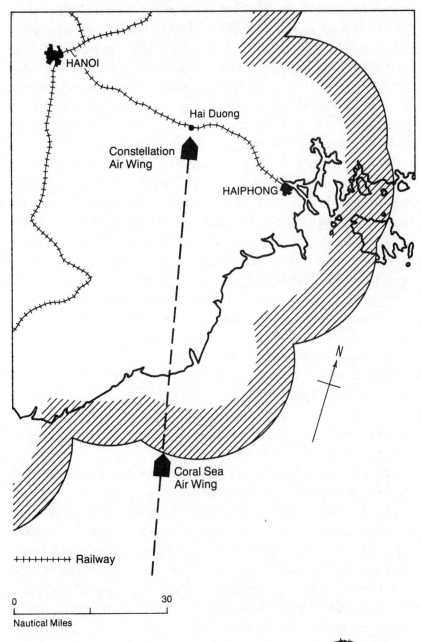

HANOI

Hai Duong

Constellation
Air Wing

HAIPHONG

N

Coral Sea
Air Wing

+++++++++ Railway

0   30

Nautical Miles

USS CHICAGO
'Red Crown'

formation leader had not seen the rail yard. "He flew exactly on course; he did everything he was supposed to, except he didn't roll in when we got to the IP [Initial Point]. It was a nice day, good visibility. The problem was that the visibility was too good. Our briefed roll-in point was over a bridge to the east of Hai Duong. On our maps was just one highly visible bridge. But up there in the real world, visibility was so good we could see a bunch of bridges. He was looking at a bridge further north thinking he hadn't reached the roll-in point yet. And he didn't roll in."

It was a potentially ticklish situation, but Eggert's crews knew what was expected of them. "When I briefed a strike the order of attacking was not sacrosanct," said the Air Wing commander later. "If the guy supposed to roll in first failed to see the target, the guy who did see it was to roll in and the others were to follow. They were not to wait around getting their fannies shot off—they were to roll in, bomb, and get out of there."

Flying in the number two position, Randy Foltz also realized what was happening. He called the leader and asked if he had the target in sight.

"You tally on the target, Boomer?"

"Negative the target yet."

"Roger, you'll have to follow us, we're gonna roll in!"

Foltz took charge of the A-6 force. He made a half barrel roll over his leader and slid into his attack dive. The other planes followed.

The delay in turning-in took the bombers farther north than planned, and instead of attacking from two separate directions they all ran in from nearly due north. The rest of the attack went according to plan, however, and the hiccup was soon forgotten.

From his flak suppression F-4 Randy Cunningham watched the A-6s and A-7s attack, "looking for all the world like a column of ants as they went down the chute. AAA puffs dotted the sky." The shell bursts were obvious enough, but Cunningham could see no muzzle flashes to betray the guns he was supposed to attack. So he and his wingman, Lieutenant Brian Grant, deposited their cluster bombs on warehouses beside the main target.

RONCO

Above, Théodore Ronco, right, Hanoi correspondent to the French newspaper *L'Humanité*, watched the attack on the Paul Doumer Bridge from a point just east of the target.

Below, the Hoan Kien lake on the center of Hanoi, photographed from a Phantom flying supersonic over the city after attacking the Paul Doumer Bridge on May 10.

MIKE VAN WAGENEN

HANOI RECON

Right, Captain Don Pickard flew Cousin 2 during the post-strike reconnaissance of Hanoi on May 10. Above, inset, Major Sid Rogers led Cousin Flight. Above, Rogers's RF-4C photographed from Pickard's plane, during the hectic dash past Hanoi. On facing page: photos taken from Don Pickard's RF-4C on May 10, 1972. Top, the Paul Doumer Bridge, all its spans still in place after the attack. Bottom left, a SAM approaching Pickard's Phantom; the missile detonated beneath the plane without causing damage. Bottom right, a MiG-17 that tried to intercept the Phantoms.

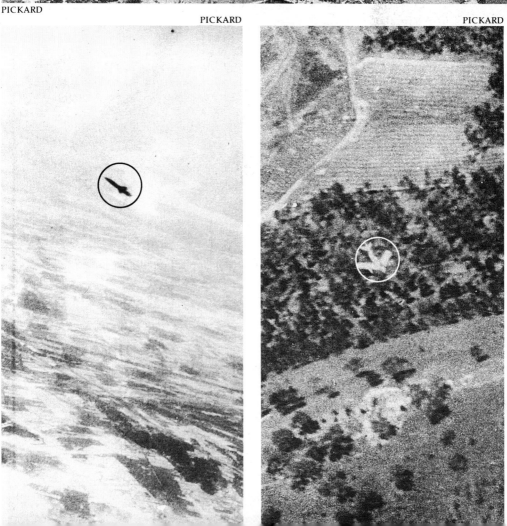

SUPPORTING THE HANOI RAIDERS
Planes that supported the attack on Hanoi on May 10, 1972. Above, a KC-135 tanker fueling F-105Gs on their way to North Vietnam. Above right, F-105G Thunderchief of the 561st Tactical Fighter Squadron; this plane, 434, flew on May 10 as Calgon 3. Below right, EC-121D airborne command plane. Below, an EB-66 radar jamming plane of the 42nd Tactical Electronic Warfare Squadron.

DONALD KILGUS

VIA HARLEY COPIC

THE NAVY'S PUNCH

Lieutenant Mike Ruth (inset) of VA-195 climbs his A-7E away from the target after releasing his bombs on the road and rail bridge near Hai Duong, on the afternoon of May 10. Note that one of the spans was already down.

EGGERT

Above, *Constellation*'s air commanders in May 1972. From left to right, standing: Cdr. J. Miller (VA-146, A-7Es), Lt. Cdr. R. Mitchell (VAQ-130 Detachment, EKA-3Bs), Cdr. Phil Scott (VF-92, F-4Js), Capt. Jake Ward (ship's captain); Cdr. Jim McIntyre (VAW-116, E-2Bs), Cdr. J. Majors (VA-147, A-7Es), Cdr. Al Neuman (VF-96, F-4Js). Kneeling: Cdr. Murph Wright (RVAH-11, RA-5Cs), Cdr. T. Conboy (VA-165, A-6As), Cdr. "Gus" Eggert (Commander Air Wing 9), Lt. Cdr. R. Lazo (HC-1 Detachment, SH-3Gs).

Below, Curt Dosé (right) with back-seater Jim McDevitt (left) and their plane captain. In the background is Phantom 211, in which they shot down the MiG-21 on the morning of May 10.

DOSÉ

CLOSE SHAVE

Above, an RA-5C Vigilante from Reconnaissance Squadron RVAH-11 based on *Constellation*.

Below, a remarkable photo of a SAM detonation, taken by the panoramic camera of one of the unit's RA-5Cs near Haiphong on the morning of May 10. The grasslike lines coming from the top right of the explosion are hot warhead fragments moving out at high velocity, several of which struck the plane that took the photo.

JOHN OLSEN

Above, Marine A-6 Intruders of VMA (AW) 224 over *Coral Sea*. Aircraft 155649, in the background, suffered severe flak damage near Hai Duong on May 10.

Below, ex–Blue Angels pilot Lieutenant Steve Shoemaker and back-seater Lieutenant Keith Crenshaw shot down a MiG-17 near Hai Duong during the afternoon action.

NAVY MIG KILLERS

Above, Phantom 100 of VF-96, the plane flow by Lieutenants Randy Cunningham and Willie Driscoll on May 10, when they destroyed three MiG-17s before being shot down themselves by a SAM.

Below, Cunningham and Driscoll leave the Sea Knight helicopter that returned them to *Constellation* after their rescue on May 10.

Right, Lieutenant Frank Pinegar (second standing from left) of HC-7 led the helicopters that rescued Cunningham and Driscoll.

USN

Above, Great to be back...Cunningham (left) and Driscoll reliving the day's events in VF-96's ready room after their return to the ship.

Below, another successful crew: Lieutenant Thomas Blonski (left) and Lieutenant Matt Connelly (center) describe the action in which they shot down two MiG-17s.

USN

RESCUED

Above, Roger Locher pictured in the cabin of the helicopter, minutes after he was picked up after twenty-three days in North Vietnam.

Below, framed by the U.S. and Thai flags, the Jolly Green Giant helicopter bearing Locher prepares to land at Udorn.

Above, Locher pictured immediately after his return to Ubon, wearing the beard he grew in North Vietnam. To his left is General John Vogt.

Below, Captain Patty Schneider, an intelligence officer at Udorn, had fallen in love with Locher and refused to believe he was killed when his Phantom was shot down.

CAPTIVITY TO FREEDOM

Above, forced to attend a press conference at Hanoi on June 29, 1972, fifty days into his captivity, Lieutenant Steve Rudloff is seated fourth from the left. Below, moment of freedom: jubilant scene inside a C-141 transport lifting off from Hanoi's Gia Lam airport on March 28, 1973, carrying released prisoners. Steve Rudloff is in the nearest row, third from the right. Right, the homecoming: three days later Rudloff arrived at Miramar, San Diego, to receive a tearful hug from his wife, Marie.

RUDLOFF

LOCHER

LATER

Above, Patty Schneider and Roger Locher on their wedding day, July 29, 1973, in the chapel at Nellis AFB, Nevada.

Below, General John Vogt explains to Jeff Ethell the planning of the mission on May 10, 1972.

USAF

DRIVING on Route 5 from Haiphong, Claude Julien's jeep was nearing Hai Duong. Suddenly and without warning a geyser of smoke and dust erupted from the ground a few hundred yards ahead. Another air attack! The driver brought the vehicle to a halt with a screech of brakes and its occupants scrambled out. Julien suddenly took in the commotion of exploding bombs and antiaircraft shells all around, which until then had been concealed by the jeep's noisy engine. Moments later he involuntarily cringed under the earsplitting, mind-numbing roar as a jet plane swept past at full power.

"A Phantom flew past us very low," the Frenchman wrote later, "just above the line of trees parallel to the road, about three hundred meters from us. Engaged by automatic fire, it was forced to climb. The sky, which earlier on had been so serene, was pockmarked with the white bursts of exploding antiaircraft shells."

Julien was ushered to a foxhole beside the road and told to get in. Crouching with just his head above ground, the Frenchman watched the air battle above.

AFTER releasing his bombs, Randy Cunningham pulled the F-4 out of the dive. Willie Driscoll glanced back at the target: "I looked over my shoulder to see where the bombs had gone and saw a lot of black dots on the horizon. I looked back at the ground, looked back at the dots and caught the flash of MiG-17s coming up the left side."

Only then did Red Crown give the first broadcast warning of MiGs airborne, and it did not refer to those now sweeping in to engage.

"This is Red Crown on Guard. Bandits! Bandits! Bullseye zero-three-six for thirty-seven, heading two-two-two, altitude unknown. Time zero-zero. Red Crown out."

Zero-zero meant the report was made on the hour. The bearing and distance from Hanoi put the "bandits" in the vicinity of Kep airfield, thirty miles north of Hai Duong and well clear of the raiders. The MiGs Driscoll could see were approaching the force unannounced.

The action that followed would later inspire the dramatized air-to-air combat scenes in the film *Top Gun.*

The MiGs had caught Randy Cunningham off guard. "I was in a starboard turn looking at the target I'd just bombed. I shouldn't have been doing that, I wasn't thinking about MiGs. I reversed port and saw two MiG-17s slashing in with guns going, inside gun range. I don't know why they didn't hit me, I could see tracers flying by the canopy." Instinctively the Phantom pilot pulled into the nearest MiG and his previous training took command of the situation: "He had a lot of closure, he was hauling, so I broke down into him and he overshot. I reversed and his wingman split over the top and shot past me. I reversed course, put my nose on his tailpipe and squeezed the trigger." The Sidewinder streaked after the MiG about one thousand feet in front in a shallow left turn. The missile smashed into the North Vietnamese fighter and it exploded in a ball of fire.

Seconds later another MiG-17 pulled in behind Cunningham, who accelerated and turned to drag it past his wingman, Brian Grant, for an easy shot. Over the radio Cunningham invited Grant to shoot down the MiG.

"MiG-17, MiG-17, MiG-17, Brian, he's on my tail. . . . Brian, I got MiGs on my tail!"

"OK, I'm dragging 'im, get 'im, baby!"

A great idea, but how? Grant had his own problems. "Just as we were maneuvering to help Randy out," he afterward explained, "somebody again yelled there was a MiG-17 'in the saddle' [in a firing position] on me and shooting. So I had to break off my attack and go into a defensive maneuver." Cunningham looked back, took in the situation at a glance and saw the only safe way out was ahead. The two Phantoms went to full afterburner and, using their huge acceleration advantage, surged away from the MiG-17s.

Commander Dwight Timm, VF-96's executive officer, was northeast of the target when the MiGs swept in beneath his

Phantom. "I saw the MiGs going across the target below us, heading south for the strike group but much lower. They had entered the area at almost exactly the same time we did; it was clear they were under GCI [ground radar] control." With his wingman, Lieutenant David Erickson, Timm curved after the MiGs. "There were so many planes around that we couldn't use the Sparrow effectively, so we had to work for a Sidewinder shot." Jim Fox, Timm's back-seater, also remembered his first sight of the enemy: "We broke starboard, our right wing went down and I saw my first MiG, a silver MiG-21. I thought, What a beautiful airplane! It was real pretty, about half a mile away diving toward the strike group. Trailing the -21 was a camouflaged MiG-17. The MiG-21 stood out, I could see it easily, but the camouflaged MiG-17s were difficult to see and I had a hard job picking them up." Things soon became hectic, Fox recalled. "With that many planes—about forty in a three-mile circle—you had to look after number one. Flight integrity was almost nonexistent. We kept flying through jet wash; if the plane shuddered we didn't know if it had taken a hit or if we had gone through someone's wash."

Patrolling the target at 18,000 feet, Lieutenant Matt Connelly was another who found it impossible to attack with a Sparrow. "I looked way down and there was an A-7 making a left turn, with two black dots going after it." Connelly rolled his Phantom into a diving turn and lined his nose on one of the "black dots," a MiG-17. He prepared to attack with a Sparrow: "I went to boresight and told Tom Blonski [the back-seater] to lock the radar on him. What did not register on me, until the third time Tom said it, was 'The scopes are black.'" Connelly glanced into the cockpit and saw what Blonski meant: there was no radar picture, the equipment was unusable and so were the two Sparrow missiles under the fuselage. Connelly switched to a Sidewinder and continued his dive after the enemy planes. "The second MiG seemed to peel away, I don't know where he went. But the first guy was still chasing the A-7 which started to roll out—I guess its pilot was looking at the second MiG and didn't see the one that was closer to him. I took a shot at the MiG, thinking it might be the only chance I would get in the whole war." The Vietnamese pilot pulled sharply into the attack and successfully evaded the missile, but in forcing him off the A-7's tail the Sidewinder had done its job.

WHILE the Phantoms tried to hold off the MiGs, Commander Gus Eggert ordered the attack planes to exit stage south:

"OK, Jasons, Boomers [A-7s of VA-147, A-6s of VA-165], get out of there!"

"We're on the way out!"

In spite of the escorts' best efforts, one or two North Vietnamese fighters succeeded in getting to the Intruders and Corsairs speeding for the coast. Lieutenant George Goryanec, flying an A-7, was speeding from the target behind his element leader when the MiGs came in. "At the bottom of our runs we were flat out. We didn't climb at all, we stayed on the deck heading for the coast at five hundred-plus knots. I saw a MiG coming in at ten o'clock, from the northeast. I turned into the MiG and it broke away. Then another MiG crossed in front of me heading towards Hai Duong, as I was getting ready to turn back out to the coast. But he didn't see me."

Lieutenant Al Junker eased his A-7 out of the dive after bomb release, but in doing so lost contact with his element leader. "I looked around for somebody else to join up with and saw what I thought was an A-6 joining on me. A few seconds later I looked back again to see how he was coming along and saw red dots coming from each side of his nose. A-6s did not have guns, and even if they did they would not be shooting at me—it was a MiG-17!" Junker punched off his empty bomb racks, concentrated on getting low and tried to outturn his pursuer. "I pulled as hard as I could, just as the MiG opened fire. His shells came over my left wing, real close, bom-bom-bom-bom-bom. . . . I felt the shock waves as they came past. I thought, I wonder how it's going to feel if this airplane comes apart at five hundred knots. . . ."

Commander Fred Baldwin, Junker's element leader, saw his wingman in trouble and barrel-rolled into a firing position behind the North Vietnamese fighter. But that was all he could do; his Corsair had no Sidewinder and his 20-mm cannon was unserviceable. Of course, the MiG-17 pilot could not know the Corsair following him was unarmed. Each time Baldwin reached a firing position he forced the MiG to break sharply away from Junker's A-7. And Baldwin found other ways to help his wingman. "As the MiG was getting a firing solution, I would tell Al to reverse his turn and that screwed up the attack. We were right down on the deck, smoking out towards the coast with balls to the wall for every knot we could get. We did a three-plane scissors tail chase for forty miles." Recorders in several aircraft taped Baldwin's calls during the 500-knot slalom over the paddy fields: "He's heading back in your four o'clock. Stand by. . . . Stand by. . . . Stand by. . . . Not yet! . . . Not yet! . . . OK, pull hard right now, he's trying to pull lead on you again!"

George Goryanec heard Baldwin's calls. "I turned and saw them behind me, they were a lot lower than I was. I could see Al Junker with an airplane behind him and Fred Baldwin, a couple of thousand feet off to one side, calling the turns. What looked like a line of 'grapefruits' was going past Al's nose. That made me mad—the guy was trying to shoot Al down."

"Jason One, I'm going with the two Bees [Busybees, A-7s of VA-146], they're in trouble."

Goryanec rolled the Corsair on its back and curved around to attack the MiG from above. He fired a long burst with his 20-mm cannon and saw what looked like a couple of hits near the wing root. "By then I was doing five hundred seventy knots, I pulled off at one thousand feet and the MiG was between me and the ground. I looked back at him, I was heading inland now and I was afraid he was going to jump me. But he leveled his wings, broke off the attack and headed north."

"Busybees, you're clean, you don't have anybody on ya."

"Roger, thank you!"

Junker's Corsair had survived without damage.

...

HAVING joined the melee after his abortive attack on the MiG-17, Matt Connelly noticed another enemy fighter to one side of him. He turned toward it, a MiG-17, and heard the tone in his earphones denoting the Sidewinder was locked on. But the MiG was in a tight turn and there was little chance of a successful shot. Had the MiG pilot held the turn he would have escaped, but perhaps the sight of the Phantom bounding in from behind made him panic. For some inexplicable reason the MiG suddenly rolled out of the turn. The tactical blunder did not go unpunished. Connelly just had time for a snap shot with a Sidewinder, from about one thousand feet. "I just stayed in that 'winder tone and then he rolled out, wings level. When I fired that missile I was real close, almost at minimum range, with an incredible overtake speed. The missile went off on the MiG's exhaust and the plane blew up in a big ball of fire. The guy ejected."

Ex–Blue Angels pilot Lieutenant Steve Shoemaker, also with VF-96, charged his Phantom through the target area from north to south, holding 600 knots at 5,000 feet. Lieutenant Keith Crenshaw, his back-seater, recalled: "Previously we had agreed that if we hassled with MiGs I would search aft of the wing line and Shoe would search forward of it. I had been looking behind, and one of the vivid memories I have of that fight is the sight of a canopy, as a MiG-17 suddenly appeared and rolled over the top of us. It was very close, about five hundred feet away, the first MiG I had ever seen. I said, 'Er, Shoe, there's a MiG just gone over the top of us. . . .' He said, 'Jesus, Keith, look around!' I glanced forward and there were MiGs all over the place, two of them in flames. We went whipping by a guy swinging on a parachute." Unable to get off a shot at any of the enemy fighters, Shoemaker maintained speed, emerged from the action to the south and went into a sweeping turn before lining up for another attack run.

HAVING OUTDISTANCED the MiGs chasing their Phantoms, Randy Cunningham and Brian Grant pulled into a steep zoom climb to 12,000 feet and banked steeply to assess the situation below.

"Back there were more MiGs than we had ever dreamed of. There were eight MiG-17s in a defensive wheel, flying in a circle," the leader recalled.

CROUCHED IN his foxhole twelve thousand feet below Cunningham, Claude Julien also watched the circling MiGs; he later wrote:

> Like conscientious geometricians they described a circle, with us in the center. . . . A worthy military historian would have counted the aircraft taking part in the fight on each side. Humbly I have to admit that I did not think of it. You do not count the dancers in a ballet, you observe their performance as a whole.

AFTER surveying the scene from their lofty perch, Cunningham and Grant swung into steep diving turns with the intention of picking off some of the circling MiGs from above. Suddenly, however, matters closer to hand led to a change of plan as a Phantom flashed past Cunningham's nose, so close that he almost collided with it. It was Dwight Timm and he was in serious trouble. From 3,000 feet behind Timm a MiG-17 was firing at him, while 3,500 feet behind was a MiG-21 tracking him and waiting to attack. Timm held a tight port turn to avoid the assailants he could see. But the greatest threat came from the MiG-17 hidden under his wing, just 300 feet away, following him in the turn. If that MiG got into a firing position it could hardly miss.

Cunningham lined up on the MiG-17 nearest Timm and prepared to launch a Sidewinder. But a heat-seeking missile does not recognize national markings, it homes on the hottest object in front of it. Such weapons had to be used carefully in a close-quarter dogfight such as this, and Cunningham could see that if he launched the Sidewinder it would go for the hottest object ahead—the jet pipes of Timm's Phantom. Over the radio Cunningham shouted to Timm to reverse his turn and go starboard. But if the executive officer did that he would make an easier target for the two MiGs he could see behind him. Oblivious to the greater danger from the third MiG, Timm held his port turn.

Willie Driscoll, Cunningham's back-seater, was keeping watch behind the Phantom and saw four MiG-17s break out of the defensive circle and start to close in. He told Cunningham, who glanced back, saw the MiGs were in no position to attack and told Driscoll to keep them in sight and call out if they moved closer. Cunningham pushed on more power and to his right, high, he saw the sun glint off a couple of MiG-19s. The North Vietnamese fighters loosed off bursts from long range, which Cunningham easily avoided. Then the Phantom pilot realigned on the MiG-17 close beside Timm.

With so many MiGs about, Cunningham could not hold position behind the threatened Phantom much longer. His next radio call bore the tone of desperation: "Showtime [VF-96 aircraft], reverse starboard. . . . goddamnit, reverse starboard!"

The call had the desired effect, and Timm reversed his turn. As the Phantom swung rapidly clear of the nearest MiG, Cunningham suddenly had a clear shot and squeezed off a Sidewinder.

Lieutenant Jim Fox, Timm's back-seater, knew nothing of the MiG nearby until after the turn. Then he caught sight of the enemy fighter to one side on a diverging heading, and moments later the missile smashed into its rear. The MiG wallowed drunkenly and its pilot ejected.

That left just two enemy fighters behind Timm's fighter, and Fox described what happened next: "The MiG-21 and the MiG-17 were staying with us, the -17 was firing his cannon and I could see the sparking gun ports and the tracer going over our canopy. Then the -21 pitched off—probably he had seen his buddy get nailed." He continued: "The other -17 stayed with us, but I knew we could maneuver away from him. We had been taught [during Top Gun] how to move away from a MiG-17: break, turn into him, then extend away. That was exactly what Timm was doing. The MiG's roll rate was extremely slow, I couldn't believe it. It was as if he was rolling in slow motion."

Meanwhile other members of the squadron were coming to Timm's aid. Brian Grant lined up on the remaining MiG-17, then he saw another Phantom pounding toward the same target. Grant had to pull away to avoid a collision. It was Steve Shoemaker, making a second charge through the "furball," sweeping in from the south. His back-seater, Keith Crenshaw, recalled: "We saw the plan form of a MiG-17 on Timm's tail, attacking with guns. We launched a snap-shot Sidewinder at the guy from inside minimum range. The missile passed very close to the MiG but failed to explode. The MiG pilot obviously saw it and pulled into a hard turn, he nearly met us head-on. But we had made him break away from the F-4." Shoemaker continued his high-speed run, emerged to the north and went into another sweeping turn.

Meanwhile Matt Connelly, having already made one MiG-17 kill, was about to make another. "The engagement was a carbon copy of the first. The guy did the same thing, he saw me coming and started turning. I went behind him, he reversed his turn and I pulled back behind him. I waited till I had a real good tone, but as I squeezed the trigger the tone dropped off. I thought, Oh shit!" The missile continued toward the enemy fighter, however, and Connelly saw it explode in a black puff beside the plane. "All of a sudden the tail came off. The missile had gone off on proximity fuse, and the expanding rod warhead had cut the whole tail off! The MiG started rolling to the left, the canopy came off, the seat fired, and there was the guy on the end of the square parachute."

At about this time Brian Grant also loosed off a Sidewinder at a MiG-17, but although the missile appeared to guide properly, it detonated well behind the target. Seemingly undamaged, the enemy fighter made good its escape.

Also at this time four MiG-21s made a halfhearted approach on Cunningham. The American pilot turned into them and they broke away. Feeling almost alone in a sky full of hostile aircraft, Cunningham selected afterburner and sped from the area.

CIRCLING Hai Duong at 14,000 feet, Commander Harry Blackburn and his wingman remained in the target area long after the last attack aircraft had disappeared to the south. Their Phantoms were in position to intercept MiGs attempting to enter or leave the fight, but their eagerness to engage enemy fighters was about to lead to the downfall of one of them.

Steve Rudloff, Blackburn's back-seater, made another radar search for MiGs but still found none. "There were no targets present, so I turned my attention back outside, to check our wingman's position and to clear his six o'clock following the change of course. He was high in our eight o'clock position, but between our aircraft and his there were ten or fifteen flak bursts." Black smoke puffs meant 85-mm rounds: the Phantom shuddered under their blast and Rudloff called the other plane intending to ask its crew to inspect his for possible damage.

"OK, we're taking some flak over here—"

The words tailed off in a short high-pitched howl as the UHF radio antenna was blown to smithereens with the rest of the vertical stabilizer.

A twenty-pound shell had exploded on or very near the tail of the American fighter, just as Blackburn initiated a hard left turn to escape from the bursts. The force of the explosion slammed the plane violently to the right and jolted Rudloff against the side of his cockpit. Then the panel in front of him erupted into a mass of flames, sparks and smoke. A glance in the rearview mirrors provided no reassurance; the entire rear of the plane was engulfed in flame. Burning fuel, fanned almost to blast-furnace heat by the airflow, produced a vibrant white flame that trailed billowing smoke. To those looking on, it appeared the plane was being devoured by an enormous black serpent.

Then something in front of Rudloff exploded in a dazzling white flash. The damage to his sight occurred in the split second before the reflex action could close his eyelids. He squinted hard a few times but everything remained black. He was blind.

It was obvious to Rudloff that nothing could be done to save the plane. He told Blackburn he thought they should eject and back came the reply: "OK! Eject!" Rudloff yanked the firing handle. "The roar of the ejection seat rockets was deafening and I was aware that I was tumbling slightly in the seat. Suddenly my parachute opened and I was swaying beneath what I hoped was a fully deployed canopy."

Shortly afterward a distinctive high-pitched stabbing note, repeated frequently, came over the radios of American aircraft in the area—the distress call from the emergency beeper. Willie Driscoll watched the Phantom go down. "It was," he later recalled, "like witnessing an auto accident late at night on a highway. It was a jolt."

For several minutes Steve Rudloff dangled from his parachute, blind and helpless, before he reached the ground. Meanwhile the action around Hai Duong continued with unabated fury.

Steve Shoemaker was on his third high-speed charge through the target area. Keith Crenshaw recalled: "We came on this MiG-17 to the southwest of the 'furball.' He appeared in front of us, he seemed to be trying to get out of the fight. We didn't make any big turn, we dived on him and I heard Shoe call, 'We got a good tone,' then he fired the Sidewinder. After that we had to pull up, we were getting too close to the ground. We lost sight of both the missile and the MiG. We got some altitude, then rolled over, and on the ground was what was obviously an airplane burning, giving off thick black greasy smoke."

ON THE ground Claude Julien's Vietnamese escort shouted that an American plane had been hit. He pointed to the sky and the Frenchman's eyes followed the line of the outstretched finger:

> The plane caught fire like a torch and started falling with incredible slowness. Accustomed to having to turn our heads rapidly to follow the flight of a Phantom, we were struck by the apparent slowness of so large a body in free-fall. . . . Beside it opened the pilot's parachute.

Observers on the ground assumed the victim was American, and since the North Vietnamese news service never admitted the loss of its own planes in combat, the assumption is understandable. But at that distance it was not possible to recognize the nationality of the falling plane. The parachutist Julien watched might have been Rudloff, but it might equally have been one of at least three MiG pilots who also ejected in the area.

...

PILOTING THE Phantom that had been flying with Blackburn and Rudloff, Rod Dilworth was also in trouble. Another exploding shell had damaged one of his engines and he had to shut it down. In the cockpit a fire-warning light was glowing. While the pilot tried to sort out the mess, back-seater Gerry Hill informed the strike leader of their plight:

"Honeybee, this is Silverkite two-oh-seven, how do you read?"

"Two-oh-seven, you're loud and clear."

"Roger, I've shut down my starboard engine, I've taken a hit, I've got a fire-warning light on."

"Roger . . . say your Posit [position]."

"Three-two-zero fifty-six miles now [position relative to *Chicago*'s TACAN beacon, about forty miles south of Hai Duong], my wingie [wingman] was hit."

"Understand your wingie was hit?"

"Roger, they went in. Two good chutes, two good chutes, that's Two-one-two. Silverkite Two-one-two went in, two good chutes."

"OK, mark the Posit."

"The Posit of the downed aircraft was directly over the target area."

"Roger."

George Goryanec was near Dilworth's position and saw the crippled Phantom. "The F-4 was about one thousand feet above and four miles in front of me, streaming fuel. Before I could join him a section of MiG-21s flew between us about two thousand feet above, heading towards Hai Duong. I guess they didn't see us because they sure didn't react. They could have had us both."

Breathing a sigh of relief, Goryanec moved closer to the Phantom. "I joined on him and checked him out. I'd never seen so many holes in a plane, ever. There was one slash, five or six inches wide and a foot and a half long, across the humpback. One engine was out, its nozzle closed down. How the other engine kept going I don't know, there were holes all over the place."

"SHOWTIMES [F-4s of VF-96] and Pouncers [Iron Hand A-7s], disengage and get out of there if you can!"

Gus Eggert could see the attack planes were safely clear of the target, and now he ordered the remainder of his force to follow. "The melee was breaking up and the F-4s were running out of gas and missiles. We didn't have any reason to stick around—we had to get ourselves back. People had got separated from each other, they headed for the beach in ones and twos."

Moving south from Hai Duong Randy Cunningham noticed a plane some distance in front, end-on and apparently stationary. The silhouette rapidly increased in size, then the high-set horizontal stabilizer betrayed it as yet another MiG-17. "I tried to meet this guy head-on, and all of a sudden he opened fire with tracer. I pulled straight up into the vertical, going up through fifteen thousand feet, pulled 6Gs going over the top. I looked back, I expected to see him moving straight through and running. But we were canopy to canopy, maybe four hundred or five hundred feet apart!" As Cunningham rolled on his back at the top of the climb the MiG pilot sent a burst of cannon fire in his direction—obviously the man was no beginner.

As the Phantom dived away the MiG slid into position behind it. "I pitched my nose up, pulled over the top, and rolled in behind his six o'clock. As soon as I dropped my nose he pulled straight up into the vertical again. I overshot, he rolled up over the top, pulled through and rolled in behind me." Each pilot seized the advantage in turn, only to lose it as his opponent pulled up and rolled in behind him. To a casual watcher it might have appeared the pilots were playing a game. But they were in deadly earnest. So long as he continued the rolling maneuver, each prevented the other from reaching a firing position. Cunningham could not afford to let the process continue too long, however; both planes were losing speed, and at low speed the MiG-17 could turn far tighter than the Phantom.

Cunningham had an ace up his sleeve—during the Top Gun course he had practiced the maneuver to extricate himself from just this situation. "The MiG was sitting at my seven o'clock. When he got his nose just a little too high, I pulled sharply down into him and met him head-on. Then I lit the burners and accelerated away from him. By the time he got his nose on me I was about a mile and a half ahead of him, out of firing range and opening."

Once clear of the MiG, Cunningham pulled into another vertical climb. And, to his surprise, the North Vietnamese pilot again followed. No enemy pilot he encountered previously had been so aggressive.

The Phantom broke out as before and pulled into yet another zoom climb. And yet again the MiG followed. This time Cunningham decided to try something different. "Each time I had gone up with this guy in the vertical, I had outzoomed him and gone higher than he had. And each time I went in front he shot at me. I figured that one time he was going to get lucky. So this time we were going up, canopy to canopy, and I pulled the throttles back to idle and selected speed brakes." Reined back by the aerodynamic drag, the Phantom decelerated rapidly and the MiG sped in front.

Cunningham closed the speed brakes and selected full thrust. The stratagem had worked: "I think that caught him by surprise because he shot way out in front of me. But a Phantom on full afterburner at one hundred fifty knots with the nose straight up in the air is not really flying, it is standing on thirty-six thousand pounds of thrust. We were hanging behind him but we were not really in a position of advantage. At those speeds a MiG-17 had about two and a half to three more Gs available than we had."

As the MiG reached the top of its climb Cunningham applied full rudder. "I stood on the rudder and got the airplane to move to his blind side, where he couldn't see us. He rolled over the top and started down, and then he made his first mistake. His nose fell through, he tried to get it out. He didn't, he started running." Possibly the MiG-17 was short of fuel and had to break off the action. Whatever the reason, its pilot dived away and made the fundamental error of opening the range and presenting his tail to

Cunningham. The American pilot made the most of the opportunity. He curved after the enemy plane, placed the gunsight pipper over it and squeezed the trigger. A Sidewinder sped away and Cunningham watched it detonate beside the tail of the North Vietnamese fighter. "It didn't blow up like most of the other airplanes, the missile just knocked off a few pieces. I didn't think I had damaged him seriously, he was still accelerating. Then I noticed flames come out of the tail. The MiG went into a thirty-degree-wing-down position and flew into the ground."

Cunningham pulled out of the dive and took stock of the situation. To his left were yet more MiG-17s, and he had begun turning into them when a warning call made him hesitate:

"Showtime heading about one-eight-zero. Heads up! You got a MiG behind you!"

"Where is he?"

"OK, he's right on your tail. Just don't let him get guns [range]. It's a -17, you can outrun him!"

The caller was Matt Connelly, also heading for the coast after a successful encounter with enemy fighters, who emphasized the point by launching a Sparrow missile without guidance in the general direction of the MiG (it will be remembered the radar on his Phantom was unserviceable).

Initially Cunningham was less than ecstatic at his colleague's action. "It looked like the Sparrow was coming right for my plane! I said, 'Matt, watch where you're shooting!' The missile went over my tail. Then I realized what Matt was doing." The missile went past the MiG, but served its purpose by making the enemy fighter break away from the F-4. Cunningham selected afterburner and again outdistanced his pursuers.

1:06 P.M. Only six minutes had elapsed since the MiGs had swept over Hai Duong. During the furious action that followed, six MiG-17s had been destroyed and one probably damaged; one Phantom was shot down by ground fire and another seriously damaged. In time and space the action was the most concentrated ever fought over North Vietnam, more akin to a barroom brawl than the long-range engagement one might expect in the missile age. And the fighting was not over yet.

"SAM, SAM, SAM. Vicinity of Haiphong. Deep Sea, out."

Deep Sea was the call sign of an EP-3B Orion Sigint plane of VQ-1, flying over the Gulf of Tonkin and monitoring the radio and radar frequencies used by the North Vietnamese. The plane's operators had picked up the distinctive signals of an impending SAM launch and broadcast a warning on the Guard channel.

From the ground Claude Julien watched the missiles streaking across the sky, and later he wrote:

> Our eyes followed the SAMs. Their flight was superbly intelli-
> gent, a will straining towards an idea they must not allow to
> escape, as they thrust towards the shining dots of aircraft seem-
> ingly beyond reach.

Climbing through 16,000 feet on their way to the coast, Cunningham and Driscoll were elated at having shot down their fifth enemy plane to reach the coveted status of aces. Then suddenly, and with no alarm from the radar warning receiver, a SAM exploded in a bright flash about 500 feet from the Phantom. The blast hurled the fighter into a steep bank to port. Jagged chunks of metal from the warhead peppered the plane, making a sound like gravel thrown at a window. Cunningham hauled the fighter back on even keel and checked his instruments. Everything seemed normal, so he continued the climb. On a previous occasion a missile had exploded closer to his plane without causing serious damage; maybe he had been lucky again.

It was a vain hope. Passing 27,000 feet about a minute later, the Phantom suddenly gave an agonized lurch and the port wing dropped. Cunningham rechecked his instruments; the main hydraulic system pressure dial was reading zero. He stared at the offending gauge, hoping the needle had stuck. But this was no false alarm. The neighboring gauge, which indicated pressure in the secondary hydraulic system, was fluctuating. Without doubt the hydraulic system had been damaged, and the precious fluid was seeping away.

As a Phantom loses hydraulic pressure the powered flying controls gradually cease to function. When the pressure approaches zero the leading edge of the stabilator goes to the fully down position, forcing down the tail. That now happened to Cunningham's aircraft, and the pilot no longer had full control. In that situation the textbook provided only one answer—eject immediately. But the plane was ten miles inside North Vietnam; if the men left it now they would certainly be taken prisoner. The only hope of avoiding that fate lay in staying with the plane and keeping it airborne a little longer. *If* they could reach the coast and parachute into the sea the chances of rescue by friendly forces would be immeasurably greater. *If* . . .

From the recesses of his mind Cunningham trawled the memory of how a pilot had brought a Phantom out of North Vietnam in similar circumstances. Following the other pilot's example, he pushed hard with his right foot. The rudder still worked, using the last vestige of hydraulic pressure. The fighter yawed to the right, the nose fell and the plane rolled steeply to the right. As the nose passed through the horizontal the pilot pulled back the throttles and opened the speed brakes to prevent the plane from going into a dive. He pushed on left rudder, selected full power and retracted the speed brakes. The fighter continued rolling and when it was right way up the nose pitched up and Cunningham repeated the process. It was a contest between velocity and gravity and, for the time being, velocity was winning. The Phantom flew a series of clumsy barrel rolls that would have won no prize in an aerobatic competition, but each carried it a few miles nearer the coast.

As if things were not bad enough, a further problem now arose within the Phantom. As a result of leaking hydraulic oil or fuel, a fire broke out in the rear fuselage and rapidly took hold. Shortly afterward the crew heard a small explosion—possibly the rocket fuel in one of the Sparrow missiles cooking off—and with that Cunningham lost his final vestige of control. The Phantom's nose pitched up once more, but this time the laws of aerodynamics asserted themselves and the fighter fell into an inverted spin. Other crews watched in horror as the plane fell slowly from the sky, their excited radio calls punctuated by another SAM warning:

"Get out! Get out! Get out!"

"Punch out! Punch out!"

"SAM, SAM, SAM, vicinity Haiphong, Deep Sea, out."

"Punch out, punch out!"

"Come on, get out of that airplane!"

"[Another voice, louder] Get out of that airplane!"

"Who are you talking to!"

"F-4 going down in a spin, off the beach!"

The reproach was timely; it would not have been the first time such panic calls, with no call sign to identify the intended recipient, had led another crew to abandon their plane unnecessarily.

Still Cunningham was reluctant to leave the crippled fighter. "On each revolution I could see land, then ocean. Incredible as it may seem, my fear kept me in the airplane. I thought we were too close to the beach. I told Irish [Driscoll] to stay with me for two more turns as I attempted to break the spin and get more water behind us." In a final effort to escape from the spin the pilot streamed the brake parachute. It had no effect. Randy Cunningham was beaten and knew it, he gave the order to eject. Driscoll went first and the pilot followed.

Hurtling from the plane upside down on his ejection seat, Driscoll became disoriented: "The sensation of ejection was of seeing blue sky, blue water, blue sky, blue water. . . ." Then the automatic systems took charge. The small drogue parachute stabilized Driscoll in space, then the seat fell away. Shortly afterward his main parachute jerked open and a semblance of normality returned to the world around. The sky, the land and the sea returned to their accustomed places. In its death throes the Phantom had performed the final task demanded of it; below Driscoll was lots of beautiful water and the coast was safely distant. His eyes followed the last moments of the fighter that had served him so well. Trailing flames and spinning like a falling leaf, it plunged into the sea and disappeared in a column of spray. Driscoll looked around and, about half a mile away, saw Cunningham hanging from his parachute.

Radios crackled into life as the relieved observers saw the two men emerge from the spinning fighter.

"There's two good 'chutes!"

"OK, stick with those."

"Roger."

"Pouncer One, headed back in." [Pouncer aircraft, A-7s on Iron Hand missions, had the secondary task of covering rescue operations.]

"How high are those 'chutes?"

"OK, they're about ten thousand [feet] now."

Sound of beeper radio.

"OK, what's their Posit again?"

"Three-two-five fifty-five miles [relative to *Chicago*'s TACAN beacon]."

More beeper signals.

Norm Birzer, piloting A-7 Pouncer 1, orbited the parachutists and assumed the duties of on-scene commander. Austin Hawkins in the escorting F-4 held position off his wing.

On its way to the coast Steve Shoemaker's F-4 also came under SAM attack. Keith Crenshaw recalled: "We heard the missile launch on the RHAW gear and picked up the SAM visually. As the missile closed in we popped several bundles of chaff and did a nose low break into it. The missile tried to follow us, then appeared to lose us."

The missile continued past the Phantom and detonated well clear.

Even when the *Constellation*'s F-4s reached the coast their problems were not over. Several of the fighters had run themselves short of fuel and now sought out the EKA-3B to take on more. The tanker had only a limited supply, however, and had to share it between several recipients. None could have the amount normally considered necessary.

Chronology demands that we now leave the rescue operation and the egress of *Constellation*'s Air Wing, and shift our attention to other concurrent events.

AT THE same time that *Constellation*'s Air Wing was fighting its furious battle around Hai Duong, a pair of Phantoms from *Coral Sea* passed south of the town heading toward Hanoi. The planes were probing deep into North Vietnam on a MiG-hunting mission, under control from "Red Crown." On this occasion the controller on the ship was Radarman First Class Nalwalker and the fighter pilots, Lieutenant Commander Chuck Schroeder and Lieutenant Ken Cannon, were being guided on to enemy fighters detected near the capital. At intervals of about twenty seconds Nalwalker passed a new range and bearing on the target:

"Bogie [unidentified aircraft] three-three-two at twenty-three miles."

"Bogie now three-four-zero at twenty."

Bent on taking their prey by surprise, the Phantoms flew in battle formation at 525 knots and 200 feet.

Suddenly Cannon sighted a plane a mile away at 1,000 feet. This was twenty miles from the Bogie the F-4s were being vectored after, but a target in sight was worth two on somebody else's radar screen. "The same time we picked him up he must have seen us, because he broke into us and I saw the plan view of a MiG-17," Cannon recalled. Both Phantoms accelerated, and while Schroeder turned after the MiG, Cannon pulled up to 6,000 feet to cover his leader. Schroeder was closing rapidly when, Cannon observed, the MiG pilot suddenly turned on his pursuer. "It looked like he did a high G barrel roll, in no time at all he was in [Schroeder's] six o'clock. I was on my back at six thousand feet, directly over the MiG."

Schroeder selected full power to accelerate out of trouble and the MiG tried to follow. Above and behind the pair, Cannon rolled his Phantom right way up and pulled around after the enemy fighter. The North Vietnamese pilot saw the new threat, broke hard to port away from Schroeder and tried to run out north in the direction of Hanoi. But yet again the Phantom's superior speed and acceleration proved decisive. Cannon lined himself up on the enemy fighter and squeezed the trigger. "It seemed like an eternity before the 'winder came off, but when it did it guided perfectly; it went right at his tail pipe. The missile exploded, I saw debris come off the tail section. The aircraft did a slow roll to the left and impacted the ground in a forty-five-degree nose-down position."

Deeper in enemy territory than any other Navy plane would go that day, Cannon turned and headed back for the coast. On the way out he rejoined Schroeder.

AS Cannon headed southeast, Coral Sea's main strike formation reached Hai Duong for the next attack. Intruders and Corsairs rolled into their dives to bomb the road and rail bridge over the Binh River, four miles northeast of the town. Again there was vigorous ground fire. A Marine A-6 took a direct hit from a 37-mm shell, which tore a two-foot hole in the starboard horizontal stabilizer. The pilot regained control of the wounded bomber, however, and it limped back to the carrier.

Throughout Coral Sea's attack an EKA-3B Skywarrior orbited at 20,000 feet near the coast giving jamming cover. Lieutenant Steve Kuhar was one of two crewmen operating the jammers. "Unlike the fighter and the bomber crews who could see the results of their labors, we couldn't. We could only surmise that if the aircraft returned safely we were doing our job, and if someone didn't return we would wonder if it was our fault. We never got any feedback on our work because we couldn't; the enemy were the only people who knew if we were effective." The jamming plane was positioned so that it, the Air Wing and the target were more or less on the same line. "If we were doing our job properly, SAMs launched at the Air Wing flew through it without detonating and we could see them streaking toward us. We were beyond the SAM radar's tracking range, but the missiles would fly beyond us and detonate high above. It was quite exciting to see that happen."

Two SAMs, probably aimed at *Coral Sea*'s Air Wing and running out to the end of their trajectories, passed high over *Constellation*'s planes circling Randy Cunningham and Willie Driscoll. The missiles raised the adrenaline level in the various cockpits but did no other harm.

AFTER HE crossed the coast Rod Dilworth decided to rid his badly damaged Phantom of its missiles. He fired the four Sidewinders in turn without difficulty. But the Sparrows were mounted under the fuselage—if fired they might ignite the leaking fuel. They would have to be jettisoned. George Goryanec, escorting Dilworth in an A-7, knew that jettisoned missiles could behave unpredictably, but nothing he had heard prepared him for what followed. The first Sparrow bumped aft down the fuselage, waggled and fell away. Then he watched the second one go. "It waggled a bit then started sliding across the [underside of the] wing. I was about fifty feet above his wing line and slightly aft. After it cleared the wing, it went nose up, flying on its fins towards me. It missed my intake by a few feet! I remember thinking, This is crazy! I'd avoided MiGs and flak, and I nearly got hit by a jettisoned Sparrow!" Although it was unpowered and its warhead was not live, the 450-pound missile would have made a nasty dent in the A-7 had it impacted. Goryanec opened out to a more respectful distance and followed the Phantom back to *Constellation*.

1:12 P.M. Soon after Dilworth got rid of his last missile, his squadron colleague floated silently to earth near Hai Duong. Steve Rudloff had spent eight minutes on his parachute after ejecting from the blazing Phantom. His blindness prevented him from seeing the air action, but the whistle of jets and the banging of antiaircraft guns told him when U.S. planes were nearby.

With no way of judging height, Rudloff was quite unprepared for the landing when it finally came. Suddenly the ground rose up and hit him with bone-jarring force. He felt a stabbing pain in his right ankle and ended up on his stomach, winded.

"As I lay on the ground I could hear sporadic rifle fire, as well as a few larger guns firing in the distance. Then I heard an approaching aircraft, and as it got closer the volume of rifle fire increased sharply. I wanted to stand up and wave my arms as an indication that I was still alive, but as soon as I put weight on my right foot I collapsed to the ground. I was momentarily stunned, but the roar of the aircraft as it passed overhead brought me back to my senses.

"I was again lying face down on the ground and the rifle fire seemed to be right on top of me. I could hear voices and the sound of numerous people approaching. There seemed no point in doing anything except remaining where I was and waiting for the inevitable. It was instantly forthcoming, in the form of what I believe was a rifle butt smashed into the small of my back."

For Steve Rudloff the war was over.

ABOUT fifty miles south of Rudloff, just off the coast, Randy Cunningham and Willie Driscoll were still descending by parachute. Gus Eggert had ordered five Corsairs and a Phantom to cover the pair, and to keep them supplied with fuel a KA-6 tanker had come north and now orbited off the coast.

A few miles from the survivors sat two junks, probably fishing and seemingly uninterested in the activity above. Lest one of the skippers started to entertain heroic thoughts, Eggert ordered three A-7s to ensure nobody reached Cunningham and Driscoll before the rescue helicopters arrived.

"Jason One, Pouncer One and Pouncer Two. Would you put up a patrol on the coastline and hit anything that comes out from the beach?"

"Roger that!"

ORBITING off the North Vietnamese coast, *Coral Sea*'s EKA-3B had reverted to its tanker role and now waited to give fuel to any plane that needed it. Most of the carrier's planes passed by without requiring the service, however; the attack had been straightforward with no fuel-consuming delays or combats. Then, some distance behind the main body of aircraft, two Phantoms closed purposefully on the tanker. It was Chuck Schroeder and Ken Cannon returning from their foray deep into North Vietnam. Steve Kuhar had no inkling of what the fighters had done. "As they came in to tank we didn't know they had engaged. One F-4, clean of external tanks, came up on the pilot's side. Mike [Lt. Mike Danosky, the EKA-3B's pilot] said, 'He's definitely been in a fight, he's clean!' I gave him the two or three thousand pounds of fuel he needed and said to Mike, 'I wonder if he got a MiG?' As the F-4 departed it did a victory roll in front of us. That was the answer!" The tanker crew were elated at having played an indirect, though vitally important, part in the fighter's success.

1:16 P.M. *Kitty Hawk*'s aircraft were running in to attack their targets. Some of the planes bombed warehouses on the coast near Quan Bac; the rest continued inland to Hai Duong to hit a road and rail bridge east of the town. Lieutenant Mike Ruth, a Corsair pilot, followed his element leader, Lieutenant Charlie Brewer, into the attack and released his two 2,000-pound and two 1,000-pound bombs in train across the bridge. As the pair climbed, Brewer's rear-facing strike camera snapped Ruth's A-7 against a backdrop of exploding bombs. The photo would become one of the classic shots of the Vietnam war.

The previous actions had exhausted the North Vietnamese fighter and SAM defenses in the area; *Kitty Hawk*'s Air Wing encountered no interference from either.

AS HE LAY on the ground near Hai Duong unseen hands stripped Steve Rudloff of his equipment, watch and flight suit. Although his captors chattered a lot, the airman could understand none of it. From time to time a plane whistled overhead and the gunfire resumed. Deep in shock, it did not occur to Rudloff that he might never see again. "I had so much on my mind that it hadn't registered that I might be permanently blind. It was not my primary concern at the time."

The airman felt his hands being tied together. Then someone pulled him to his feet, a rope was tied around his waist and another was placed loosely around his neck. One captor tugged at the waist rope and as Rudloff stepped in the required direction he felt excruciating pain from his right ankle whenever he put weight on it. The airman limped away from the landing place, the occasional backwards jerk on the neck rope reminding him there was someone behind holding that one. He guessed he was being led along embankments between rice paddies, because from time to time he slithered sideways and squelched into wet mud. Whenever that happened his captors would pull him back up the slope and the trudge continued.

The raiders had left behind a Phantom crewman shocked and sightless, in pain and feeling very lonely, stumbling toward a fate he did not care to think about. "Meanwhile, I was on the ground wishing the Wright brothers had stuck with the bicycle!" Rudloff later quipped, with a cheerfulness he certainly did not feel at the time.

NOT FAR from Rudloff, Claude Julien had watched the departure of *Kitty Hawk's* planes. For a few minutes the surrounding countryside was still. But then, as he climbed from his hole, he was surprised to see men, women and children emerge from other hiding places all around. One moment the area was deserted, the next there seemed to be movement everywhere. Afterward he wrote:

> The planes had gone but we could not resume our journey straight away because of the danger of delayed-action bombs. Bus passengers joined us under the young pine trees giving us their shade. We were overwhelmed by the heat from the sky and the paddy fields. A young mother remained in a shelter to breast-feed her baby.

1:23 P.M. Off the mouth of the Red River the operation to rescue Randy Cunningham and Willie Driscoll was entering its final phase. Four minutes earlier the airmen had splashed into the sea. Now the three Sea King helicopters from HC-7 that had been waiting off the coast (Big Mother 61, 62 and 65) were clattering toward the survivors from the southeast. A Corsair circled protectively over the choppers, giving directions:

"Recommend [you steer a heading] three-two-zero, Big Mother."

"Big Mother, you'll notice the slope up from the shore where it joins the blue-water ocean. The deepest indentation of the blue water is about where the survivors are."

"Roger, what do you indicate, how far off the beach?"

"About eight miles off the beach. It ought to be no problem and there are no surface vessels in the area."

"The one furthest to sea, and they are only separated by two or three hundred yards, has got a green dye marker. The second one is on a bearing of about three-four-zero for three hundred yards with no dye marker at this time."

"We got red smoke flare from the far one and green dye from the close one."

Then, in a more concerned voice: "Honeybee, we got a couple of Bogies out at twelve o'clock, fast-moving, our altitude."

"That's affirmative, both in sight."

The unidentified aircraft turned out to be friendly, probably egressing planes from *Kitty Hawk.*

Leading the rescue in Big Mother 62 was Lieutenant Frank Pinegar. He told Big Mother 65 to pick up the nearer survivor (Cunningham) while he went for the other. Holding the helicopter at forty feet, Pinegar flew slowly past Driscoll in his life raft, and the swimmer, Elvin Milledge, dropped into the sea beside the airman.

Pinegar moved a short distance away so that the rotor wash would not hinder the swimmer, who reached the raft and cut away a line wrapped around Driscoll's leg. Milledge's report continued with what was probably a tactful understatement of how an enlisted man handled an officer in a state of shock: "Upon trying to move into position to inspect his [Driscoll's] back and other side, I realized he had hold of me. So I got a firm hold on him and he released his hold. . . ."

Milledge completed his check of the survivor, then, satisfied they were ready to be picked up, indicated this by splashing the water. The helicopter moved over the survivor and the rescue sling was lowered. Though hindered by the rotor wash, the swimmer slid the rescue sling around the survivor's shoulders, then placed the "D" rings on both their life vests into the spring loaded hook on the end of the line. Now all was ready for the lift. "I gave the first crewman a 'thumbs up' and we came out of the water. We came up alongside the aircraft swinging, and I used my left arm and right leg to cushion the blow and keep the survivor's back from hitting the aircraft," Milledge continued. "The first crewman got a hold on the survivor and I got a hold on the door and the overhead. With my feet on the deck the first crewman brought us aboard the aircraft. I asked the survivor if he was OK; he gave me a 'thumbs up' and I disconnected both of us from the rescue hook as the first crewman inspected him for injuries."

Simultaneously, Big Mother 65 hoisted Cunningham from the sea. With the survivors safely on board, the helicopters lifted their tails and sped from the area. With A-7s circling overhead they headed back to *Okinawa.*

AGAIN the air wings returned to Yankee Station and aircraft began landing on their carriers. *Constellation*'s planes, split up during the action, returned in small groups or singly. "People had become grossly separated and were streaming back, some very low on gas. A bunch of different types would arrive together, others came back singly and minutes apart. There was no way we could have an orderly recovery. The ship ran an open deck; when people got back they just went in and landed," remembered John Olsen. Matt Connelly, returning from the hectic fight in which he destroyed two MiGs, had particular reason to remember that land-on: when he slammed his Phantom down on the carrier's deck, it had only 500 pounds of fuel left.

After watching the landing from the deck of *Constellation,* Garrett Olinde noted in his diary: "The ship's crew poured on deck minutes after the last engine had been shut down and the flight deck secured. Everyone walked around the parked aircraft, especially the damaged F-4 that had returned on one engine. The underside of the plane, shredded like an old tin can, was touched, poked at and photographed by hundreds of people." The Phantom never flew again.

George Goryanec described the mood felt by most crews after the mission: "When we were debriefed everybody was high. We knew it had been a good day. We knew Randy had got three, Matt Connelly had got two and Steve Shoemaker had got a probable. People were shouting and hugging each other, it was unbelievable. Everybody was telling his little bit and piece." Assembling a coherent account of the air battle proved difficult, however, as Jim Fox recalled: "Everybody wanted to tell what had happened, but it was real hard to put together the story. Our crew's version was different from the other crews', mine was even different from Dwight Timm's [his pilot]."

Some had come close to death during the encounter, and now needed to recover their thoughts. Al Junker, a member of the same A-7 squadron as Goryanec, recalled his feelings after the one-sided brush with the MiG: "After I landed I just wanted to be alone. I went out to the catwalk and stood there quietly looking out to sea, thanking God for bringing me back from the mission alive."

2:15 P.M. The midday air strike was over, and with it the most intensive single air action of the Vietnam war. Seven MiGs had been shot down and one probably damaged. Two Phantoms had been destroyed; a Phantom and an A-6 had returned with serious damage. Later it was assessed that *Constellation*'s Air Wing had fought and defeated a total of twenty North Vietnamese fighters: fourteen MiG-17s, two MiG-19s and 4 MiG-21s.

Those on the carriers would be allowed little time to brood on the day's events. Four hours of daylight remained and yet another Alpha Strike was planned. On the decks there was more hectic activity to reposition, refuel and rearm the planes. The elevators carried damaged or unserviceable machines to the hangars and brought up replacements. The next launch was due to begin in just over an hour's time.

THE AFTERNOON ACTION, AND LATER

3:15 p.m.–Midnight

Human beings, like plans, prove fallible in the presence of those ingredients that are missing in maneuvers— danger, death, and live ammunition.

—Barbara Tuchman

3:15 P.M., YANKEE STATION. USS *Constellation* turned into the wind and began launching aircraft for her third Alpha Strike of the day. At 3:45 her Air Wing set out and at 4:30 P.M. the planes began attacking facilities at the port of Hon Gai. The 3,000-ton Soviet collier *Grisha Akopyan,* tied up at the jetty, was hit by two 500-pound bombs, which killed the bosun, injured the captain and caused severe damage. Other bombs started fires in the port area. Hon Gai lay outside the main belt of North Vietnam's air defenses, and the planes attacking the port encountered relatively little return fire.

The escorting Phantoms operated over a wide area, however, and some had memorable brushes with the defenses. Curt Dosé and Jim McDevitt of VF-92, the crew which shot down the first MiG that day, were escorting an Iron Hand A-7 north of the target when they heard signals from a SAM control radar tracking them. Dosé informed the A-7 pilot, but the latter, though only 300 yards away, said his equipment showed no such signals. Then the Phantom's warning receiver picked up missile guidance signals and showed a strobe at nine o'clock—the attack was from the west. As luck would have it, the late afternoon sun sat low in the sky to the west, its rays diffused by a bank of haze.

Curt Dosé was worried. A Phantom could outmaneuver a SAM relatively easily, but only if it was seen early and the evasive maneuver was started in good time. "We couldn't see any missiles and that made us real nervous. We peered into the setting sun trying to see where they were, but visibility was lousy." Ideally the A-7 should now have been delivering a counterattack with Shrike missiles, but still its pilot had not picked up signals from the missile control radar.

Suddenly Dosé saw the two SAMs "busting out of the haze in our nine o'clock, doing about Mach 3." He rolled the Phantom on its back and pulled into a dive trying to outmaneuver the missiles, but the robot weapons corrected to a new collision course. Disconcerted, the pilot rolled out and pulled into a maximum G climb. With contemptuous ease the missiles readjusted their trajectories and continued after the fighter.

By now the SAMs were too near for any evasive maneuver to be effective, and closing fast. Curt Dosé steeled himself for death. "One missile came past the nose, the other went over my canopy. It looked like a killer shot. Those missiles had 280-pound warheads, they had us cold. They were so close I could see the control surfaces moving. I gritted my teeth and waited for the explosion. I was looking at 'em, tensed up, ready to die. And they just continued on past, they didn't go off!"

The missiles continued beyond the Phantom until they were out of sight. The narrow escape left Dosé in a cold sweat: "As soon as they were past we rejoined the A-7 and got the hell out of there—he was doing no good, he couldn't see anything. And I wasn't ever that fond of Iron Hand escort anyway."

During this incursion there were few encounters with MiGs.

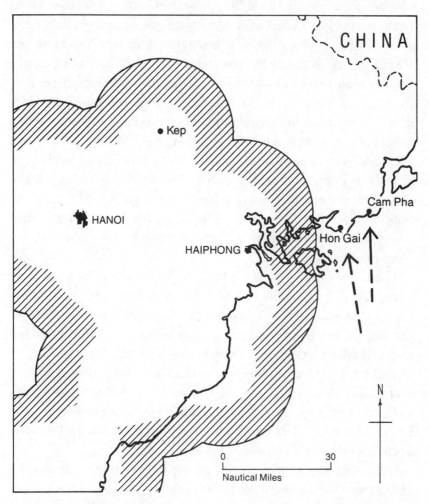

During the late afternoon action planes from USS *Constellation* raided the port of Hon Gai, those from *Coral Sea* attacked the railroad and highway bridge at Cam Pha and those from *Kitty Hawk* flew an armed reconnaissance of the Cam Pha area.

Lieutenant John Anderson, piloting a Phantom of VF-96, was on patrol near Hon Gai when he received vectors from Red Crown to engage incoming Blue Bandits—MiG-21s. "Meeting them head-on, we got 'clear to fire.' We both got radar lock, closing at a lot of speed. We got rid of our tanks and were ready to go. About ten miles ahead the two guys turned." Everyone thought the Phantoms would be able to overhaul the enemy fighters easily, but in fact they were the new MF version that were faster low down than earlier models. Anderson continued: "We were seven miles behind them heading north, doing Mach 1.2 to 1.3 at fifteen thousand feet. And Les [Lt. Les Roy, his back-seater] reported the range was opening. I said, 'I don't believe this!' Steve [Lt. Steve Queen, the element leader] said, 'Keep it going!' I said, 'Sure, they're gonna hit the border, they're gonna have to turn. And when they turn they're ours.' We were in perfect position, we were ready to go."

Then, just south of the Chinese border, the tables were suddenly turned as a couple of SAM sites joined in the fight. Anderson explained: "It was a SAM trap! I beat the pair of missiles coming for me, Steve beat the pair that were on him. I beat one more, then suddenly my back-seater shouted, 'Break right!' I pulled hard right and there was a missile about a thousand feet away and closing. It exploded behind us and shook the plane. Les's call saved us, otherwise the missile would have been right up our rear end." The two Phantoms pulled around and headed south away from the area.

Following the midday action many Navy fighter crews had "MiG fever," the urge to get at the enemy planes and knock them down. One of *Constellation*'s crews allowed these feelings to cloud their judgment, with near-disastrous results. Having located two unidentified planes on radar near the target, they failed to get clearance from Red Crown or to identify visually before launching a Sparrow at one of them. The "MiGs" turned out to be A-7s, but fortunately for all concerned the missile failed to guide and passed well clear of its intended target. Understandably the incident caused considerable bitterness among the attack pilots, and the matter would finally be settled in the course of a fistfight some weeks later, in a bar at Cubi Point!

Meanwhile, planes from *Coral Sea* attacked and damaged the railroad and highway bridge at Cam Pha, twelve miles east of Hon Gai. *Kitty Hawk*'s Air Wing flew an armed reconnaissance over the coastal area and bombed buildings near Cam Pha.

Compared with the day's previous actions, the final Alpha Strike was largely an anticlimax. Only two MiGs had tried to engage and relatively few SAMs had been launched. With the exception of those mentioned above, hardly any of the crews taking part in the action had reason to remember it. The comments of Lieutenant Mike Stansel, radar intercept officer in a Phantom patrolling off the coast, were typical of those on the mission recorded by the authors. "What with Harry Blackburn getting shot down and the great battle with MiGs earlier in the day, that mission was overshadowed. And, as I recall, there really wasn't much of anything there [Hon Gai]."

5:00 P.M., HANOI. As the last of *Kitty Hawk*'s planes cleared Cam Pha and headed for their carrier, Claude Julien finally reached the capital at the end of his interrupted journey. Because the air attacks had rendered unusable the road bridge at Hai Duong and the Paul Doumer Bridge at Hanoi, he had been unable to return by the main Route 5. But roads and tracks crisscrossed the area, and his Vietnamese driver had no difficulty finding another route, crossing the rivers by ferry or pontoon bridge. On the way the French journalist saw long convoys of military trucks on the move, some towing artillery or SAM transporter trailers. He saw dispersed under trees or almost any bit of cover small collections of oil drums and other supplies. In contrast to this warlike activity, the peasants went about their work much as they had always done. Julien wrote:

> The region we passed through had been shaken by the attack, but the peasants resumed work on the dikes and dug ditches. Again children paddled in the water with the buffaloes. Peasants

pushed barrows or carried baskets on yokes; draft animals and overloaded bicycles seemed in harmony with the surface-to-air missiles and the rest of the arsenal which nobody attempted to hide from the visitors.

When the vehicle reached Hanoi the Frenchman saw workmen erecting large panels stating that fourteen American planes had been shot down that morning; the figure would later be amended to sixteen to include those claimed downed during the afternoon action.

5:00 P.M., YANKEE STATION. When Julien reached Hanoi, Randy Cunningham and Willie Driscoll were on their return journey to *Constellation.* The Sea King helicopters had carried the pair to USS *Okinawa,* where they received thorough medical examinations. Pronounced fit to travel, the new-made fighter aces boarded a Marine Sea Knight to fly back to *Constellation.*

Captain Ward had broadcast to *Constellation*'s company the news that Cunningham and Driscoll had become the first fighter aces of the Vietnam war, that they had been shot down into the sea and rescued, that they were on their way back to the ship by helicopter and gave the time they were expected. By then the planes from the last Alpha Strike had landed and been secured, allowing many of the ship's company on deck to watch the heroes' return.

Signalman Greg Slavonic watched from his post on *Constellation*'s signal bridge when the Sea Knight approached. "The helicopter came in and landed in the middle of the flight deck. Captain Ward and another officer [Al Neuman, the commander of VF-96] went to meet Cunningham and Driscoll as they stepped from the helicopter. It was just like a political rally. Everybody was cheering and clapping, Cunningham and Driscoll waved to everyone and Captain Ward and the other officer shook them by the hand. Everybody was still cheering and clapping as Captain Ward and the other officer escorted them from the flight deck to the island."

The crew's achievement would be the main topic of discussion throughout the ship for the rest of the day and many that followed.

11:00 A.M. TO 7:00 P.M., YEN BAI. When darkness fell Roger Locher was still at liberty in North Vietnam, not far from the point where he landed by parachute after ejecting from his blazing Phantom eight hours earlier. Around him the terrain was hilly, with ridge lines separated by canyons ("a bit like the Blue Ridge Mountains near Front Royal"). When he heard the search party approaching, the airman hid in a small depression and covered himself with leaves, brush and rotting vegetable matter. "It was wet and uncomfortable—but better than the alternative!" he recalled. "They took about two hours to get from the crash site to where I was. When I first heard them I thought they were tracking me; it sounded like they were coming straight for me. Of course, you imagine that. They had a good search party of adult men; starting at about noon they searched fairly thoroughly. People yelled and screamed to get me to move, and once every fifteen minutes somebody fired three rounds from an automatic rifle into the ground."

Locher thought it would be only a matter of time before he was found, but until somebody stood over him with a gun he resolved to remain still. He later explained his philosophy. "If they wanted me, they would have to stand on me. I grew up in Kansas and spent a lot of time hunting pheasants. A lot got killed because they got nervous. They would sit among cover on the ground and you could walk past without seeing them. But if you stopped for a cigarette one might flush out from just behind you, three feet away, and you would get it. Had it sat tight it would have lived." Roger Locher had no intention of imitating the birds' error.

At dusk the searchers assembled noisily and went home. Stepping quietly in case someone had stayed behind, the fugitive moved a few hundred yards before dark. Then he picked out a relatively soft piece of ground, stretched out and began his first fitful night's sleep in North Vietnam.

• • •

2:15–7 P.M., HAI DUONG. Now a prisoner of the North Vietnamese, Steve Rudloff suffered the fate Cunningham, Driscoll and Locher had avoided. The captive's painful, sightless stumble lasted about twenty minutes before the party reached a village. There the airman was taken into a house and sat on a chair; someone untied his hands and gave him a cup of weak tea. Rudloff made a motion to his lips as if to smoke, and a cigarette was lit and placed between his fingers. During the next couple of hours Rudloff's sight returned in stages: first he made out vague outlines, then he recognized colors, then his full vision returned. But the ankle got progressively worse, and he was unable to walk more than a few feet without collapsing.

The villagers left the airman in no doubt about their feelings toward him. Men shook fists, others delivered punches. But if things started to get out of hand the Vietnamese in charge of Rudloff would stand protectively in front of him and yell at assailants until they backed off.

Eventually a truck arrived with troops to collect the prisoner, who was blindfolded and pushed into the back. The vehicle drove off, but at the next village it stopped, the prisoner's blindfold was removed and he was placed on exhibition. The process was repeated three or four times, Rudloff recalled. "At the village which turned out to be our last stop the population was extremely hostile. Following the standard scenario I was blindfolded again and placed in the back of the flatbed truck. While waiting to move I was struck on the side of the head with a blunt instrument and fell to the floor dazed. I could hear the angry voices of the military men in the truck with me, it sounded as though they were verbally chastising the individual who had struck me. I'm sure they felt they would be held responsible if any serious harm came to me and I was grateful for their 'humanitarian' concern."

Following the incident the truck completed the journey without further stops to show off the prisoner. When it reached Hai Duong the vehicle drove into a military compound, where soldiers led the captive into a sparsely furnished room.

Rudloff's blindfold was pulled away and the interrogation began almost immediately. U.S. Navy orders stated that prisoners should divulge no information other than their service number, rank and name. But the people who had drafted the order had probably never been in this predicament. The airman thought it better not to anger his captors unnecessarily, and decided to answer unimportant questions or those to which his captors probably had the answers.

Steve Rudloff's inquisitor began innocuously enough and asked if he was married and had children. The airman replied he had a wife and three children. Then the questioner asked the names of his ship and his pilot and again Rudloff answered truthfully. He figured the North Vietnamese were clever enough to read "USS Constellation" on items of his equipment, and they had probably captured Harry Blackburn. But when Rudloff refused to divulge the identity of his squadron the interrogator's tone changed in an instant. "He clenched his fist, banged the table and stood over me. He slapped me once or twice on the temple but not on the face—they were not hard blows." The line of questioning changed. "He handed me a piece of chalk and told me to draw on the floor the layout of my formation. When I hesitated he whacked me twice and clenched his fist. So I drew a diamond formation of four planes, pointed to one and said that was my plane. That seemed to satisfy him." (In fact Rudloff's F-4 had been one of a pair.)

Then the interrogator was called away and the questioning ceased. Rudloff remained in the room until after dark, when he was taken to a jeep outside and motioned to get in the back. The vehicle nosed out of the compound and sped away. The captive did not know the destination, but it required no clairvoyant skill to realize this trip had not been laid on for his pleasure.

7:00 P.M., YANKEE STATION. When darkness fell, Steve Kuhar was dining in *Coral Sea*'s "dirtyshirt mess," where aircrew were allowed to eat in their flight suits. The shrill note of a bosun's whistle on the ship's address system announced that the captain was about to deliver his daily bulletin. The chatter stopped immediately—the men were more hungry for news than for food. Kuhar recalled: "Everybody stopped what they were doing and moved closer to the nearest loudspeaker. The captain began with a description of accomplishments of our Air Wing and said Lieutenant Ken Cannon had shot down a MiG. Then he said it had been a historic day for the U.S. Navy, it had gained the first Vietnam war fighter aces! We were stunned by that statement; ace meant five kills. He told us Lieutenant Cunningham and Lieutenant Driscoll from the *Connie* had shot down their third, fourth and fifth MiGs that day. A great roar went up; it was like a lightning bolt went through the ship. I thought, Can that really be? Until then it had been unusual to see a MiG, and to engage one was even rarer. But three kills on one mission, I could hardly believe it! The captain went on to say that Cunningham and Driscoll had lost their aircraft, but both had been rescued from the sea uninjured."

7:00 A.M., WASHINGTON, D.C. (7:00 P.M. HANOI TIME). While Kuhar ruminated on his captain's words, Admiral Elmo Zumwalt was waiting to go on the air on the *Today* television show. Wearing full uniform, the admiral was introduced to viewers and invited to describe the operation to mine the North Vietnamese ports. After giving an outline of what had happened, Zumwalt described it as a "passive" act. It left to the other side the option of whether or not to risk damage or casualties; ships that remained clear of the mined waters would be perfectly safe. Ducking a couple of political questions, Zumwalt went on to talk about the hot news story of the morning: Cunningham and Driscoll's feat in shooting down five MiGs—three in one engagement—to make them the first aces of the Vietnam war. That item would occupy the nation's headlines for the rest of the day.

EVENING, THAILAND. The mood in the officers' clubs at the USAF bases in Thailand reflected the fortunes of each Wing during the day. At Udorn there was a morose air, as colleagues of the four missing men drank silently to their memory. "People were drinking but not enjoying the drinks," Tommy Feezel recalled. "Our minds were on the events of the day, the friends we had lost and the possibility that Bob Lodge and Roger Locher might still be alive."

At Ubon and Korat the mood was entirely different. Their planes had all returned safely—a perfect excuse for a party. As the evening wore on they became progressively wilder. Don Kilgus, a Wild Weasel pilot at Korat, described one of the party games played during such celebrations called GCA (ground controlled approach, the radar landing system at airfields): "The Stag Bar in the officers' club at Korat was about twenty-five feet long. Guys would get the candles in ornate holders from the dining room and set them out in two parallel lines across the floor. These were the 'runway lights.' Other guys would spread four or five buckets of ice on the 'runway' to make it good and slippery.

"When the 'runway' was ready a guy would stand a few feet from the end, take a short run to get up speed, then launch himself on his stomach with arms outstretched and slide across the ice. The idea was to go the full twenty-five feet to the end of the 'runway,' which terminated at an open door. Outside the door was a porch with a small drop to the ground, where there would be a steadily growing pile of drunken bodies.

"We worked hard, and when we were done we played hard. If you don't have a sense of humor in a stressful environment such as a war, people will break."

Later that evening there was a damper on the enjoyment of some of the partygoers when they learned they were assigned to the next day's mission and would have to be up early for the briefing. Only a few of them could be told that the Paul Doumer Bridge was still intact, and Headquarters Seventh Air Force had ordered a repeat attack on the following day. "The toughest and bravest guys in the world were a bunch of fighter pilots that have just come back from Hanoi," remembered James Allen. "The next bravest were the guys who just found they were not on the next day's schedule. But it was amazing how tough people ceased to be when the next day's schedule went up and they were on it; very quickly they became very quiet."

EVENING, YANKEE STATION. The official U.S. Navy prohibition of alcoholic drinks on its warships did not prevent celebratory parties there, too. Among carrier aircrew flying operations this rule was honored more in the breach than in the observance, and one of the participants recalled the modest soirée held that evening in VF-92's area on *Constellation*. "Drinking was common on carriers but it was confined to the aviators and we had to stay in our spaces. Senior officers either turned a blind eye or joined in. That evening there was a pretty hair-raising party at the squadron for everyone except the Alert 5 guys, to give people a chance to cut loose." The men's thoughts were with the two friends who had not returned that day, Harry Blackburn and Steve Rudloff. But two parachutes had been seen to open and there was reason to believe both had survived.

The rest of the Navy appreciated that in this conflict the aviators did nearly all the fighting, gained nearly all the victories and suffered nearly all of the losses; it was tacitly accepted that these men had a right to let rip if the occasion demanded.

EVENING, BETWEEN HAI DUONG AND HANOI. Steve Rudloff would have given anything to be at the VF-92 party that evening. Instead, he was being bounced around in the back of a Vietnamese army jeep speeding away from Hai Duong. Still his twisted ankle was giving him intense pain. With him in the vehicle were a driver and two other Vietnamese, one of whom covered him with an automatic rifle. During the journey Rudloff's mind wandered to the possibility of escape. "My hands were not tied. The guy with the gun nodded off from time to time and it crossed my mind that I might grab the gun, blow away the guard, then the driver and the other guy. Then I thought to myself, Yeah, that'd be real smart—*then* what the hell are you going to do?"

There was little traffic on the road, but in the jeep's headlights the prisoner saw military vehicles of all types drawn up under trees lining the route. Rudloff started counting the vehicles but gave up when he reached 300. The Vietnamese escorts treated their captive well and kept him provided with cigarettes. On the outskirts of Hanoi the vehicle stopped while one of the soldiers visited his girlfriend. She came out of the house giggling, with a cup of tea for the prisoner.

The jeep drove farther into the city and through the gates of the Hoa Lo prison—the notorious "Hanoi Hilton." On arrival the previously affable guards became different men. Eager not to appear soft in front of superiors, the three hustled Rudloff from the jeep into the building with a maximum of shouting and general unpleasantness.

At about 11:00 P.M., soon after Rudloff arrived at the prison, the grilling began. Two men came into the room, one in uniform and the other in civilian attire; the former knew no English but the latter had a functional command of the language. "Like the guy at Hai Duong, they wanted immediate military information. The first thing they asked was where U.S. aircraft were going to strike next." Rudloff played the dumb guy. He said he was only a very junior officer, not even a pilot; nobody told him anything.

After a short period of verbal foreplay the captors produced the flying map Rudloff had stowed in the cockpit as he crossed the coast of North Vietnam. He surmised the map must have blown out of the plane when he ejected.

"It came as a shock when they showed me my map, I figured everything like that had been destroyed. Now I didn't know what they might have. The map bore our route to the target and I had circled the positions of SAM and flak sites. They said 'Why do you have this place circled on your map?' I said some trucks had been seen there.

"They kept pushing me—where were American planes going to strike next? I told them I didn't know, I was just a lieutenant, nobody told me that sort of information, I received my orders just an hour before takeoff. Then they got to the ridiculous point of saying, 'Well, where do you think they might go?' I pointed to a bridge ringed to the northwest of Hanoi, where a SAM site was, and said 'Well, that's a bridge, maybe they'll go there.' Immediately I said it I realized that was a mistake. They said, 'Why are they going there, what's there?' It was as though I had confirmed that our aircraft were about to attack the place!"

Next, Rudloff's interrogators demanded to know about the mines dropped outside Vietnamese harbors. What patterns had been laid? How did the timing and detonation systems work? How could they be made safe? The questioners had found an area about which Rudloff, a fighter radar operator, really did know nothing: "I wouldn't have known what a mine looked like if I walked into one!"

When midnight chimed in Hanoi and the day reached its end, Steve Rudloff's interrogation was still in its opening stages. The exhausted airman's questioners had all the time in the world, and would use as much of it as they thought necessary. The inquisition would continue with scarcely a break for another twenty-seven hours.

MAN ON
THE RUN
May 11–June 2

By trying we can easily learn to endure adversity.
Another man's, I mean.

—Mark Twain

NIGHT OF MAY 10/11, YEN BAI. Sitting alone on a
wooded hillside deep in enemy territory, Roger
Locher made a mental inventory of his posses-
sions. He had a stout pair of boots, underwear,
flight suit, G suit, life preserver, and a survival
vest and its contents: two beeper radios and four
batteries, survival knife, .38-caliber Browning pis-
tol and ammunition, mosquito net, a small medical kit and various signaling devices—flares,
smoke markers, signal mirror and whistle. Following the loss of the survival pack his only means of
sustenance was two pints of water and a couple of
Pillsbury "Space Stick" snacks, none of which
survived his first meal in North Vietnam.

The airman thought it unlikely that helicopters
would come that deep into enemy territory to pick
him up, but if he could reach the sparsely inhab-
ited mountainous area to the west his chance of
rescue would be much greater. The distance was

ninety miles in a straight line. In a Phantom in a hurry it would take about five minutes; if he could advance an average of two miles per day it would take about six weeks. On the way he needed to cross the Red River, so he decided to take his life preserver. For food he would "live off Mother Nature." Whatever it lacked, Roger Locher's evasion plan certainly had the merit of simplicity.

Any attempt to move across North Vietnam would have been doomed from the start had the airman been injured, but in this respect Roger Locher had been extremely lucky. Apart from the shock, which soon wore off, during the ejection he had suffered only minor burns ("no worse than a bad case of sunburn") to unprotected skin on his neck and wrists.

After first light on the second day the airman covered the first couple of hundred yards of the planned ninety-mile journey. But then the searchers returned and again he hid in a patch of rotting foliage. "Again they had the whole village out to look for me, even women and kids. Fortunately they didn't bring dogs or they probably would have found me. Some little kids came within thirty feet of me, but they were there to get away from the adults and take it easy. After about an hour they went back to join the search party."

The airman lay still until the children had gone; then he took out a radio and listened for calls from American aircraft in the area. What he heard brought no comfort. A Phantom was providing cover for a downed crew while rescue helicopters moved in, and Locher could hear snatches of the fighter-bomber pilot's calls. "He said, 'Understand they are getting closer?' Then, later, 'Understand you think they see you, understand you want me to strafe your position?' From the code words I knew they were well to the south of me. I thought if they couldn't be rescued from there, what chance would I have? That was a dark time, my lowest psychological point."

At dusk on the second day the search ended and again Locher moved a few hundred yards before nightfall. On the morning of the third day it was raining when the search resumed, though again the fugitive was able to move short distances in the morning before sunrise and in the evening after sunset.

Rain was falling at dawn on the fourth day as Locher resumed the scramble to get as far as possible and establish himself in a new hiding place. But this time the area remained quiet; the hunt had been called off. Locher decided to stay where he was for the rest of the day and start moving west at dusk. During the morning the airman heard a noise like someone running toward him. He risked a peep and the "someone" turned out to be a five-foot-long monitor lizard on its way to some forest assignation. If the animal noticed Locher, it respected his wish for privacy. The airman returned the courtesy.

CAPTAIN PATTY SCHNEIDER, one of the intelligence officers at Udorn, was distraught when she heard that Roger Locher had been shot down. They had never dated, but now she realized she had fallen in love with him. "We always seemed to end up together at parties and he would usually walk me to my barracks. When I had good or bad news from home he was the first one I told. I decided that when he came back he wasn't going to get away from me again!"

Patty's reason for saying "when" rather than "if" Locher came back rested on slender evidence. After the May 10 action the intelligence staff at Udorn had painstakingly reviewed all available evidence on the loss of the two Phantom crews. Those who had been in the area reported hearing no beeper signals from either downed plane. But a playback of the tape from a Harlow Flight F-4 revealed a weak but clear beeper transmission lasting thirty seconds, with no voice transmission, on the Guard frequency (the fighter's crew had deselected Guard because of the volume of traffic on the main MIGCAP frequency). Further analysis established that the transmission was made at 10:06 A.M. The time was significant; it was twenty-two minutes *after* Oyster Leader was hit but eight minutes *before* Harlow Flight lost its aircraft.

In fact the transmission had come from Locher's beeper. His

voice call had not been radiated because, still in shock after the ejection, he forgot to press the "voice transmit" button. To those examining the evidence, the beeper signal posed more questions than it answered. It *could* have come from Locher's or Lodge's radio; but equally well it could have been made by someone shot down days or weeks before. Or it might even be part of a North Vietnamese attempt to lure rescue helicopters into a trap. Patty did not allow such doubts to dampen her faith, however. She "just knew" Locher was alive.

YEN BAI. Roger Locher was alive, but famished. Initially he had been too busy evading capture to worry about lack of food. But once he had shed the pursuers he entered a phase where his rumbling stomach dominated all thoughts. Locher ate wild fruit and shoots, when he could find them, but it was early spring and there was not a lot of new growth around. "My stomach was growling, I was always thinking about eating. I found a few dariens, small pods about the size of an apricot which contained edible kernels. Another fruit looked like a pithy cherry, it too had an edible inside. And there were weed shoots. They had no taste, they were just a bland blah. And that was it," the airman recalled. "I avoided meat. There were plenty of gray squirrels about; I could have shot them, but I figured somebody might come to investigate. And I had no way to cook the meat; I didn't want to catch parasites I couldn't handle." Fortunately for Locher several streams ran through the area and provided a plentiful supply of fresh water.

Day followed day in a regular pattern: get up at first light and walk a mile or so away from the rising sun and then hide; at dusk walk a few hundred yards toward the setting sun, then bed down for the night. By day mosquitoes were bothersome and Locher found it necessary to wear a mosquito net over his head. The hilly terrain varied between relatively lightly wooded areas and thick primary jungle with trees eighty feet high forming a dense canopy beneath which was perpetual twilight. In places the hills were steep and sometimes he had to take a circuitous route to move in the required westerly direction. There were few trails and he kept clear of those he did find.

At irregular intervals Locher switched on a radio and listened for calls from U.S. aircraft, but after the abortive rescue operation on the second day he heard nothing. Sometimes he switched on the beeper and made a brief voice call, keeping the transmission short so as not to betray his position to North Vietnamese listeners. Nobody replied.

Getting comfortable at night was always a problem. "It was tough to sleep on sloping ground, because as your body relaxes you start to slide down the hill. You end up with a heel dug in, then you get a cramp in that leg. At the end of about the eighth day I decided to find a nice flat spot on which to sleep. I found a place that leveled out by a creek and lay down there. The next thing I knew, I had leeches all over me. . . ." Frantically the airman shed his clothes and plucked the loathsome bloodsuckers off his body. From then on he slept on dry sloping ground each night and accepted the occasional bout of leg cramp.

On the thirteenth day Roger Locher's desire to make progress overcame some of his initial caution, and nearly cost his freedom. That morning he was trudging west buried in his thoughts when he suddenly realized he had blundered into a village. There were people all over the place, and if he went out the way he had come he thought he was sure to be seen. The airman crawled into a patch of foliage, covered himself with brushwood and leaves and resolved to stay put until dark. Everything went well until late in the afternoon.

"The kids were bringing in the cattle and this water buffalo must have smelled me. He stopped, standing on one of the saplings covering me, and refused to go on. The kids shouted and hit him, but he wouldn't budge. Then one of the kids went running off to the village. I thought they'd seen me, and were going to get dad with his gun. A little while later the kid came back with his bigger brother who hit the animal hard enough to make it go. As they went off I looked up and there was the butt of the water buffalo, first kid, second kid, and a little kid who ran after them, tripped and fell down, got up and ran on. The animal had knocked the camouflage off my right leg; if they had been looking for me they would certainly have found me. It's a good thing water buffaloes can't speak!"

The airman replaced the camouflage, waited until dark, then crept quietly away from the village.

By the final week in May food ceased to dominate Locher's thoughts; it was as though his body had given up caring. He could feel himself getting weaker; even standing up required inordinate effort. On the thirty-first he reached the end of the high ground; ahead lay the flat cultivated plain of the Red River Valley beyond which was the high ground he was making for. The airman faced a miserable choice—he was between the proverbial rock and a hard place: if he went forward into the populated area there was an increased risk of capture, but if he stayed put he could starve to death and perhaps nobody would know. He decided to start at first light the next day, get as far across the valley as he could, then hide before the peasants came to work the fields.

That night a long fall of rain kept the fugitive awake. The following morning, June 1, he overslept. When he awoke the sun was high in the sky and peasants were working in the fields through which he had to pass. There was no point in starting out now, so he decided to set out at dusk. He thought it was a bad omen, but in fact Lady Luck was smiling on him.

Midway through the morning a thunderous *whooooosh* rent the air: the SAM battery near Yen Bai had launched a missile. The significance of the reverberations did not escape Locher: "If they were firing, there had to be American aircraft nearby. I monitored Guard frequency on my radio but heard nothing. So I waited about five minutes, then I came up: 'Any U.S. aircraft, if you read Oyster One Bravo, come up on Guard.' "

To the south of Yen Bai, Phantoms of the 8th Tactical Fighter Wing were on the way home after bombing a target near Hanoi. One of the flights was using the call sign Oyster on that day and, by a remarkable coincidence, it was Oyster 2 that picked up Locher's transmission. Lieutenant Jim Dunn (who flew an F-4 chaff bomber during the May 10 mission) heard Locher's voice come through weakly. The survivor's use of the same Oyster call sign struck Dunn as "kinda spooky." He informed his flight leader, but by then Oyster Flight was beyond range of Locher's transmitter, so another flight was asked to reply to the call.

At this stage the downed airman's aim was simple; he merely wanted to say he was still alive. Fletch Flight (an F-4 unit on this occasion) made contact and Locher repeated the earlier call and gave more detail. "About five minutes later Fletch Leader came back and said, 'We passed the word, and the Jollies and Sandies are on their way.' That put a big weight on my shoulders. I thought there was no way a rescue force would come in so far for me . . . but I didn't tell them not to come!"

NORTHERN LAOS. Captain Dale Stovall of the 40th Rescue and Recovery Squadron was on airborne standby in his Jolly Green Giant helicopter when he heard about Locher's call. "One of the F-4s coming out called King Bird [the HC-130 Hercules search-and-rescue control aircraft] and said 'We have a guy on the radio who says he is Oyster One Bravo, he went down on May ten and tell everyone he is OK.'" As always, there was a risk the North Vietnamese had made the call, or even that a captured airman had been coerced into luring a rescue force into a trap. But after a short discussion it was decided to investigate the transmissions further. Cautiously the search-and-rescue force, two Jolly Green Giants with four A-1 Sandies and four Phantoms providing cover, advanced into North Vietnam.

It took the leading pair of A-1s about twenty minutes to reach the Yen Bai area and establish radio contact with Locher. Next the A-1s had to complete an important item on the agenda for rescue. The crews of the Jolly Green Giants were brave but they were not foolhardy. Before the vulnerable helicopters entered the area, the A-1 pilots had to ascertain that the caller really was Locher. Each U.S. airman flying on operations in the theater left behind four questions and answers personal to himself. A question and answer from Locher's list were passed on secure radio link from Headquarters Seventh Air Force near Saigon to the

Rescue Coordination Center at Nakhon Phanom, thence to the HC-130 airborne command post over northern Laos, thence to the A-1 Leader. Locher was asked for his mother's maiden name, and answered correctly. The operation could proceed.

Escorted by a second pair of A-1s the two big helicopters clattered low over the ground toward Yen Bai. Despite the deep penetration into enemy territory, initially it seemed the rescuers would have a clear run. As the aircraft passed over villages people stood in the open and watched, thinking that the unfamiliar machines that deep in North Vietnam had to be friendly.

Then things started to go wrong.

The SAM battery near Yen Bai launched a missile at one of the A-1s without success, then switched its attention to the Phantoms high above. A missile caused serious damage to one of the fighters, forcing it and its flight to break away. Worse followed, in the shape of a MiG-21 that closed on the rescue force. Dale Stovall described what followed: "Just as Ron Smith [the A-1 Flight Leader] was starting in the direction Roger Locher was, the MiG made the first pass on us. The A-1 covering us, Sandy Two, started screaming at us Jollies, 'Get down! Get down! MiG! MiG!' So we dumped our helicopters toward the deck. As I pulled out of a semi-split 'S' I saw this MiG-21 go by the other helicopter, about a thousand feet away."

For some reason the MiG did not open fire, but surprise was lost and without fighter cover the helicopters had to abandon the rescue attempt. The Jolly Green Giants headed southwest and, after another inconclusive brush with a MiG, began the long flight back to Thailand.

Roger Locher was dismayed that the rescue attempt had come to nothing, but throughout he had fought not to let his hopes run too high. And at least people knew he was alive. The airman stayed in his hiding place, relieved he had not set out at dawn for the sparsely covered floor of the valley.

UDORN, THAILAND. The news of Locher's radio call left Patty Schneider euphoric. "My knees went shaky, I couldn't concentrate on my other work anymore." Recording tapes of conversations between the F-4 crews and Locher were brought into the Intelligence Center and she was one of several present when they were played and replayed. "We listened to see if it was his voice and if he was under duress. We were all of the opinion that it was his natural voice and he did not seem to be under duress," she recalled.

SAIGON. It was one thing for a bunch of relatively junior intelligence officers at Udorn to establish the identity of an airman down in North Vietnam and conclude that he was not speaking under duress. It was quite a different matter to secure authority to mount what would now have to be a major operation to get him out, involving risk to a large number of planes and crews. That particular buck stopped on the desk of General Vogt, the Seventh Air Force Commander.

"The Wing at Udorn called me and said they wanted to get him [Locher] out," General Vogt recalled. "The problem was that it was going to involve a substantial effort. Choppers would have to be sent up there; they would have to have enough support to deal with the possibility that when they got up around the air base at Yen Bai, the MiGs would come swarming in. There could be a major air battle, we might lose aircraft.

"I had to decide whether we should risk the loss of maybe half a dozen airplanes and crews just to get one man out. Finally I said to myself, Goddamn it, the one thing that keeps our boys motivated is the certain belief that if they go down, we will do absolutely everything we can to get them out. If that is ever in doubt, morale would tumble. That was my major consideration. So I took that on myself. I didn't ask anybody for permission, I just said, 'Go do it!' "

Like many a senior commander before him, John Vogt had made a brave decision and now had to live with it. If losses were incurred during the operation, there would be no shortage of Monday-morning quarterbacks to tell him how he should have handled the problem differently.

· · ·

YEN BAI. Locher rose at first light on June 2 and began listening to the pocket-sized radio that was his lifeline to the outside world. Still he fought to keep down his hopes of rescue; he could not believe helicopters would again come so far into enemy territory for him.

THAILAND. While the downed airman pondered on his chances of rescue, he had no idea of the size of the effort sparked off by his radio call. General Vogt had willed the end, he also willed the means. All other Air Force operations scheduled against North Vietnam that day were postponed and the forces released made available to support the rescue.

Soon after dawn the two helicopters and four A-1s took off from Nakhon Phanom for the three-and-a-half-hour flight to Yen Bai, accompanied to northern Laos by the HC-130. Then the huge supporting operation began to take shape around the rescue force. Sixteen Phantoms were to attack Yen Bai airfield, to crater the runway and prevent the MiGs based there from interfering with the rescue. A further sixteen Phantoms were to hit antiaircraft gun positions in the area. The rescue force and the bombers, plus their attendant F-4 escorts, radar-jamming EB-66s, F-105 Wild Weasels and KC-135 refuelers, totaled 119 aircraft. About as many planes would take part in the rescue of Locher as had been involved in the original May 10 attack on Hanoi!

As on the previous day, Captain Ron Smith was in tactical command of the four A-1s and two helicopters heading in to collect Locher. At a prebriefed point over the mountains to the southwest of the survivor, the two helicopters and two of the A-1s went into an orbit. They were to wait there until called forward. The two leading A-1s, piloted by Smith and his wingman, continued to the rescue area.

Locher had correctly answered his authenticating question the day before, but there still remained an outside possibility that the helicopters were heading for a trap—the airman might have been answering with a gun pointed at his head. So Smith had a new question, devised by an officer who had attended the same college as Locher. Locher described what happened after he made radio contact with the rescuers. "Ron Smith said 'Hey, Oyster, I got a question for you and you'd better answer it right.' I'd been studying my other three questions all night, I knew the answers to those. But it wasn't one of them. He said 'What's Kite's?' Kite's? Everybody at Kansas State University knew the drinking haunt frequented by students. I said, 'It's a place to drink beer.' He said 'Drink what?' 'Beer!' He said, 'You sound like the one I want.' I said, 'You're damn right I'm the one you want!' " Locher's snap reply and indignant quip established beyond doubt that there was nobody telling him what to say.

Sitting on the hillside, the downed airman heard the whistle of distant jets, then the wail of sirens at Yen Bai. Four F-4s rolled in and attacked the south end of the airfield; another four went for the north end. Simultaneously, more F-4s dive-bombed antiaircraft batteries in the area, causing secondary explosions that sent columns of smoke high into the sky.

Ron Smith also saw the attack: "Everything was going like clockwork. As I crossed the last hill before the Red River, with my wingman, the bombs went off at Yen Bai. We could see that clearly, a few miles away. I told Roger to get out his mirror and signal flares, and to have his radio ready. I said he would not hear from us for thirty to forty-five minutes, and when he next heard us we would be right on top of him. He was to flash his mirror at the first A-1 he saw. He acknowledged that he had the instructions." That done, the two A-1s headed back to the waiting area to pick up the rest of the force.

The rescue force re-formed and advanced toward the survivor with Dale Stovall again flying the lead helicopter. As the planes crossed the Red River they came under machine-gun fire from the ground. The helicopters' gunners replied in kind. Smith directed the second helicopter and two of the A-1s to orbit just north of the survivor. Then Stovall moved his helicopter in for the pickup, with Smith and his wingman in A-1s flying close cover.

A few minutes later Locher heard an A-1 roar past. By the time

2 came in he had his signal mirror pointing at the approaching aircraft. The A-1 pilot saw the bright flash of the sun off the mirror, called "Tallyho!" on the radio, and began circling the survivor. Then the A-1s laid a smoke screen between the downed pilot and the Red River Valley.

The rescue helicopter swept in behind the A-1s, clattered over the survivor, pulled into a tight semicircle and nosed toward him in a slow hover. The pickup went exactly according to the book, but, as Stovall explained, the same could not be said for the first part of the egress: "It took less than two minutes to get Roger on board the helicopter, and we were all on our way over the ridge line. Jerry [Captain Jerry Shipman, pilot of the backup helicopter] was waiting for us, and we started back in formation. Every village had been alerted and we started taking small arms fire on the way back.

"As we came over a ridge line before we dropped into the Red River [Valley] we had the surprise of our lives. A train coming down that railroad from China had seen the smoke at Yen Bai and had stopped exactly at our crossing point. We came over the ridge line in formation, and sitting in front of us was a fourteen-car train. Two cars had sandbagged gun positions, similar to what you see in the World War Two movies. Their gunners were looking down the Red River Valley. They tried to get their guns cranked around to fire at us, our gunners were trying to get a shot at them. Meanwhile I was trying to jink and the Sandies were all hollering and yelling. It was like a kids' parade. We went right over them and pressed on at low level across the valley."

A-1s made several strafing runs on the train, then rejoined the helicopters heading southwest. Shortly afterward one of the A-1 pilots spotted a MiG-17 some distance away. Apparently its pilot did not see the rescue force, however; he turned away and the fighter was not seen again.

During these events Locher sat in the fuselage of the helicopter, oblivious to what was happening outside. Someone had passed him a box of C rations and, like an orphan who had found the key to the treats cupboard, he gobbled cookies as fast as he could.

When he could get no more in his mouth he stuffed them into his pockets. "I still didn't think I was getting out of North Vietnam, and I'd be damned if I was going to go down a second time without eating!" he explained. He worked his way through a can of apricots and a few other items before his stomach, unaccustomed to such largess, issued a stab of protest.

After a three-hour flight the rescue formation reached Udorn to deliver Locher to his home base. A large crowd was waiting at the airfield to greet him, and the reception committee included General Vogt, who had flown in from Saigon especially. Stovall described the rescuers' arrival: "The A-1s broke out and got ahead of us a little ways. Then all made a low pass on the field, pitched out and landed. We came in behind them, made a low pass down the flight line, popped our red smokes [smoke markers] and came back in, landed and taxied in. We had been in the aircraft about eight hours and we were hot and sweaty and extremely excited."

As Locher stepped from the helicopter, loud cheers and yells rose from the several hundred service people standing on the ramp. Patty Schneider watched excitedly as the gaunt, unshaven, filthy, ecstatic man she loved shook hands with the general and with his friends. Weak from lack of food, Locher walked like an old man; he had left the base weighing 180 pounds, now he was down to 150 pounds. Willing hands helped him into the waiting ambulance. It was the moment Patty had prayed for, yet now she was at a loss what to do. "All the other guys knew how I felt, but Roger really didn't. When he got in the ambulance I didn't want to get in. I felt I had no right to be in there; we had not dated or anything. But the other guys pushed me towards the ambulance and said 'Get in there!' So I did. That was how Roger found out he was special to me."

The Israeli leader Moshe Dayan once commented that the person who deserves most credit for a military operation that succeeds is the one who would have had to take the blame if it failed. In the case of Locher's rescue that man was General Vogt, who had risked his reputation in allowing the operation and in switching massive resources from other tasks to support it. Now that the operation had succeeded, his reward was written all over the grinning faces around him.

ROGER LOCHER'S feat—for an aircrew survivor, unassisted, to remain at liberty for twenty-three days in enemy home territory and initiate a successful rescue—established a record for the Vietnam war and ranks with the most successful combat evasion episodes in history. The remarkable rescue also set a record for those who retrieved him, for the operation took the Jolly Green Giant helicopters deeper into North Vietnam than on any other such mission. Ironically, the airman's determined effort to ease the task of his rescuers achieved virtually nothing. During the three-week trudge he moved only about twelve miles to the west; had he stayed put after the Vietnamese gave up the search, the helicopters would have needed to spend only a few minutes more over enemy territory to reach him.

THE MAY 10, 1972, ACTION ANALYZED

In battle nothing is ever as good, or as bad,
as the first reports of excited men would have it.
                    —Field Marshal Sir William Slim

HAVING followed each of the air actions over North Vietnam on May 10, 1972, in some detail, let us now consider the day's events as a whole. U.S. planes flew a total of 414 sorties to attack, or support attacks on, targets in North Vietnam: 120 by the Air Force and 294 from carriers. Of this total an estimated 338 sorties, 88 by the Air Force and about 250 by the Navy, penetrated North Vietnamese airspace.

The sorties may be divided into two categories: the bombers sent to attack the primary targets; and the supporting planes taking part in the operation in all other roles—fighter escort, defense suppression, radar countermeasures, reconnaissance, air-to-air refueling, search and rescue and airborne command and control.

Air Force planes flew thirty-one bomber sorties (due to an administrative foul-up, a laser-marking F-4 had to go to Hanoi without bombs), Navy planes flew about 110 bomber sorties. For each Air Force bomber there were 2.8 supporting planes, for each Navy bomber there were 1.7 supporting planes. The reason for the discrepancy was that the Air Force's targets were farther from base, and more heavily defended, than those attacked by the Navy; as a result the Air Force raiding forces required a higher proportion of tankers, fighters and defense-suppression aircraft.

The most elaborate attack of the day was the Air Force's set-piece operation against the Paul Doumer Bridge. Four F-4s aimed seven electro-optical guided bombs at the bridge, all of which missed. When questioned about this weapon, General Vogt did not mince his words; he told the authors: "It wasn't worth a shit. . . ." Eleven F-4s then attacked the bridge with twenty-two laser-guided bombs. Poststrike analysis, based on video recordings of the TV pictures produced by the laser designator pods, credited the LGBs with twelve hits and four probable hits. Smoke and spray made it impossible to plot the impact points of the other six bombs. After the attack the Paul Doumer Bridge was still standing, though two spans at its eastern end were seriously damaged and the bridge was unusable.

The other Air Force target was the rail yard at Yen Vien, attacked by sixteen Phantoms, which dropped 140 free-fall 500-pounders. Poststrike photos showed widespread damage, and all through tracks had been cut.

Navy aircraft attacked four major bridges: two near Hai Duong, one at Haiphong and one near Cam Pha. The raiders dropped spans at each of the first three, but that near Cam Pha survived the attack. Thus, with the Paul Doumer Bridge put out of action by Air Force planes, four bridges between Hanoi and Haiphong were unusable. All rail traffic between the two cities was halted.

Navy aircraft also attacked rail yards at Hai Duong and Haiphong, the Haiphong petroleum storage area, and warehouses in the Quan Back and Cam Pha areas. In each case widespread damage was reported.

. . .

THE TARGETS attacked by U.S. planes on May 10 were all associated with the movement of supplies and equipment to Communist forces fighting in South Vietnam and were legitimate military objectives. The raids were well planned and carried out with a high degree of professionalism, but that did not prevent damage being caused outside the target areas and deaths and injuries to civilians.

Some damage and casualties were almost certainly caused by SA-2 missiles fired by the North Vietnamese defenses. As each missile completed its initial boost phase it automatically released its booster rocket. Falling from several thousand feet, the hefty booster would flatten anything it hit. Also, SA-2 missiles would often go out of control after launch and fly into the ground, or fall intact after reaching the end of their trajectories. Weighing up to two and a half tons, depending on how much fuel had been burned, a missile detonating on the ground could cause as much devastation as any bomb.

During the May 10 action there was a large explosion in Gia Lam village about a mile from the Paul Doumer Bridge, probably caused by a falling SAM or one of the electro-optically guided weapons that failed to guide. Thirty-two civilians were killed and many others wounded.

Other reports of "indiscriminate bombing" during this attack probably resulted from the operations by the Wild Weasel and Iron Hand aircraft. The F-105Gs launched more than thirty Shrike and Standard antiradiation missiles in the general direction of Hanoi, most of which went their own way after the radars they were aimed at shut down. Probably it was one of these missiles that rammed into the Huu Nghi Viet-Xo hospital in the east side of Hanoi. A French reporter who inspected the damage later wrote: "A fragmenting rocket went through a wall 20 cm [8 in] thick and exploded in the pharmacy. A missile which projects ten thousand steel cubes over 50 meters is an 'antipersonnel' weapon and can in no way be intended to destroy strategic objectives." That description exactly fitted the type of warhead carried by U.S. antiradiation weapons.

ANALYSIS OF AIR-TO-AIR ATTACKS BY U.S. PLANES, MAY 10, 1972

Time of Action (1)	Initial Pickup (2)	Forces Engaged (3)	Firing Aspect (4)	Weapons Fired (5)	Remarks
8:58 A.M.	Red Crown	2N v 4	rear	7 Sidewinder	1 MiG-21 shot down (6).
9:42 A.M.	Red Crown	4AF v 6	5 head-on 3 rear	8 Sparrow	3 MiG-21s shot down (7). 1 F-4 shot down by MiG-19, from the rear with cannon (8).
10:01 A.M.	Visual	4AF v 1	1 rear	1 Sparrow	Disruptive shot, forced MiG to break off attack on F-105.
10:01 A.M.	AI radar	2AF v 2	2 side 1 rear	3 Sparrow	Inconclusive engagement, no hits (6).
10:04 A.M.	Visual	2AF v 3	1 head-on	1 Sparrow	Inconclusive engagement, no hit.
10:14 A.M.	Visual	2AF v 1	rear	1 Sidewinder 2 Sparrow	1 F-4 shot down by MiG-19, from the rear with cannon. No U.S. hits (6).
1:00 P.M.	Visual	11N v 20	rear	10 Sidewinder 3 Sparrow	6 MiG-17s shot down, all by Sidewinders, in large-scale turning fight.
1:05 P.M.	Visual	3N v 1	rear	20-mm cannon	A-7 engaged MiG-17 and probably damaged it.

| 1:09 P.M. | Visual | 2N v 1 | rear | 1 Sidewinder | Target found visually, by F-4s being radar vectored on to another enemy aircraft. 1 MiG-17 shot down. |
| 5:00 P.M. (approx.) | AI radar | 2N v 2N | head-on | 1 Sparrow | Missile fired at A-7 misidentified as hostile. No hit. |

COMMENTS

(1) Time of Action. Time the first U.S. missile or cannon was fired.

(2) Initial Pickup. Means by which the U.S. fighter crew first knew of the presence of the enemy aircraft they attacked. This came from Red Crown (radar or other surveillance from USS *Chicago*, two cases), visually from the cockpit (six cases), or by the fighter's own airborne intercept radar (two cases).

(3) Forces Engaged. First number gives the U.S. aircraft involved and their service. Second number gives North Vietnamese aircraft known or believed to have been involved.

(4) Firing Aspect. Aspect, relative the MiG, from which U.S. fighter(s) launched missile(s).

(5) Weapons Fired. Figure includes each occasion a U.S. pilot squeezed the trigger to fire a missile, whether or not the missile left the fighter or guided properly.

(6) Two or more missiles fired from near to or outside the limit of their engagement envelope.

(7) In two cases pairs of Sparrows were ripple fired at the same target, without waiting to see if the first missile guided properly. In both cases the target aircraft was destroyed.

(8) F-4 came under attack while one Sparrow was in flight. Forced to take evasive action, break radar lock on the target and leave the missile without guidance.

Air attacks, even with high-tech weaponry, are rarely as precise as some of their proponents would like us to believe.

THE DAY saw the heaviest aerial fighting of the Vietnam war, with eleven MiGs and two Phantoms shot down in air-to-air combat. According to one official U.S. source the North Vietnamese People's Army Air Force put up forty-one fighter sorties. The authors believe this figure refers to the number of MiGs seen from U.S. planes, however, and is probably an underestimate. Those forty-one sorties—or sightings—can be split between the various actions approximately as follows:

Against the early morning attack on Haiphong: four MiG-21s.

Against the midmorning attack on Hanoi: five MiG-19s, nine MiG-21s.

Against the early afternoon attack on Hai Duong: fourteen MiG-17s, three MiG-19s and four MiG-21s.

Against the late afternoon attack on Hon Gai and Cam Pha: two MiG-21s.

The table on pages 168–69 was compiled by the authors to show the circumstances in which U.S. fighters attacked MiGs during the May 10 action. In six of the ten engagements the target plane was first picked up visually; in two cases the initial warning that led to the engagement came from the Red Crown controller on USS *Chicago;* and on two occasions the target was first seen on the U.S. fighter's airborne intercept radar (in one case the target was an A-7, which was then attacked in error).

The table underlines the importance of maintaining a good visual lookout in the combat area. Electronic aids can assist a fighter crew to find the enemy, but in a daylight engagement the human eye remains the primary means of searching for the enemy. Significantly, in half the aircraft shot down in air-to-air combat on May 10 (two Phantoms and four MiG-17s) their crews appear not to have known they were under attack before their plane was hit, even though their assailant came within visual range to deliver the lethal blow.

The authors believe that U.S. fighters launched nineteen Sidewinders and a similar number of Sparrows during the day's actions. Sidewinders destroyed eight MiGs; Sparrows destroyed three. Seven Sparrows were fired head-on and destroyed two MiGs; all the other missiles that scored hits were fired from the rear. The Sidewinder demonstrated an operational effectiveness of 42 percent; the Sparrow, 15 percent. The Soviet-made Atoll air-to-air missiles fared worse: at least four were fired but none hit, giving an operational effectiveness on that day of zero percent.

Those figures are far removed from the "near 100 percent" kill rate predicted for guided missiles before the Vietnam war. Why the discrepancy? One U.S. missile expert summed up the reason in these words:

> [Before the conflict] we defined a 90 percent reliability at the 90 percent confidence level in a white-gloves, filtered-air test range where most failures were considered as a "no test." In combat there is no such thing as a no test. Missiles are reliable when the target is destroyed and unreliable when it isn't.

There were, moreover, several cases where pilots launched missiles under conditions that gave individual weapons little or no chance of scoring a hit. For example, during the early morning action Curt Dosé and Austin Hawkins launched or attempted to launch seven Sidewinders. At the time both the F-4 and the target MiG were in a high G turn at very low altitude, and to score a hit under such circumstances was a creditable achievement. During the midmorning action John Markle and Steve Ritchie both ripple-fired pairs of Sparrows at single targets (both targets were destroyed). Twice Sparrows were fired with no chance of scoring a hit, solely to force MiG pilots to break off attacks on U.S. planes; the stratagem was successful on both occasions. On the other side of the coin, the day saw Randy Cunningham's exemplary performance in shooting down three MiG-17s for an expenditure of three Sidewinder missiles.

The strict rules of engagement imposed on U.S. fighter crews, requiring the target plane to be identified positively as hostile before missiles could be launched, were a constant source of irritation. Under operational conditions the "see and identify" range was usually below four miles, significantly less than the maximum engagement range of the Sparrow missile. Only the radar controllers on Red Crown (USS *Chicago*) or Disco (the EC-121 radar plane) could clear fighter crews to engage planes outside visual identification range. The rules negated the Sparrow's long-range engagement capability and cost several victories. But, irksome though the rules were, there were sound reasons for enforcing them. At times on May 10 the U.S. planes outnumbered their opponents over North Vietnam by more than ten to one. Had there been no requirement for positive identification before missile launch, a few gung-ho fighter crews bent on amassing high personal scores could have rained mayhem on friend and foe alike. Late on the afternoon of May 10 we saw an instance where an F-4 crew disregarded the rules, mistook a pair of A-7s for MiGs and launched a Sparrow at one of them. Fortunately for everyone involved the missile failed to home. Overall, the "identify first" rule saved many U.S. planes. And even with the strict rules of engagement there were occasions (though not on May 10, 1972) when U.S. aircraft were shot down over North Vietnam by missiles from "friendly" fighters.

None of the F-4s assigned to the air-to-air role carried cannon, although this weapon was fitted to A-7s, F-4Es and F-105s that operated in the air-to-ground role on this day. An A-7 probably damaged a MiG-17 with cannon fire. Had the F-4s flown by Dosé and Hawkins carried this weapon they would probably have shot down the second MiG-21 they chased, and there would almost certainly have been more MiG kills during the Hai Duong action.

During air-to-air combats on May 10, the eleven MiGs that were shot down for the loss of two F-4s gave a kill ratio in the American pilots' favor of 5.5 to one. Both of the F-4s lost were "bounced" from behind by MiG-19s, and shot down by cannon from short range.

For the most part the North Vietnamese fighters were properly handled and employed the correct tactics for a numerically weaker, less well-equipped and less well-trained force: they endeavored to fight only on their own terms, usually delivering snap attacks and breaking off the action once they had lost the element of surprise.

During the early afternoon MiG-17s attempted a different type of combat, when they remained in the target area for *six* minutes trying to lure *Constellation*'s Phantoms into a low-altitude turning fight. Three years earlier the ruse might have worked; the reason it did not succeed on May 10 can be stated in two words: Top Gun. Using the skills they had learned during the course, Randy Cunningham and other pilots quickly took the measure of their more nimble but slower opponents. Then, making it seem almost easy, VF-96 proceeded to carve up the MiGs. Whenever the Navy pilots found themselves at a disadvantage during the combat, they used the F-4's superior acceleration to break out the fight, move to a position of advantage and rejoin the action on their terms. In the course of the multiplane hassle *Constellation*'s Phantoms shot down seven MiG-17s in rapid succession without loss to themselves. That afternoon, in a space of just eight minutes, the cost-effectiveness of the Top Gun training course was established beyond possible doubt.

THE NORTH VIETNAMESE ground defenses—missiles and guns—shot down two U.S. planes to bring the total U.S. loss to four (1.1 percent of the sorties that penetrated North Vietnamese airspace). Five aircraft (1.5 percent) returned with damage, which in one case led to the plane being scrapped.

The most reliable U.S. source states that on May 10 North Vietnamese missile batteries launched ninety-three SAMs, forty-one at Air Force planes and fifty-two at Navy planes. It is clear that the combination of special tactics, electronic countermeasures and defense suppression forces effectively contained this threat. Only one aircraft was lost to a SAM (giving a SAM firing-to-kill ratio of 1.07 percent), and three suffered minor damage.

Antiaircraft artillery fire shot down one U.S. plane, damaged another beyond repair and inflicted major damage on a third. The main effect of such fire was to deter U.S. aircraft from flying

PAVNAF AIRCRAFT DESTROYED AND DAMAGED, MAY 10, 1972

Time	Type	Location	Cause	Details
8:58 A.M.	MiG-21	About 5 mi. N of Kep airfield	AAM Sidewinder	Shot down by F-4J of VF-92, Lt. C. Dosé and Lt. Cdr. J. McDevitt. Seen to crash.
9:43 A.M.	MiG-21	40 mi. NW Hanoi	AAM Sparrow	Shot down by F-4D of 555TFS, Maj. R. Lodge and Capt. R. Locher. Pilot seen on parachute.
9:43 A.M.	MiG-21	as above	AAM Sparrow	Shot down by F-4D of 555TFS, Lt. J. Markle and Capt. S. Eaves. Seen falling with part of wing missing.
9:44 A.M.	MiG-21	as above	AAM Sparrow	Shot down by F-4D of 555TFS, Capt. S. Ritchie and Capt. C. DeBellevue. Seen hit, pilot seen on parachute.
1:00 P.M.	MiG-17	Near Hai Duong	AAM Sidewinder	Shot down by F-4J of VF-96, Lt. R. Cunningham and Lt. W. Driscoll. Seen to crash.
1:03 P.M.	MiG-17	as above	AAM Sidewinder	As above. Exploded, pilot seen to eject.

Time		Location	Weapon	Notes
1:03 P.M.	MiG-17	Near Hai Duong	AAM Sidewinder	Shot down by F-4J of VF-96, Lt. M. Connelly and Lt. T. Blonski. Pilot seen to eject.
1:04 P.M.	MiG-17	as above	AAM Sidewinder	As above.
1:04 P.M.	MiG-17	10 mi. NE Hai Duong	AAM Sidewinder	Shot down by F-4J of VF-96, Lt. S. Shoemaker and Lt. K. Crenshaw. Explosion observed on ground in vicinity of combat; kill later confirmed from intelligence sources.
1:05 P.M.	MiG-17	40 mi. S Hai Duong	20 mm cannon	Attacked by A-7 of VA-147, Lt. G. Goryanec, chasing another A-7. Probably damaged.
1:08 P.M.	MiG-17	Near Hai Duong	AAM Sidewinder	Shot down by F-4J of VF-96, Cunningham and Driscoll. Seen to crash.
1:09 P.M.	MiG-17	20 mi. S Hanoi	AAM Sidewinder	Shot down by F-4B of VF-51, Lt. K. Cannon and Lt. R. Morris. Seen to crash.

Information from U.S. sources.

U.S. AIRCRAFT DESTROYED AND DAMAGED, MAY 10, 1972

Time	Type	Unit	Location	Cause	Details
8:45 A.M.	F-4J NG-205	VF-92 Constellation	Haiphong	SAM	Minor damage from SAM. Blast caused temporary loss electrical power. Pilot Lt. J. Olsen.
8:45 A.M.	RA-5C	RVAH-11 Constellation	Haiphong	SAM	Minor damage from SAM.
9:40 A.M. approx.	F-4	433TFS 8TFW Dingus Flt	Near Hanoi	SAM	Minor damage from SAM. Pilot Maj. R. Blake.
9:44 A.M.	F-4D 65-784 OY	555TFS 432TRW Oyster Flt	30 mi. NW Hanoi	MiG-19 cannon	Shot down. Maj. R. Lodge killed, Capt. R. Locher rescued after 23 days in North Vietnam.
10:14 A.M.	F-4E 67-386 SA	334TFS 432TFW Harlow Flt	70 mi. NW Hanoi	MiG-19 cannon	Shot down. Capt. J. Harris, Capt. D. Wilkinson killed.

Time	Aircraft	Unit / Carrier	Location	Cause	Remarks
10:15 A.M. approx.	RF-4C 68-604 OZ	14TFS 432TFW Cousin Flt	Near Hanoi	Operational accident	Minor damage when jettisoned fuel tank. Pilot Capt. D. Pickard.
1:03 P.M.	F-4J 1555797 NG-212	VF-92 Constellation	Hai Duong	85-mm AAA	Shot down by AAA, Cdr. H. Blackburn killed, Lt. S. Rudloff prisoner.
1:03 P.M.	F-4J 155560 NG-207	VF-92 Constellation	Hai Duong	85-mm AAA	Damaged beyond repair by AAA. Pilot Lt. R. Dilworth.
1:10 P.M.	A-6A 155649 NL-502	VMA-224 Coral Sea	Hai Duong	37-mm AAA	Damaged AAA, 2-ft. hole in stbd. horiz. stabilizer.
1:10 P.M.	F-4J 155800 NG-100	VF-96 Constellation	Southwest of Haiphong	SAM	Shot down. Lt. R. Cunningham and Lt. W. Driscoll ejected, both rescued from the sea.

through defended areas below 14,000 feet, unless it was necessary for a particular part of the mission.

OF eight men in the four F-4s shot down that day, there is evidence that five (62 percent) ejected. Two were rescued from the
sea, one evaded capture on land and one was taken prisoner. The
fate of the fifth ejectee, Commander Harry Blackburn, is unclear,
though his parachute was seen to open. After the war his body
was returned by the Vietnamese authorities and he is officially
listed as having died in captivity. Concerning the remaining three
crew members, the authors have no evidence that any of them
ejected from their planes before they crashed. In the case of the
eleven MiGs shot down, eyewitness evidence suggests that at
least five of their pilots ejected and parachuted to safety.

OPERATION Linebacker continued through the spring, summer and
fall of 1972, during which U.S. planes knocked out all the major
bridges in North Vietnam and kept them out of action. The
attacks effectively strangled the nation's rail network, while mining of the channels leading to ports prevented further supplies
from coming in by sea. The North Vietnamese replied by employing convoys of trucks to bring supplies overland from China,
circumventing the broken bridges by the use of pontoon bridges
or ferries. The carriage of supplies and war materials, though
rendered more difficult, was never prevented altogether.

On January 15, 1973, following agreement between the U.S.
and North Vietnamese representatives on a cease-fire in South
Vietnam and a release of prisoners, President Nixon ordered an
end to offensive action against North Vietnam. The air war over
the North had lasted more than three thousand days, with peri-
ods of heavy fighting interspersed with times of calm as the
diplomats tried repeatedly to reach a settlement. May 10, 1972,
saw the most intensive air-to-air combat, and the greatest loss of
aircraft, of any single day. Yet no decisive effect can be ascribed
to it, it was simply "one day in a long war."

AFTERWARD

He that outlives this day, and comes safe home,
Will stand a-tiptoe when this day is named.
—Shakespeare, *Henry V*

FOLLOWING the launch of Operation Linebacker the Soviet government was loud in its condemnation of the bombing; at the same time, however, it went out of its way to state that the President's visit to Moscow should still go ahead. Secretary Brezhnev was unwilling to allow his support for North Vietnam to jeopardize the new relationship with the United States. The summit meeting between the two leaders began on May 22 and was publicly dominated by the final negotiations on the SALT treaty and agreements on scientific cooperation and economic matters.

THE ATTACK on the Paul Doumer Bridge on May 10, 1972, failed to drop any of its spans, though the structure was damaged and rendered unusable. On the following day Phantoms of the 8th Tactical Fighter Wing made a repeat attack with laser-guided bombs and dropped a damaged span. A few days later People's Army of Viet Nam engineers erected a pontoon bridge a few hundred yards downstream, which, surprisingly, was never attacked; it would carry the majority of traffic entering Hanoi from the east, until the U.S. bombing finally ceased early in 1973. Repairs of the Paul Doumer Bridge began in earnest at the end of January 1973. On March 4 the bridge was ceremonially reopened and a flag-bedecked steam engine bearing a large portrait of Ho Chi Minh pulled the first train to cross it since May 10, 1972.

IN LATER years, what became of some of those involved in the air battle over North Vietnam on May 10, 1972?

Steve Rudloff remained in captivity in North Vietnam for 322 days. Then, on March 28, 1973, a bus arrived at the "Hanoi Hilton" to drive his batch of prisoners over the newly repaired Paul Doumer Bridge and on to Gia Lam airport. There the men boarded an Air Force C-141 transport and took off for Clark Field in the Philippines. Three days later he arrived at his home base, the Naval Air Station at Miramar, San Diego. Press photographers snapped the reunion hug with his wife, Marie, and one of the shots made the front pages of newspapers all over the country. Steve stayed in the Navy until 1980 and rose to the rank of commander. When interviewed he was living at Cooperstown, New York, where he was executive director for the Southern Oswego County Red Cross.

After Randy Cunningham returned to the United States, it was appropriate that he should spend a tour as instructor at Top Gun and pass on his experience to other fighter crews. Then he spent a tour in the Navy fighter planning office at the Pentagon. Following promotion to lieutenant commander, he served as executive officer on an F-14 squadron. He was promoted to commander and returned to Miramar, where he assumed command of the Pacific Fleet's aggressor squadron, a unit operating F-5s and A-4s using Soviet tactics in mock combat against Navy fighters. In January 1987 he retired from the Navy and became dean of aeronautics at the National University, San Diego, with plans to run for Congress.

Willy Driscoll, Cunningham's back-seater on May 10, is also out of the Navy and sells real estate for Coldwell Banker in Carlsbad, California.

Matt Connelly, who shot down two MiGs on May 10, now flies for Pacific Southwest Airlines. So, does Steve Shoemaker, who shot down one MiG on that day. Tom Blonski, Connelly's back-seater, is an engineer for Contel in Vermont. Keith Crenshaw, Shoemaker's radar intercept officer, still flies for the Navy with the rank of commander.

Curtis Dosé, pilot of the Phantom that shot down the first MiG to fall during the May 10 action, later became a Navy test pilot. He now flies for the Flying Tiger Line, which merged with Federal Express.

Fred Baldwin, the A-7 pilot who took part in the three-aircraft chase over the Red River delta with a MiG in the middle, went on to command the air wings on *Constellation* and *Ranger.* He retired from the Navy in 1978 and became general manager of the Flat Iron Paving Company at Boulder, Colorado.

Roger Locher quickly regained strength after his rescue from North Vietnam. He returned to the United States in July 1972 and began pilot training in September. In July 1973 he married Patty Schneider, and the best man was Chuck DeBellevue. When interviewed, both Roger and Patty were still in the Air Force, both serving at Nellis AFB, Nevada. Roger was a lieutenant colonel commanding the 4450th Tactical Fighter Squadron flying A-7s. His ordeal left no scars other than one common among people who have experienced real hunger: "Whatever I take on my plate I eat. I really hate to see food thrown away. I don't waste food—ever." Patty is a lieutenant colonel and still in intelligence.

Another Oyster Flight member, Steve Ritchie, made his first MiG kill on May 10 and thereafter his score mounted steadily. On August 28 he gained his fifth victory to become the first Air Force ace of the conflict. In the spring of 1974 he left the service to run for Congress. "People from my home district in North Carolina asked me to run for Congress on a Republican ticket. Senator Barry Goldwater convinced me I should leave the Air

Force and go into politics—he promised to help," Ritchie explained. "I went home to start campaigning—as Watergate blew up. There I was, running as a Republican in the South against a very popular Democrat incumbent. That was an experience— worse than flying over Hanoi!" The fighter ace was not elected. After that he worked for six years as special assistant to Joe Coors, lecturing throughout the nation on the free-market economy and its importance to the American way of life. When the Reagan administration took office, Ritchie accepted the post of director of the Office of Child Support Enforcement in the Department of Health and Human Services. "I took the post to get a different view of how governments operate, and I really got that. It was another learning experience." At the time of the interview Ritchie was vice president of business development at Barlows, Inc., in Falls Church, Virginia, providing computer security services. He was philosophical about what his future might hold. "I've quit trying to plan for the future. At high school I never thought of being a fighter pilot. When I went back to Southeast Asia in 1972 I never thought I'd see a MiG, much less shoot down five. I never imagined I would run for Congress, I didn't anticipate any of the things I've done. I never thought I'd live this long anyway, so, what the hell, every day is a plus!"

Chuck DeBellevue flew as back-seater with Ritchie during four of the latter's five victories, and continued on operations after the latter returned to the United States. DeBellevue's big day came on September 9, 1972, when, flying with another pilot, they downed two MiGs to bring his total to six. That figure was unequaled by any other American who fought over North Vietnam. At the end of 1972 he returned to the United States and began pilot training. Afterward he flew Phantoms with the 43rd Fighter Interceptor Squadron at Elmendorf AFB, Alaska, and when interviewed he held the rank of colonel and was serving at the U.S. Army War College at Carlisle, Pennsylvania.

Barry Morgan, the rookie pilot who flew on the chaff-dropping mission to Hanoi, left the Air Force in 1975 and was ordained into the Baptist Church. When interviewed he was assistant professor at the Hannibal Le Grange College, Hannibal, Missouri.

Carl Miller commanded the 8th Tactical Fighter Wing and led the Phantoms that attacked the Paul Doumer Bridge. After his return from Thailand he advanced steadily through the ranks, and his final post, with the rank of general, was commander, 21st NORAD Region U.S. Air Defense. He retired in 1979, and in 1981 became national administrator of the Civil Air Patrol.

D. L. Smith led the attack on the Paul Doumer Bridge by Phantoms carrying laser-guided bombs on May 10. Later in his service career he was appointed leader of the Air Force aerobatic team, the Thunderbirds. He was killed in a tragic accident at Cleveland in 1981, when, taking off after a display, his T-38 ran into a flock of birds and crashed.

Bill Driggers flew on Smith's wing during the attack. When interviewed he was working at the Washington office of Texas Instruments, Inc.

Mike Van Wagenen piloted the last F-4 to attack the Paul Doumer Bridge on May 10, and took part in the attack on the following day that dropped the damaged span. Fourteen years later he was still flying, but his plane was quite different from the Phantom he flew over Vietnam. Now he flies one of the four Pitts biplanes of the Holiday Inn Aerobatic Team, dedicated to reviving the spirit of the barnstorming era. Not that he feels there is much money to be made that way. "To make one million dollars in the air-show business," he confided, "start with three million dollars and know when to quit!" In fact his main renumeration comes from his post as executive director of the South Tahoe Gaming Alliance.

Don Pickard, who took part in the hectic poststrike reconnaissance of Hanoi on May 10, continued flying RF-4Cs and later commanded the 1st Tactical Reconnaissance Squadron based at Alconbury in England. From there he went to Eglin AFB, in Florida, and became director of reconnaissance test and evaluation at the Tactical Air Warfare Center. Early in 1987, holding the rank of lieutenant colonel, he left the Air Force to become manager, Advanced programs, with Fairchild Western, Inc., at Syosset, New York.

After he returned to the United States, Brewster Shaw became an F-4 instructor; then he attended the Test Pilots' School at Edwards AFB, California, before becoming an instructor there also. Early in 1978 he joined NASA and began training for the space shuttle program. He has flown twice in space: as pilot of *Columbia* in November 1983, during the first space laboratory mission; and as commander of *Atlantis* in November 1985, when it deployed three communications satellites and the crew made extravehicular excursions.

After leaving Vietnam in 1973, General John Vogt became commander of Allied Air Forces, Central Europe. Now retired from the Air Force, he lives in Annapolis and continues to be active as an elder statesman within the U.S. defense community. He serves in an advisory capacity on the Technical Policy Panel of the Strategic Defense Initiative program, the Defense Policy Advisory Board and the CIA Intelligence Advisory Board. In his free time he and his wife enjoy sailing their ten-ton yacht, *Olympia,* in the waters off the U.S. east coast.

Joe and Pat Wright left the British consulate in Hanoi later in 1972, and their next posting could hardly have been more different—they spent a couple of years in Geneva, Switzerland. In 1975 Joe was appointed Her Majesty's Ambassador to the Ivory Coast, Upper Volta and Niger in central Africa. He left the British Foreign Service in 1978, and when interviewed he and Pat were living in retirement at St. Leonards on the south coast of England.

Claude Julien became editor of the Paris-based newspaper *Le Monde Diplomatique.* When interviewed, Théodore Ronco was still reporting for *L'Humanité,* living at Toulon in the South of France.

Harry Blackburn's remains were returned by the Vietnamese government in April 1986 and, after identification, were flown to Travis AFB, California. He is buried at Fort Rosecrans military cemetery, in San Diego.

11

CONFLICTING EVIDENCE

A battle is a swirl of "ifs" and "ands."
—General Sir Ian Hamilton

ALTHOUGH the authors believe that this account of the events of May 10, 1972, is accurate in all essentials, the dictates of U.S. security and the non-availability of Vietnamese official records have left a few gray areas. Moreover, some published U.S. official accounts include information that is at variance with the authors' findings. This chapter sets out the main items of conflicting evidence so that the reader may judge their relative value.

Were spans of the Paul Doumer Bridge dropped during the attack on May 10, 1972?

In its description of the action on May 10, 1972, the book *The Tale of Two Bridges,* published by the Office of U.S. Air Force History, stated on page 165:

> The aircraft carrying guided-bombs dropped four spans of the Paul Doumer Bridge, knocked out one abutment, and severed an adjacent rail line.

This statement has been repeated in several later accounts, official and unofficial, on the action. But it is clear from Don Pickard's poststrike reconnaissance photograph, as well as Joe Wright's observations on the ground, that all spans of the Paul Doumer Bridge were in place on the evening of May 10, 1972.

How many SAMs were launched against the raiding forces on May 10, 1972?

The same book states, on page 90, that ". . . 160 SAMs were fired at the strike force that day [May 10, 1972]." The account left it unclear whether that figure referred to the number of missiles fired at the Paul Doumer attack force, or at the two U.S. Air Force forces attacking that day, or at all U.S. planes over North Vietnam that day.

Almost certainly the 160 refers to the number of SAMs reported seen by all U.S. crews that day, but the figure should be treated with caution. Wild Weasel crewmen have told the authors that such reports of SAM firings were invariably swelled by the inclusion of *all* missiles seen in flight, including Shrikes and Standard ARM weapons launched at the enemy radars. A separate U.S. intelligence document, declassified before release to the authors, stated that forty-one SAMs were fired at Air Force planes and fifty-two at Navy planes on that day. In the absence of official Vietnamese records, the authors believe these to be the most reliable figures available.

How many MiG sorties were flown on May 10, 1972?

The Tale of Two Bridges states, on page 90, that the defenders flew forty-one MiG sorties that day. Almost certainly that is the number of North Vietnamese fighters reported seen by U.S. crews in the course of the various actions, rather than the number that took off. In the absence of official Vietnamese records, or a figure from a more reliable source, the authors feel this should be treated with caution. It is unlikely that every North Vietnamese fighter that took off was seen from a U.S. aircraft.

How many U.S. aircraft were lost on May 10, 1972?

After the action the U.S. government announced that three U.S. planes had been shot down that day. On May 11 the official North Vietnamese government newspaper *Nhan Dan* stated that fourteen U.S. planes had been shot down over North Vietnam, plus two more near the Demilitarized Zone. Later the Hanoi Military History Institute publication *The People's Struggle Defeated the Sabotage War of the Imperialist Americans* stated that eighteen U.S. planes had been brought down that day. The detailed research and interviews conducted for this book indicate that four U.S. planes were destroyed and one more was damaged beyond repair, making a total of five planes lost. The authors are confident this figure is accurate.

How many North Vietnamese aircraft were lost on May 10, 1972?

In accordance with its official policy, the North Vietnamese government never admitted that it suffered any aircraft losses on May 10, 1972. U.S. fighter crews were credited with eleven MiGs shot down after being hit by missiles; one other was claimed damaged by cannon fire. In the absence of official Vietnamese figures, the authors offer this as the best available evidence.

What part did Sigint play during the action on May 10, 1972?

Although full details of the role played by Sigint, tactical signals intelligence, in the air battle on May 10, 1972, remain classified even after seventeen years, there is no doubt that information from this source played a significant part in the action.

Readers with knowledge of radar might have wondered how, during the early morning action, *Chicago*'s radar operators could possibly have known that a pair of MiG-21s was taxiing out to take off at Kep airfield, more than 120 miles away. It will be remembered that a bandit warning broadcast by Red Crown led to the MiGs being intercepted immediately after takeoff and the destruction of one of them by Curt Dosé. The same readers might have asked how, during the midmorning action, Larry Nowell could have directed the F-4s of Oyster Flight into action against the MiGs when both sides' planes were 180 miles away from *Chicago* and the Phantoms were flying at 2,000 feet. Or how, during the early afternoon action, Ken Cannon and Chuck Schroeder flying at 200 feet could have been vectored toward MiGs near Hanoi, more than a hundred miles from the ship. In each case the planes were well below the cruiser's radar horizon. Nobody has been willing to give official confirmation that Sigint provided the information on which these interceptions were made, but the authors are almost certain it was the source.

At its best Sigint gave very detailed information on the movements of enemy planes, but at its worst it gave no information at all. If a MiG made no transmission of any sort, it was very difficult for U.S. Sigint planes to track it. Hence the sudden and unannounced appearance of MiG-19s on two occasions during the midmorning action, which in each case led to the loss of an Air Force Phantom. And the ability, during the early afternoon action, of a pack of MiG-17s to get within gun range of *Constellation*'s strike force near Hai Duong without so much as a peep from Red Crown. Even the most elaborate intelligence backup did not absolve fliers of the need to maintain a careful search of the sky while they were over enemy territory.

Which MiG-19 pilots shot down the two Phantoms on May 10, 1972?

The only North Vietnamese account of the action available to the authors that throws any light on the subject comes from the government publication *Shooting Down the B-52s, on the Spot,* a collection of personal memoirs from PAVNAF senior officers. In his account, Colonel Ta van Duy stated:

> After studying the situation and anticipating the enemy's intentions, senior officers of the Party Executive Committee and Air Force agreed to launch an aerial counteroffensive committing all types of aircraft.
>
> The campaign opened on May 10, 1972. Our planes took off and fought the enemy at all altitudes and from all directions, attacking in several waves. The enemy also changed his tactics in order to engage our air force more effectively.

Shortly after it took off from its base at Kep, the section led by Dang Ngoc Ngu engaged a number of attacking enemy aircraft. The enemy planes had the advantage of speed and altitude, but calmly and bravely Dang avoided the missiles fired at him. Skillfully he brought his aircraft into a firing position, and shot down an F-4 due east of his base.

On the same day a section led by Le Thanh Dao also engaged the enemy, over Hoa Binh Province. No sooner had Le and his wingman, Vu van Hop, dived on the enemy planes than their adversaries broke formation. A few seconds later Le and Vu found themselves in a dogfight with the pack of wolves. Together, Le and Vu succeeded in shooting down two American F-4 Phantoms. The crews bailed out and were captured on the ground. The Central Military Committee commended both men highly, because until then both had been young and inexperienced pilots.

As historical evidence the account leaves a lot to be desired, and in places the information conflicts with the known pattern of events. However all three pilots are thought to have belonged to the 3rd Company, the only unit operating MiG-19s, and both U.S. planes lost in air-to-air combat were shot down by this type. The account suggests—the authors put it no stronger—that Le Thanh Dao and Vu van Hop shot down Bob Lodge's Phantom, Oyster 1 (though only one Phantom went down, its crew was not captured and the action did not take place over Hoa Bihn Province); and Dang Ngoc Ngu may have shot down Captain J. Harris's Phantom, Harlow 4 (though the action took place west, not east, of Kep and the missiles were fired at the MiG after, not before, it shot down the Phantom).

Who piloted the MiG-17 that engaged Randy Cunningham so aggressively before the latter shot it down?

Several Western accounts have stated that the pilot of the third MiG-17 shot down by Randy Cunningham and Willie Driscoll on May 10 was Colonel Tomb or Toon, said to have been the top-scoring North Vietnamese fighter ace. The source of this information is said to be so sensitive that it cannot be revealed even after seventeen years. (If all of the stories about the colonel are to be believed, he was in action three times on May 10, flying a different type of MiG on each!)

Despite an intensive search of Vietnamese open literature the authors have found no reference that can be linked to a Colonel Tomb or Toon, however. Accounts of exploits of famous pilots were often published and it is unlikely in the extreme that so successful a North Vietnamese pilot would not have received public recognition. (By May 1972 all the MiGs sent into action over North Vietnam were flown by North Vietnamese pilots.)

Photographs have been published in the West of a Vietnamese People's Army Air Force MiG-21 4326 bearing thirteen victory stars, and non-Vietnamese writers have linked this fighter with Colonel Tomb. However, it was normal Vietnamese practice to paint on fighters victory stars indicating the claims made by all pilots while flying that plane. A photograph of MiG-21 4324 was published in the official magazine *Vietnam* with the caption:

> With this MiG 21 No. 4324, our pilots brought down 14 US planes, the largest number of aircraft ever downed by a Vietnamese jet. Six of the 9 airmen *who took turns in piloting the MiG* [authors' emphasis] have been awarded the title "Hero of the People's Armed Forces."

Almost certainly the victories claimed for aircraft 4326 were achieved by several different pilots.

The authors believe there was no Colonel Tomb or Toon, and no North Vietnamese pilot achieved thirteen victories. Probably Tomb or Toon was a nickname given to a Vietnamese pilot often heard by U.S. radio monitors, whose real name was not known. The real name of the pilot of the third MiG-17 shot down by Cunningham and Driscoll remains a mystery.

Were the North Vietnamese air defenses more effective than those encountered by U.S. planes over Germany in World War II?

Several writers have compared the North Vietnamese defenses with those encountered over Germany in World War II, and judged the former to have been far more effective. The line has been repeated so many times that it is part of the received wisdom on the Vietnam conflict. For example, in his book *People's Army of Vietnam* Douglas Pike wrote that the North Vietnamese air defenses "were the most effective and sophisticated the world had ever seen in action—far surpassing the primitive defenses of London, Berlin, and Tokyo during World War II."

Certainly the North Vietnamese air defenses were more sophisticated than those protecting London, Berlin and Tokyo during World War II. But sophistication and effectiveness are not the same thing, and it should be remembered that the U.S. attack forces operating over North Vietnam also employed equipment and tactics considerably more sophisticated than those used in earlier conflicts.

The main measure of the *effectiveness* of an air defense system is the percentage of planes in an attacking force it shoots down or damages. On May 10, 1972, the North Vietnamese defenses shot down just over 1 percent of the U.S. planes that penetrated their airspace and damaged 1.5 percent. During attacks on North Vietnam by U.S. tactical aircraft in 1972, such losses were well above the average.

The authors have conducted an in-depth study, similar to this one, of the first large-scale U.S. daylight attack on Berlin on March 6, 1944.* On *that* day, of the 702 U.S. heavy bombers which penetrated enemy airspace, 9.8 percent (69) were lost and 53 percent (339) returned with battle damage. U.S. forces attacking Germany suffered similarly heavy losses on several occasions.

Measured as a percentage of attacking U.S. planes shot down, the German air defenses in World War II were roughly *nine times* more effective (in terms of planes damaged, they were thirty-five times more effective) than those met over North Vietnam. When it came to dogged bravery and determination in the face of pow-

---

*Jeffrey Ethell and Alfred Price, *Target Berlin: 6 March 1944* (Arms and Armour Press, London; Sterling Publishing, New York, 1989).

erful air defenses, those who flew the B-17s and B-24s over Germany still have no equal. And to say so is no slur on the bravery of those who operated over North Vietnam.

It is not the authors' case that the North Vietnamese air defense system was ineffective. The high proportion of supporting aircraft to bombers during the attacks on May 10, 1972, testifies to the respect given it. But when sufficiently strong supporting forces were present—and they were during 1972—the American tactics, fighter escorts, electronic countermeasures and defense suppression forces were able to prevent the North Vietnamese defenses from inflicting severe losses.

AAA (or Triple-A). Antiaircraft artillery (fire).

Atoll. NATO code name for the Soviet K-13 infrared homing air-to-air missile.

Bandit.* Enemy aircraft.

Blue Chip. Code name for Seventh Air Force Operational Headquarters at Tan Son Nhut airfield near Saigon.

Bogey.* Unidentified aircraft.

Bullseye.* Reference point for broadcast reports on the position of North Vietnamese fighters. On May 10, 1972, this was the city of Hanoi.

CBU. Cluster Bomb Unit.

Combat Tree. Electronic system fitted to U.S. fighters to enable them to identify enemy planes from their IFF (q.v.) signals.

EOGB. Electro-optical guided bomb.

Fansong. NATO code name for Soviet fire-control radar associated with the SA-2 missile system.

Firecan. NATO code name for Soviet fire-control radar used to direct antiaircraft guns.

IFF. Identification Friend or Foe. Electronic system to identify aircraft on radar.

Iron Hand. Operations against enemy ground fire-control radars for guns and missiles, usually with radar-homing missiles.

LGB. Laser-Guided Bomb.

Linebacker. Name of operation to attack targets in North Vietnam from May 10, 1972.

MIGCAP. MiG Combat Air Patrol. Type of patrol mounted by U.S. fighters seeking to engage enemy fighters in combat.

Pave Knife. Laser marking pod, to designate targets for attack with laser-guided bombs.

PAVNAF People's Army of Viet Nam Air Force.

Pickle.* Release ordnance.

RHAW. Radar Homing and Warning (receiver).

Rolling Thunder. Name of operation to attack targets in North Vietnam prior to May 10, 1972.

SAM. Surface-to-air missile. (In the context of this book, the Soviet-built Dvina (NATO code name SA-2.)

Shrike. Radiation homing missile, used during Iron Hand (q.v.) missions.

Sigint. Signals intelligence. Intelligence derived from all types of enemy electromagnetic signal, including those from radar and communications systems.

Splash.* Aircraft shot down.

Squawk.* Transmit IFF (q.v.) signals.

Standard ARM. Radiation homing missile, used during Iron Hand (q.v.) missions.

Tallyho.* (Sometimes shortened to "Tally.") Target in sight.

Top Gun. Course to train U.S. Navy fighter pilots in the latest techniques of air-to-air combat.

Wild Weasel. USAF code name for units involved in Iron Hand (q.v.) missions.

Winchester.* Out of ordnance.

RIO. Radar Intercept Officer.

WSO. Weapon Systems Officer.

Yankee Station. Operating area for U.S. aircraft carriers mounting air strikes into North Vietnam. Situated off the coast at the extreme south of the country.

AIRCRAFT TYPES IN ACTION, MAY 10, 1972

Note: The armament loads given were typical of those carried by the type in action on that day.

A-1 Skyraider (Douglas). Single-seat attack aircraft powered by a single reciprocating engine, used for search-and-rescue helicopter support. Built-in armament four 20-mm cannon, carried various underwing loads.

A-6A Intruder (Grumman). Subsonic two-seat twin-engined carrier-based all-weather attack aircraft. Typical load carried: eighteen 500-pound bombs.

A-7E Corsair II (LTV). Subsonic single-seat single-engined carrier-based attack aircraft. One internally mounted 20-mm cannon. Typical loads carried during the action: six 1000-pound bombs; or ten 500-pound Mk 82 bombs; or two AGM-45 Shrike radiation homing missiles and ten Mk 20 Rockeye cluster bombs; sometimes carried one Sidewinder missile for self-defense.

E-2B Hawkeye (Grumman). Twin turboprop airborne early warning radar plane. Crew five. No armament carried.

EB-66E Destroyer (Douglas). Subsonic three-seat twin-engined radar countermeasures aircraft, based on the B-66 bomber. No armament carried.

EC-121D Constellation (Lockheed). Airborne Command and Control Center carrying long-range search radar, using the airframe of the Constellation airliner. Four piston engines. Crew of about fifteen. No armament carried.

EKA-3B Skywarrior (Douglas). Subsonic three-seat carrier-based twin-engined radar countermeasures and tanker aircraft, modified from the A-3 bomber. Aircraft performed both roles during a regular mission. No armament carried.

EP-3B Orion (Lockheed). Four turboprop Sigint collection plane, a converted Orion patrol plane that was itself based on the Electra airliner. Crew about thirty. No armament carried.

F-4D Phantom (McDonnell). Mach 2 performance two-seat twin-engined land-based fighter-bomber. Typical loads carried during the action: (air to air) three AIM-7 missiles, plus three AIM-9 or one AIM-4.

F-4E Phantom. As above, built-in armament of one 20-mm cannon. Typical loads carried: two 2,000-pound laser-guided or electro-optically guided bombs; or nine 500-pound Mk 82 bombs; or nine 450-pound chaff-bombs. In each case the aircraft carried three AIM-7 missiles for self-defense.

F-4J Phantom. Carrier-based version of the F-4. Typical loads carried: (air to air) four AIM-7 and four AIM-9 missiles; (air-to-ground operations) ten 500-pound Rockeye cluster bombs plus two AIM-7 missiles plus four AIM-9 missiles.

F-105G Thunderchief (Republic). Supersonic two-seat defense-suppression fighter-bomber. Built-in armament one 20-mm cannon. Typical load carried: one AGM-78 Standard ARM plus two AGM-45 Shrike missiles.

HC-130 Hercules (Lockheed). Four turboprop transport aircraft, modified to support and coordinate search-and-rescue operations. Carried equipment to refuel helicopters in flight. No armament carried.

HH-3A Sea King (Sikorsky). Twin-turboshaft helicopter, used for search and rescue. Crew of four. No armament carried.

HH-53B Jolly Green Giant (Sikorsky). Twin-turboshaft heavy-lift helicopter used for long-range rescue. Crew of five. Armament: two electrically powered 7.62-mm miniguns.

KA-6D Intruder (Grumman). Tanker version of the A-6 Intruder. No armament carried.

KC-135 Stratotanker (Boeing). Four-engined air-to-air refueling tanker based on the airframe of the Boeing 707 airliner. Crew of four. When fully laden, carried 75 tons of fuel, about half of which could be passed to other aircraft. No armament carried.

MiG-17 (Mikoyan-Gurevich). Soviet-designed subsonic single-seat interceptor fighter, NATO code name Fresco. Built-in armament varied, typically one 37-mm and two 23-mm cannon.

MiG-19 (Mikoyan-Gurevich). Soviet-designed supersonic single-seat interceptor fighter, NATO code name Farmer. It is possible that some, maybe all, fighters of this type encountered by U.S. aircraft on May 10 were the Chinese-built version, the Shenyang F-6; to avoid confusion, throughout this book the aircraft is referred to as the MiG-19. With half its fuel burned, this aircraft had a thrust-to-weight ratio exceeding unity, the only plane in action on May 10 to achieve this. This gave the MiG-19 an excellent dogfighting capability, as U.S. crews discovered. Built-in armament varied, typically three 30-mm cannon. Some carried two K-13 (NATO code name Atoll) air-to-air missiles.

MiG-21 (Mikoyan-Gurevich). Soviet-designed Mach 2 performance single-seat interceptor fighter, NATO code name Fishbed. Built-in armament varied, typically one 23-mm cannon. Carried two K-13 (Atoll) air-to-air missiles.

RA-5C Vigilante (North American). Supersonic two-seat twin-engined carrier-based reconnaissance aircraft. No armament carried.

RC-135M (Boeing). Using an airframe similar to that of the KC-135, this plane operated in the Sigint collection role. Crew thirty-five. No armament carried.

RF-4C Phantom (McDonnell). Dedicated reconnaissance version of the F-4 fighter, operated by the USAF. No armament carried.

RF-8C Crusader (LTV). Supersonic single-seat single-engined carrier-based reconnaissance aircraft, converted from the F-8 fighter. No armament carried.

U-2R (Lockheed). Single-seat single-engined ultrahigh altitude reconnaissance plane, used for the collection of communications intelligence. No armament carried.

8TH TACTICAL FIGHTER WING F-4 CREWS WHO TOOK PART IN ATTACKS ON THE HANOI AREA ON MAY 10, 1972

Chaff-Dropping Force (All planes carried chaff bombs)
Dingus Flight, 433rd Tactical Fighter Squadron
   Ldr. Maj. Robert Blake
      Capt. Samuel O'Donnell
   2 Lt. James Dunn
      Lt. Richard Houser
   3 Capt. Larry Honeycutt
      Lt. Charles Crisp
   4 Lt. Barry Morgan
      Capt. Michael White

Hitest Flight, 435th Tactical Fighter Squadron
   Ldr. Maj. Phillip Mentesana
      Capt. Gregory Krosnoff
   2 Capt. William Byrns
      Lt. Charles Hostenske
   3 Lt. Ronald Moore
      Capt. Ryan Cobb
   4 Capt. Michael Suhy
      Lt. Lanny Toups

Paul Doumer Bridge Attack Force
Goatee Flight, 435th Tactical Fighter Squadron, EO-Guided Bombs
   Ldr. Col. Carl Miller
      Maj. David Sommers
   2 Capt. Kenneth Hall

Lt. Lance Roberts
3 Capt. Richard Carmichael
Lt. Harry Jensen
4 Capt. Norris Bohm
Lt. David Ladurini

Napkin Flight, 433rd Tactical Fighter Squadron, Laser-Guided Bombs
Ldr. Col. Richard Horne
Capt. Worrall Wilson
2 Maj. Donald Rigg
Maj. Earl Johnson
3 Capt. David (D.L.) Smith
Lt. Wayne King
4 Maj. William Driggers
Lt. Richard Bates

Biloxi Flight, 25th Tactical Fighter Squadron, Laser-Guided Bombs
Ldr. Capt. Lynn High
Capt. Lawrence Todd
2 Lt. Gordon Seuell
Lt. Michael Pomphrey
3 Capt. James Allen
Capt. David Tatman
4 Capt. James Carder
Maj. Jesse Burington

Jingle Flight, 433rd Tactical Fighter Squadron, Laser-Guided Bombs
Ldr Lt. Col. Richard Hilton
Capt. William Wideman
2 Lt. James Hale
Capt. Harold Edwards
3 Capt. Thomas (Mike) Messett
Lt. James Bryant
4 Capt. Michael Van Wagenen
Capt. Roger Cooper

Yen Vien Rail Yard Attack Force (Planes carried 500-pound bombs)
Gopher Flight, 25th Tactical Fighter Squadron
Ldr. Maj. Albert Munsch

Capt. Robert Segars
2 Lt. James McCarty
Lt. Laird Johnson
3 Lt. David Hamilton
Capt. Francis Perella
4 Maj. Charles Pratt
Capt. James Shaw

Icebag Flight, 334th Tactical Fighter Squadron
Ldr. Lt. Col. Dumitru Tokanel
Capt. Joe Daniel
2 Capt. Stuart Alton
Maj. Stanley Miller
3 Maj. Daniel Nesbett
Lt. Henry Goddard
4 Capt. Mickey Baity
Maj. Sidney Walton

Gigolo Flight, 25th Tactical Fighter Squadron
Ldr. Maj. Lawrence Irving
Lt. Raymond Henley
2 Capt. Brewster Shaw
Lt. Scott Bergren
3 Maj. Roger Baki
Lt. Gary Reed
4 Capt. Douglas Nix
Lt. Johnny Wyatt

Bertha Flight, 336th Tactical Fighter Squadron
Ldr. Lt. Col. Daniel Blake
Lt. Timothy Fisher
Capt. James Foth
Lt. John Walsh
Maj. Walter Varablic
Capt. Richard Reynolds
Capt. William Looke
Maj. Franklin Blum

U.S. NAVY TASK GROUPS OFF NORTH VIETNAM
ON MAY 10, 1972

Carrier Task Group 77.4
   USS *Constellation* CVA-64
   USS *Badger* DE-1071

Carrier Task Group 77.6
   USS *Coral Sea* CVA-43
   USS *Hammond* DE-1067

Carrier Task Group 77.7
   USS *Kitty Hawk* CVA-63
   USS *Worden* DLG-18
   USS *Larson* DD-830

NORTH SAR (Search and Rescue)
   USS *Sterett* DLG-31
   USS *Ozbourn* DD-846

PIRAZ (Positive Identification Radar Advisory Zone)
   USS *Chicago* CG-11 (Red Crown)
   USS *Long Beach* CGN-9

Task Group 77.0
   USS *Lockwood* DE 1064

Task Group 77.1
   USS *Newport News* CA-148 (bombardment of coastal targets,
   supported by TG 70.1 and 77.1.2)

Task Group 77.1.2
   USS *Hanson* DD-832

USS *Buchannan* DDG-14
USS *MC Fox* DD-829

Task Group 70.1
USS *Oklahoma City* CTG-5

Amphibious Task Group 76
USS *Okinawa* LPH-3 (helicopters for search and rescue)
USS *Blue Ridge* LCC-19

NORTH VIETNAMESE FIGHTER AND ANTIAIRCRAFT DEFENSE UNITS ON MAY 10, 1972

Information mainly from U.S. intelligence estimates

IN 1972 all North Vietnamese armed forces, including air and naval units, were subordinated to the People's Army of Viet Nam (PAVN).

Fighters

On the morning of May 10, 1972, the North Vietnamese fighter force was believed to possess seventy-five MiG-21s, thirty-two MiG-19s and eighty-five MiG-15s and MiG-17s (the former and most of the latter used for operational training). Most of these fighters were based at airfields within seventy-five miles of Hanoi.

Some MiG-19s and all MiG-21s carried the Soviet-made K-13A (NATO code name Atoll), a first-generation infrared air-to-air missile effective only if fired from a relatively narrow cone to the rear of the target aircraft. This weapon was greatly inferior to the AIM-9D and E versions of the Sidewinder carried by most U.S. fighters during the action. All MiGs carried heavy cannon.

North Vietnamese fighters were directed into action under close control by ground-controlled intercept (GCI) radars (NATO code names Big Bar and Barlock).

Surface-to-Air Missiles

Only one type of surface-to-air missile (SAM) system was encountered by U.S. aircraft operating over North Vietnam, the Soviet-made Dvina (NATO code name SA-2). This weapon dated from the late 1950s and was obsolete by 1972. Each Dvina firing unit comprised four to six launchers and a fire-control radar (NATO code name Fansong). There were about two hundred missile-firing sites in North Vietnam in the spring of 1972, but only about thirty-five Dvina firing units operational at any time. To reduce their vulnerability to air attack the firing units moved position from day to day, playing a lethal version of the shell game with Air Force and Navy defense suppression planes. At the beginning of May 1972 it was estimated there were about thirty-five SAM sites active at any one time, the densest concentrations being around Hanoi (thirteen) and Haiphong (ten).

The SA-2 missile (NATO code name Guideline) had a maximum range of about nineteen miles, and its 280-pound warhead was lethal against aircraft within 150 yards of the point of detonation. It was estimated that ninety-three of these missiles were launched on May 10, 1972.

Antiaircraft Guns

In May 1972 it was estimated that defending North Vietnam were 3,300 guns of all calibers, most of them positioned north of the 20th parallel. The antiaircraft gun units, like the SAM firing units, frequently shifted position between sites. There were five main types of antiaircraft gun in use:

100 mm, maximum effective altitude with radar control 39,000 feet. Maximum practical rate of fire 30 rounds per minute. Projectile weight 35 pounds.

85 mm, maximum effective altitude with radar control 27,000 feet. Maximum practical rate of fire 20 rounds per minute. Projectile weight 20 pounds.

57 mm, maximum effective altitude 20,000 feet with radar control, 13,000 feet with optical fire control. Maximum practical rate of fire 70 rounds per minute. Projectile weight 6 pounds.

37 mm, maximum effective altitude 8,000 feet with optical fire control. Maximum practical rate of fire 180 rounds per minute. Projectile weight 1.6 pounds.

23 mm, maximum effective altitude 6,500 feet with optical fire control. Maximum practical rate of fire 800 rounds per minute per barrel (twin-barreled and four-barreled weapons were common). Projectile weight .4 pounds.

The main type of antiaircraft gun control radar encountered by U.S. aircraft over North Vietnam was the Soviet-made SON-9 (NATO code name Firecan).

In addition to the above, numerous smaller-caliber automatic weapons were available at all defended targets. These weapons were ineffective against planes above 3,500 feet, but provided an effective deterrent below that altitude.

Bowman, John, et al. *The Vietnam War: An Almanac.* New York: Pharos Books, 1985.

Cunningham, Randy, with Jeff Ethell. *Fox Two.* Mesa, Ariz.: Champlin Fighter Museum, 1984.

Davis, Larry. *Wild Weasel, the SAM Suppression Story.* Warren, Mich.: Squadron/Signal Publications Inc., 1986.

Dorr, Robert. *McDonnell Douglas F-4 Phantom II.* London: Osprey Publishing, 1984.

Drendel, Lou. *. . . And Kill MiGS,* Warren, Mich.: Squadron/Signal Publications Inc., 1974.

Futrell, R. Frank, et al. *Aces and Aerial Victories.* Washington, D.C.: U.S. Government Printing Office, 1976.

Giap, Vo Nguyen. *People's War Against U.S. Aeronaval War.* Hanoi, Vietnam: Foreign Languages Publishing House, 1975.

Gunston, Bill. *Aircraft of the Soviet Union.* London: Osprey Publishing, 1983.

———. *Illustrated Encyclopedia of the World's Rockets and Missiles.* London: Salamander Books Ltd., 1979.

———. *Military Aircraft of the World.* New York· Hamlyn Publishing, 1981.

Hanoi Military History Institute. *The People's Struggle Defeated the Sabotage War of the Imperialist Americans.*

———. *Shooting Down the B-52s, on the Spot.*

Hersh, Seymour. *The Price of Power.* New York: Summit Books, 1983.

Karnow, Stanley. *Vietnam: A History.* New York: Viking Press, 1983.

Lavalle, Major A., et al. *Air Power and the 1972 Spring Invasion.* Washington, D.C.: U.S. Government Printing Office, 1976.

————. *The Tale of Two Bridges and the Battle for the Skies over North Vietnam.* Washington, D.C.: U.S. Government Printing Office, 1976.

Marolda, Edward, et al. *A Short History of the United States Navy and the Southeast Asian Conflict 1950–1975.* Washington, D.C.: Naval Historical Center, 1984.

Mersky, Peter, and Norman Polmar. *The Naval Air War in Vietnam.* Annapolis, Md.: The Nautical and Aviation Publishing Company of America, 1981.

Momyer, General William. *Air Power in Three Wars.* Washington, D.C.: U.S. Government Printing Office,

Nixon, Richard. *The Memoirs of Richard Nixon.* New York: Grosset & Dunlap, 1978.

————. *No More Vietnams.* New York: Avon Books, 1985.

Pike, Douglas. *PAVN: People's Army of Vietnam.* Novato, Calif.: Presidio Press, 1986.

Richardson, Doug, and Mike Spick. *F-4 Phantom II.* London: Salamander Books Ltd., 1984.

Spick, Mike. *Fighter Pilot Tactics.* Cambridge: Patrick Stephens, 1983.

Truong Nhu Tang. *A Viet Cong Memoir.* New York: Random House, 1986.

Newspaper and Magazine Articles

Nhan Dan newspaper, Hanoi, various issues.

Vietnam magazine, Hanoi, various issues.

A-1 Skyraider (Douglas), 52, 195
A-4 Skyhawk (Douglas), 12
A-6A Intruder (Grumman), 20,
    32, 37, 47, 106, 195
A-7E Corsair II (Vought), 20, 32,
    34, 38–39, 138, 195
  attacked in error, 140, 170, 172
A-37 Dragonfly (Cessna), 4
aces, 124, 142, 146, 182
Agence France Presse, 28
air battles:
  analysis of, 168–69
  descriptions of, 43–46, 55–62,
    72–75, 109–23, 124, 128–29
Airborne Warning and Control
    Wing, 552nd, 27
Air Force, U.S., 12, 23
  aircraft involved on May 10,
    1972, 50–51
  Navy compared with, 49, 52,
    166
  number of aircraft in
    Southeast Asia, 4
  Route Packages of, 8, 9
  Seventh, 5, 8, 14, 99, 101, 147
Allen, Hank, xi
Allen, James, xi, 98–99, 147–48

Alpha Strike, 27, 32, 102, 136,
    141
ALQ-87 electronic
    countermeasures pod, 68
analysis of action on May 10,
    1972, 165–178
  air-to-air attacks, 168–69, 170
  bomber sorties, 165–66
  bridges attacked, 166
  ceasefire, 178
  civilian casualties, 167
  downed pilots, 178
  ground defenses, effectiveness
    of, 173, 178
  lack of cannons on F-4s, 172
  missile effectiveness, 171
  North Vietnamese aircraft
    losses, 174–75
  North Vietnamese fighter
    sorties, 170
  Operation Linebacker, 178
  rail yards attacked, 166
  rules of engagement, 171–72
  U.S. aircraft losses, 176–77
Anderson, John, xi, 140
antiaircraft guns, 14, 37, 65, 86,
    101, 206

anti-radar missiles, *see* Shrike
  missile; Standard ARM
Army, U.S., withdrawal of, 4
ARVN (Army of Republic of
  Viet Nam), 4
Atoll missile, 46, 75, 171

B-52 Stratofortress (Boeing), 4,
  5, 101
Babouchkine, 16
Bac Mai airfield, 101
Badger, USS, 31
Bai Thong airfield, 23
Baldwin, Fred, xi, 113, 181
Balter flight, 52, 61, 74
"bandits," 41
Bates, Rick, xi, 88
battles, air, *see* air battles
Bidwell, Loren, xi, 26, 104
Birzer, Norman, xi, 104, 105,
  106, 127
Blackburn, Harry, 104, 117–19,
  141, 148
  fate of, 178, 184
Blake, Bob, 66–68, 70
Blonski, Tom, 111, 181
Blue Angels, 114
"Blue Chip," 14, 25, 53, 91
Boeing 707, 21
Bolier, Michael, xi, 34, 37
bombs:
  chaff, 66, 70, 73
  cluster, 34
  electro-optical guided, 11, 82,
    84, 166, 167
  free-fall, 10, 23
  laser-guided, 11, 85–86, 87,
    166
  smart, 23
Brewer, Charlie, 132
Brezhnev, Leonid, 15, 179

British Residence, 64, 72, 85,
  96
Buchanan, USS, 19
"Bullseye," 41
Byrns, William, xi, 71

CAG (commander air group),
  104
Campbell, Jim, xi
Cam Pha, 16
  U.S. air raids on, 139, 141,
    166
Cannon, Kenneth, xi, 128–29,
  132, 146
ceasefire, 178
Central Highlands, 4
chaff, 77, 88, 127
  bombs, 66, 70, 73
  definition of, 66
Chicago, USS, 27, 28, 41, 75, 81,
  93, 109, 128, 140
China, People's Republic of, 7
CinC (Commander in Chief)
  Pacific, 14
civilian casualties, 167
clock code, 40
Combat Tree, 12, 13, 57
Connelly, Matt, xi, 111–12, 114,
  117, 123, 135, 136
  later career of, 181
Constellation, USS, 5, 20, 26, 27,
  30–32, 47, 102, 104, 137
  Air Wing of, 32, 33, 34, 35,
    36, 105, 106, 135–36, 137
  party on, 148
Cooper, Damon, 8
Coral Sea, USS, 5, 16, 20, 27, 31,
  32
  Air Wing of, 33, 34, 46,
    128–32, 141
C rations, 162

Crenshaw, Keith, xi, 114, 117, 119, 127, 181
Crisp, Charles, xi, 70–71, 99
Cunningham, Randall, xi, 27, 103, 108, 109–10, 114–15, 116, 117, 121–23, 124–27, 136, 171, 173
  ace status of, 124, 142, 146
  later career of, 180
  sea rescue of, 131, 133–35

Dang Ngoc Ngu, 94, 189
Danner, Brent, xi
Danosky, Mike, 132
Dayan, Moshe, 163
DeBellevue, Charles, xi, 55, 57, 60–61, 62, 181, 182
  ace status of, 182
Dien Bien Phu, battle of, 7
Dilworth, Rod, 120, 130
Dingus flight, 66, 68–71, 73
DMZ (Demilitarized Zone), 3, 5
"Don't Send Me to Hanoi," 78
Dosé, Curtis, xi, 41, 43–46, 47, 137–38, 170, 172, 181
Driggers, William, xi, 79, 84, 183
Driscoll, Willie, 103, 109, 116, 119, 124–27
  ace status of, 124, 142, 146
  later career of, 181
  sea rescue of, 131, 133–35
Dunn, James, xii, 24–25, 69, 156–57
Dvina (SA-2) missile, vii, 13–14, 167, 205–6

E-2B Hawkeye (Grumman), 27, 31, 41, 195
Eaves, Steve, 58

EB-66E Destroyer (Douglas), 5, 21, 52, 65, 195
EC-121D Constellation (Lockheed), 27, 55, 195
Echo Tango, 91
Edwards, Harry, xii
Eggert, Lowell "Gus," xii, 103, 104, 108, 112, 121, 131
Eisenhower, Dwight D., 7
EKA-3B Skywarrior (Douglas), 20, 32, 34, 46, 105, 127, 129, 131
Electronic Warfare Squadron, 42nd, 65
EP-3B Orion (Lockheed), 27, 124, 196
Erickson, David, 111

F-4 Phantom (McDonnell), 4, 5, 11, 32, 47, 106, 172, 196
F-8 Crusader (Vought), 12
F-105G Thunderchief (Republic), 5, 20, 52, 54, 65, 167, 196
F-106 Delta Dart (Convair), 12
Fansong radar, see radar, Fansong
Feezel, Thomas, xii, 56, 57, 58, 61, 62, 146–47
Fishbed J, 13
Foltz, Randy, xii, 106, 108
Fox, Jim, xii, 111, 116, 136
Fox, USS, 19
France, 7
"furball," 117

Gabriel, Charles, 99
GCA (ground controlled approach) game, 147
GCI (ground radar) control, 111
Gia Lam:
  airfield of, 86, 93, 101
  civilians killed in, 167

Goddard, Henry, 90–91
Goldwater, Barry, 181–82
Goryanec, George, xii, 112, 113, 120, 130, 136
Grant, Brian, xii, 108, 110, 114, 115, 116–17
Gravely, Tom, 106
Great Britain, 28
Griffiths, Ralph, xii
Grisha Akopyan, 137
Guam, 4
Guard frequency, 39, 153, 156
Gulf of Tonkin, 35

Hai Duong, 102, 141
    U.S. air raids on, 105–136, 107, 166
Haiphong, 8, 19, 29
    U.S. air raids on, 6, 27, 30–48, 166
    U.S. mining of harbor of, 15–17
Hamilton, Ian, 185
Hancock, USS, 5
Hanoi, 7, 8
    code name for, 41
    U.S. air raids on, 6, 50–101, 76
"Hanoi Hilton" (Hoa Lo prison), 25, 72, 149
Hanson, USS, 19
Harris, J., 95
Hawkins, Austin, 41, 43–46, 47, 103, 106, 127, 170, 172
HC-130 Hercules (Lockheed), 52, 196
Henry V (Shakespeare), 179
HH-3A Sea King (Sikorsky), 52, 133–35, 196
HH-53B Jolly Green Giant (Sikorsky), 52, 157, 196

High, Lynn, xii, 79, 86
Hill, Gerry, 120
Hilton, Ann, 22
Hilton, Rick, xii, 22–23, 81–82
Hitest flight, 66, 68–72, 73
Hoa Lo prison ("Hanoi Hilton"), 25, 72, 149
Ho Chi Minh, 180
Honeycutt, Larry, 70–71
Hon Gai, 16
    U.S. air raids on, 137, 139, 141
Humanité, L', xiv, 21
Huu Nghi Viet-Xo hospital, bombing of, 167
hydraulic systems, 60, 124–25

IFF, *see* radar, identification friend or foe equipment
India Zulu, 54
"in the saddle," 110
Iron Hand missile suppression, 34, 38, 105, 138
Irving, Kelly, xii, 88, 90
Irwin, Chuck, 93, 97

Joel, Henri, 28, 73
Johnson, Laird, xii, 90
Johnson, Lyndon B., bombing halted by, 4
Joint Chiefs of Staff, U.S., 7, 14
Jordan, Dave, xii
Julien, Claude, xii, 21, 36, 37–38, 46, 48, 109, 115, 119, 124, 133, 141–42, 184
Julius Caesar (Shakespeare), 30
Junker, Al, xii, 112, 113, 136

KA-6D Intruder (Grumman), 32, 196
Kansas State University, 161

KC-135 Stratotanker (Boeing), 21, 52, 54, 95, 196–97
Kep airfield, 41, 43, 44, 45, 103, 109
Kien An airfield, 39
Kilgus, Donald, xii, 25, 65–66, 147
King, Robert, xii, 89
King, Wayne, 85, 86
Kissinger, Henry, 5, 15
Kite's, 161
Kitty Hawk, USS, 5, 20, 27, 31, 32
  Air Wing of, 33, 34, 46, 132, 141
Kontom, 6
Korat, officers' club in, 147
Korea, Democratic People's Republic of (North), pilots from, 13
Kraut, Al, 39
Kuhar, Steve, xii, 129, 132, 145–46
Kursograf, 34

Laos, 11, 27, 52, 56
Lee, Robert E., 64
Le Thanh Dao, 59, 189
Locher, Roger, xii, 58–61, 62–63, 147
  capture evaded by, 143, 151–56
  later career of, 181
  rescue of, 156–58, 159–64
Lodge, Bob, 54, 56–57, 58, 59, 60, 147
Long Bien Bridge, *see* Paul Doumer Bridge

McCarty, James, 90
McClung, Lonny, xii

McDaniel, Eugene, xiii, 72
McDevitt, Jim, 43, 46, 137–38
Mack, William, xii, 19
McNamara, Thomas, xiii
Marecic, Terry, xii
Markle, John, xii, 57–58, 59, 95, 171
May 10 action, *see* analysis of action on May 10, 1972
Messett, Thomas "Mike," xiii, 24, 86, 87
MiG-15, 13, 205
MiG-17, 13, 170, 197, 205
MiG-19, 13, 170, 172, 197, 205
MiG-21, 13, 170, 197, 205
MiG-21MF, 13, 46, 62, 140
MIGCAP (anti-MiG combat air patrols), 15, 81, 103
MiGs, 12, 13
  "trolling for," 103
Milledge, Elvin, 134–35
Miller, Carl, xiii, 66–67, 78, 79, 84, 88, 183
Miramar Naval Air Station, 12
missiles:
  effectiveness of, 171
  radar-directed, 23
  see also specific missiles
Monde, Le, xii, 21
Moore, Ron, xiii, 71
Moorer, Thomas H., 14
Morgan, Barry, xiii, 24–25, 69–70, 72–73, 182
Mulligan, Jim, xiii, 72

National Security Council, U.S., 15
"Nav-lofting," 105
Navy, U.S., 5, 23

Air Force compared with, 49, 52, 166

bomber sorties by, 165–66

Haiphong bombed by, 30–48

North Vietnamese harbors mined by, 8, 14, 15, 146

Route Packages of, 8, 9

Top Gun course of, 11–12

Navy Task Force 77, 8, 15

Nesbett, Daniel, xiii, 90–91

Neuman, Al, xiii, 40, 142

Newport News, USS, 19–20

Nhan Dan (Hanoi), 69, 85, 187

Nix, Douglas, xiii, 53, 91

Nixon, Richard M., 179

air strikes ordered by, 5–6

ceasefire and, 178

mining of North Vietnamese harbors ordered by, 15, 16

nuclear option rejected by, 7

troops withdrawn by, 4

No More Vietnams (Nixon), 7

North Korea, pilots from, 13

North Vietnam, *see* Vietnam, Democratic Republic of

Nowell, Larry, xiii, 55–56

nuclear option, 7

officers' club (Korat), 147

Okinawa, 21

Okinawa, USS, 33, 36, 135

Oklahoma City, USS, 19

Olinde, Garrett, xiii, 31–32, 135–36

Olsen, John, xiii, 39, 41, 47, 135

O'Neil, James, xiii, 66, 74

Operation Linebacker, 7–8, 15–17, 178, 179

aims of, 7–8

effect of, 178

Oyster Flight, 50, 52

air battle of, 54–62

parachutes, North Vietnamese and U.S. compared, 61

Paris, peace negotiations in, 15

Paul Doumer Bridge, 8, 10, 21, 24, 72, 79, 96, 141, 147, 179–80

analysis of reconnaissance photos of, 99, 101, 166

civilians killed during raid on, 167

conflicting reports of damage to, 185–86

U.S. bombing of, 10, 23, 50, 53, 78, 80, 83, 84–87

Paulhan, Jean, 49

Pave Knife laser designator pod, 11

PAVN (People's Army of Viet Nam), 3–4, 13, 170, 205

Pearson, Ron, xiii, 106, 108

People's Army of Vietnam (Pike), 191

People's Struggle Defeated the Sabotage War of the Imperialist Americans, The, 187

Pettit, Larry, xiii, 56, 62

Pevek, 16

Phan thi Tran, xiii

Phantom, *see* F-4 Phantom

Phuc Yen airfield, 101

Pickard, Don, xiii, 92–94, 97–98, 101, 183

pickle, 70

Pike, Douglas, 191

Pinegar, Frank, 134

PIRAZ (Positive Identification Radar Advisory Zone), 27

Poland, 28

Pomphrey, Michael, xiii, 88
pontoon bridges, 178, 180
Potter, Jerry, xiii
Pratt, Bud, 89
Providence, USS, 19
proximity fuses, 44, 117

Quan Back, 166
Quang Tri Province, 4, 6
Queen, Steve, xiii, 140

RA-5C Vigilante (North
    American), 20, 34, 39–41,
    47, 197
radar, 27–28, 36
    airborne intercept, 12
    early warning, 34, 35, 54, 105
    Fansong, 38, 66
    identification friend or foe
        (IFF) equipment, 12, 13, 28,
        57
    jamming of, 68, 105, 129
RC-135M (Boeing), 21, 27, 197
reconnaissance photos, 99, 101
Red River, 8, 21, 82, 105, 156,
    161
Reed, Gary, xiii, 91
Rescue and Recovery Squadron,
    40th, 157
Rescue Coordination Center, 158
RF-4C Phantom (McDonnell),
    22, 52, 197
Ridge, Bill, xiii, 74–75
Rigg, Don, xiv
Ritchie, Steve, xiv, 58, 60, 61–62,
    171, 181–82
Rockeye cluster bomb, 34
Rogers, Sid, 92, 94, 101
Ronco, Théodore, xiv, 21, 73, 85,
    86, 184
Roscoe, 25

Route 5, 21–22, 48, 109, 141
Route Packages, 8, 9
Roy, Les, 140
Rudloff, Steve, xiv, 26, 102–3,
    104, 105, 118–19, 120,
    148
    blinding of, 118
    capture of, 131, 132–33
    eyesight returns, 144
    interrogation of, 145, 149–50
    as prisoner, 144–45, 148–50
    release of, 180
rules of engagement, 171–72
Ruth, Michael, xiv, 132

SA-2 (Dvina) missiles, vii,
    13–14, 167, 205–6
Saigon, 4
SALT treaty, 179
SAM (surface-to-air missiles),
    vii, 13, 79, 105, 129, 138,
    140, 186, 205–6
Schneider, Clara "Patty," xiv,
    153, 154, 158–59, 163, 181
Schroeder, Chuck, 128–29, 132
Scott, Phil, xiv
Seventh Air Force, U.S., 5, 8, 14,
    99, 101, 147
Shakespeare, William, 30, 179
Sharp, Brad, xiv, 23, 24
Shaw, Brewster, xiv, 24, 91,
    183–84
Shaw, Jim, xiv, 89–90
Shipman, Jerry, 162
Shoemaker, Steve, xiv, 114, 117,
    119, 127, 136
    later career of, 181
Shooting Down the B-52s, on the Spot,
    188
Shrike missile, 34, 38, 65, 66,
    105, 167

Sidewinder missile, 34, 44, 45, 104, 171
Sigint (signals intelligence), 28, 187–88
Silver Star, 24
Simmons, David, xiv, 64, 87
Slavonic, Greg, xiv, 26, 142
smart weapons, 11
Smith, D. L., 84, 86, 183
Smith, Ron, xiv, 160–61
sonic booms, 87–88
South Vietnam, see Vietnam, Republic of
Soviet Union, 7, 28
  advisors from, 13
  merchant ships fired on, 16, 29
Sparrow missile, 13, 34, 44, 45, 57, 58, 130, 171
  long-range capability of, 13, 172
Standard ARM (anti-radar missile), 65, 66, 167
Stansel, Mike, xiv, 47, 141
Stovall, Dale, xiv, 157, 158, 161
strap-on guidance systems, 11
Strategic Reconnaissance Squadrons:
  82nd, 21
  99th, 22
Suhy, Mike, 72
summit meeting (Moscow, 1972), 15, 179

T-38, 12
TACAN, 120, 127
Tactical Fighter Squadrons:
  25th, 23, 53
  433rd, 22, 24
  561st, 25
Tactical Fighter Wings:

8th, 20, 23, 78, 98, 156, 179
388th, 20, 25, 98
Tactical Reconnaissance Squadron, 14th, 22, 92
Tactical Reconnaissance Wing, 432nd, 20, 98
Tale of Two Bridges, The (Lavalle), 185, 186
Tan Son Nhut, 14, 25, 53, 91
TARCAP (TARget Combat Air Patrol), 102, 103
Ta van Duy, 188
Thailand, 48
  U.S. air bases in, 4, 5, 20–21, 22, 27, 52–53, 146–47
Thanh Hoa, 16
Thanh Hoa bridge, 23
Thomas, Guy, xiv, 28
Thunderbirds aerobatic team, 183
Timm, Dwight, xiv, 110–11, 115–16, 136
Tinker, Charles, xii, 41, 44, 103
Today, 146
Tomb (or Toon), Colonel, 189–90
Top Gun, 12, 110
Top Gun course, 11–12, 116, 173, 180
Toups, Lanny, xiv, 24, 71–72
Townsend, William, xiv
"trolling for" MiGs, 103
Tuchman, Barbara, 137

U-2R (Lockheed), 21, 22, 27, 197
United States:
  intelligence agencies of, 8
  losses of, 123, 136, 170, 176–77, 187

Thailand air bases of, 4, 5, 20–21

Van Wagenen, Mike, xiv, 79, 81, 86–87, 183
Vietnam, 190
Vietnam, Democratic Republic of (North), 28
air defenses of, effectiveness of, 190–92
early warning radar of, 34, 35, 54, 105
fighter sorties by, 170, 186
ground defenses, effectiveness of, 173, 178
identification of pilots of, 188–89
import requirements of, 8
losses of, 123, 136, 170, 174–75, 187
national anthem of, 3
SAM zone of, 35
South Vietnam invaded by, 5, 6
U.S. mining of harbors, 8, 14, 15, 146
Vietnam, Republic of (South):
army of, 4
guerrilla activity in, 3
invaded by North Vietnam, 5, 6
smart bombs tested in, 11
Vinh, 16
visual lookout, importance of, 170, 188
Vogt, John W., Jr., xiv, 5, 6, 14–15, 25–26, 53–54, 91, 99

later career of, 184
Locher rescue decision and, 159, 163
Voltaire, 102
Vu Van Hop, 59, 189

Waller, Jim, 66
Walsh, John, xv
Wayne, John, 106
Weaver, Warren, xv, 95–96
White, Donald "Dean," xiv, 61, 74, 75
Wideman, Bill, 81–82
Wild Weasel, *see* F-105G Thunderchief
Wilkinson, D., 95
"Winchester," 70
"Winchester Cathedral," 78
Wright, Joe, xv, 6, 64, 72, 85, 87, 96, 184
Wright, Pat, xv, 64, 72, 85, 87, 96, 184
Wyatt, Johnny, 53

Yankee Station, 20, 27, 30, 32, 48, 102, 105, 135, 137, 142
air squadrons of, 33
Yen Bai, 74, 75, 143, 156, 160
Yen Vien railroad yard, 23, 50, 53, 92–93
analysis of reconnaissance photos of, 99, 101, 166
U.S. bombing of, 89–91

Zumwalt, Elmo R., Jr., xv, 146

ABOUT THE AUTHORS

JEFFREY ETHELL, the son of a U.S. Air Force fighter pilot, was taught to fly before he learned to drive a car. He now holds a commercial pilot's license with an instructor's rating, and has logged over 3,300 flying hours. He has flown several of the high-performance aircraft currently in service with the USAF and the USN, as well as several preserved World War II combat planes. He has long been interested in aviation history and has conducted research for the Smithsonian National Air and Space Museum. His previous books include *Komet, Escort to Berlin* and *F-15 Eagle;* with Alfred Price, *The German Jets in Combat, Target Berlin* and *Air War South Atlantic;* and, with Vincent Loomis, *Amelia Earhart, the Final Story.*

ALFRED PRICE served as an aircrew officer in the Royal Air Force, and in a flying career spanning fifteen years he logged some four thousand flying hours in several combat aircraft, including the Vulcan bomber. He was an instructor in electronic warfare, aircraft weapons and air-fighting tactics. Now working full time as an author, he has written more than thirty books on aviation subjects. His works include *Instruments of Darkness, Aircraft versus Submarine, Battle of Britain: The Hardest Day, The Spitfire Story* and *Panavia Tornado.* He holds a PhD in history from Loughborough University in England and is a Fellow of the Royal Historical Society.